The Enterprise Cloud

Best Practices for Transforming Legacy IT

James Bond

Beijing · Cambridge · Farnham · Köln · Sebastopol · Tokyo

The Enterprise Cloud

by James Bond

Copyright © 2015 James Bond. All rights reserved.

Printed in the United States of America.

Published by O'Reilly Media, Inc., 1005 Gravenstein Highway North, Sebastopol, CA 95472.

O'Reilly books may be purchased for educational, business, or sales promotional use. Online editions are also available for most titles (*http://safaribooksonline.com*). For more information, contact our corporate/institutional sales department: 800-998-9938 or corporate@oreilly.com.

Editor: Brian Anderson	**Indexer:** Wendy Catalano
Production Editor: Shiny Kalapurakkel	**Interior Designer:** David Futato
Copyeditor: Bob Russell, Octal Publishing, Inc.	**Cover Designer:** Karen Montgomery
Proofreader: Jasmine Kwityn	**Illustrator:** Rebecca Demarest

May 2015:   First Edition

Revision History for the First Edition

2015-05-15:   First Release

See *http://oreilly.com/catalog/errata.csp?isbn=9781491907627* for release details.

978-1-491-90762-7

[LSI]

Contents

Foreword

In 1905 George Santayana observed that, "Those who cannot remember the past are condemned to repeat it." That observation also applies to information technology.

James Bond has painstakingly and methodically written what I consider to be one of the definitive books on the subject of the Enterprise Cloud. It includes an excellent chronology of how we got here, the myriad of implementation variations that exist and what each is good for, and most importantly, lessons learned along the way that can enable readers to avoid many of the pitfalls that negatively affected early adopters. The material that James lays out can be likened to a Systems Development Life Cycle for Enterprise Cloud that includes strategic planning, straight through to a step-by-step roadmap for implementation and operation.

"I have personally spent over four decades as an information technology practitioner, and the best compliment I can give James's book is that I learned a great deal from reading the manuscript, and I would buy this book myself. I highly recommend it!"

—Dennis Devlin, Chief Information Security Officer and Sr. Vice President of Savanture, Distinguished Fellow of the Ponemon Institute, Former Assistant Vice President of Information Security and Compliance Services for The George Washington University, Former VP Thomson-Reuters, Former IT Director for Harvard University

Preface

Despite the significant momentum and industry buzz about cloud computing, only a fraction of organizations have an enterprise cloud. Most organizations are still planning their cloud transition strategy while incrementally improving traditional IT services and modernizing data centers. Consolidating enterprise datacenters and implementing server virtualization and automation are critical components of any modernization initiative; however, virtualization and automation are only part of the transition to a cloud environment. Although shifting workloads and commodity information technology (IT) services to a third-party hosting provider is not a new trend, cloud computing is a new style of delivering IT that provides on-demand elastic computing capacity through self-service ordering and automated provisioning systems. We have seen our first generation of public cloud providers, enterprise customers building private clouds, and more recently, a shift toward the *hybrid cloud*. With only a fraction of worldwide organizations already migrating to the cloud, the migration of internal enterprise IT to the cloud will be the most significant transformation within the IT industry.

The shift of traditional on-premises enterprise IT systems (e.g., server farms, storage, networks, and applications) to hosted cloud-based datacenters and providers will dominate the industry over the next 10 years. Cloud-based virtual machines (VMs), storage, and mobile applications are now common and widely available to customers; however, the available public cloud services are still in the childhood years of sophistication and feature depth. *The Enterprise Cloud: Best Practices for Transforming Legacy IT* will provide insider knowledge and lessons learned regarding planning, architecture, deployment, security, management, and hybrid and cloud brokering—technologies and processes that are now the dominant concerns and focus for enterprise IT organizations. As a cloud subject matter expert with significant hands-on experience, I am constantly asked for more information on what I've learned, the necessary business process changes, and the best practices to transition from enterprise IT to a cloud-computing environment. Based on real customers and providers, in commercial and public sector industries, this book also chronicles some of the many successes as well as the less-than-successful cloud deployments, and provides valuable lessons from which we can all learn.

What Is Included in This Book

This book will help you understand the best practices based on actual field experience transitioning on-premises enterprise IT services to a cloud-based environment. Whether you are still planning or ready to implement your long-term cloud strategy, this book will help you evaluate existing cloud technologies and service providers. I cover the cloud from two perspectives: as a consumer of cloud services and as an owner/operator of your own enterprise private or hybrid cloud. Knowledge acquired in the real world is analyzed from the perspectives of operations, security, billing and finance, application transformation, and deployment. Each of these learned lessons are then converted into best practice checklists to save you and your organizations countless dollars and time.

Here is a glance at what is in each chapter:

Chapter 1: *Planning and Architecture*

In this first chapter, I discuss the basic characteristics, definitions, deployment models, and foundational knowledge necessary to plan your transition from enterprise IT to the cloud. It is essential to understand how IT is transforming from traditional datacenters and IT departments to cloud-centric computing. I take you back in time and discuss the roots of the IT industry to demonstrate how cloud computing is really just a new style of IT service delivery that takes advantage of many computing techniques that were created more than 30 years ago. I analyze key technologies that are used in cloud computing environments, such as virtualization, application transformation, and automation. Concepts and definitions of the cloud, widely accepted since 2010, will be updated and refreshed based on real-world cloud deployments, customer experiences, and challenges encountered.

Chapter 2: *Operational Transformation*

In this chapter, I explore lessons learned in the area of cloud operations and management. I discuss challenges that were not foreseen when many service providers and customers began their cloud transition over the past years. Topics include virtualization, automation, continuous monitoring, capacity management, operational personnel, Information Technology Infrastructure Library (ITIL) process changes, and best practice checklists.

Chapter 3: Deploying Your Cloud

Moving to a cloud computing environment requires significant planning; careful selection of cloud models and decisions on governance; build versus buying a cloud service; and systems architecture. I analyze experiences gained in the areas of building your own private or hybrid cloud, as well as handling scope creep, customer expectations, release management, automated patching, and modernized backup and disaster-recovery techniques. Detailed guidance and examples are provided for selecting and deploying cloud-enabled datacenters and servers, and network, storage, and software management tools. These experiences are converted into best practices.

Chapter 4: Application Transformation

The first generation of cloud services focused heavily on basic infrastructure VMs and storage services. The assessment, porting, and migration of legacy applications is really where the most time and effort will be in the coming years. Although you can port some applications easily to the cloud, others will require significant assessment, refactoring, replacement, or reprogramming to truly take advantage of the cloud; but that effort will result in better resiliency, performance, elasticity, and long-term supportability. This chapter also describes cloud native applications and introduces you to a style of continuous application development and delivery.

Chapter 5: Billing and Procurement

Although planning and deployment of the cloud are foremost concerns of many IT executives, first-generation cloud adopters discovered significant challenges in the way organizations handled procurement and chargeback of cloud services that often surprised senior business managers. Whether consuming a public cloud offering or managing your own private cloud, you will need to adapt traditional procurement, ordering, and billing processes to this new style of IT. This chapter analyzes what these early-adopter customers and cloud providers learned, providing an extensive set of best practices so that you can better prepare your organization for the transition to the cloud.

Chapter 6: Cloud Security

I will compare traditional datacenter and IT security with the unique threats to and vulnerabilities of a cloud environment. Recommendations for mitigating cloud-centric security threats are discussed as well as security trends and future threat predictions. I also provide an introduction to the numerous security accreditation and industry standards published by government and international organizations. In Chapter 6, I convert the knowledge gleaned from these experiences into best practices for security governance, precertification in an automation cloud environment, and continuous monitoring.

Chapter 7: Cloud Management

One of the most important components of cloud computing is a robust cloud management system. Many organizations have learned the hard way that building or buying a cloud management platform must be done early and with careful evaluation and planning. Delaying the automation and orchestration of cloud ordering, billing, provisioning, and operational tools has proven to be extremely difficult to add later—the cloud management platform is actually one of the first things that you need to determine because it provides the foundation and sometimes the architecture of the cloud environment. In this chapter, I provide more experience-based education, example software architectures, evaluation criteria, and best practices in selecting or building your own cloud management platform.

Chapter 8: Hybrid and Cloud Brokering

Throughout this book, I cover numerous cloud deployment models such as public and private, but hybrid clouds and cloud brokering is increasing in popularity and will be a dominant aspect in the next generation of cloud computing. In this chapter, I detail and analyze hybrid clouds and cloud management platforms as well as the newer term, *cloud broker*, and its role. The technologies and concepts behind hybrid cloud and cloud brokering did not exist at the inception of cloud computing. I discuss the definition, purpose, and roles of a cloud broker and the differences between hybrid cloud and brokering.

Chapter 9: Industry Trends and Future Cloud Computing

In this concluding chapter, I discuss trends in the cloud computing industry and the key technologies for managing and deploying future clouds. Both cloud providers and organizations operating their own clouds need to understand the critical technologies and challenges that will be the core of modern cloud services: hybrid cloud management, service brokering, self-service control panels, and application transformation.

How to Read This Book

Each chapter in this book provides an analysis of knowledge acquired by industry-leading cloud providers and early-adopter enterprise customers. The chapters are organized by topics such as planning and architecture, deployment, finance and procurement, security, cloud management, and hybrid/brokering. At the end of each chapter, a summary of recommended best practices is provided to help you incorporate all of this amassed experience into your cloud transition. Finally, the last chapter provides an analysis of industry trends and how the industry is expected to evolve over the next few years.

Who Should Read This Book

This book is designed for business and IT executives. I focus on real-world best practices and guidance for planning, deploying, migrating, and managing IT in a cloud computing environment. I provide the knowledge and guidance necessary for executives to make decisions on how best to adopt cloud services and transform from traditionally managed datacenter services to a service-oriented cloud environment. Primary focus is placed on the following:

- Real-world lessons learned and how to apply them to your organization's adoption and transformation from internal enterprise IT to cloud.

- Converting lessons learned into best practices in key areas such as operations, security, billing, deployment, application transformation, cloud management systems, and brokering.

- Providing an understanding of hybrid cloud computing and the future of datacenter modernization.

- Defining cloud brokering and Anything as a Service (XaaS) aggregation and arbitration across multiple cloud providers.

- Projecting the future of cloud computing: we'll review the challenges of the early years of cloud computing and pinpoint where organizations need to focus for the next-generation clouds.

Conventions Used in This Book

The following typographical conventions are used in this book:

Tip

This element signifies an industry trend for enterprise clouds and is labeled as such.

Note

This element signifies a key take-away from the text and is labeled as such.

Citing This Book

This book is here to help you get your job done. In general, if examples are offered with this book, you may use it in your programs and documentation. You do not need to contact us for permission unless you're reproducing a significant portion of the system design examples, diagrams, or best practices checklists. For example, writing documentation that uses several chunks of examples from this book does not require permission. Selling or distributing a CD-ROM of examples from O'Reilly books does require permission. Answering a question by citing this book and quoting system design examples, diagrams, or best practice checklists does not require permission.

We appreciate, but do not require, attribution. An attribution usually includes the title, author, publisher, and ISBN. For example: "*The Enterprise Cloud* by James Bond (O'Reilly). Copyright 2015 James Bond, 978-1-491-90762-7."

If you feel your use of code examples falls outside fair use or the permission given above, feel free to contact us at *permissions@oreilly.com*.

Safari® Books Online

 *Safari Books Online* is an on-demand digital library that delivers expert *content* in both book and video form from the world's leading authors in technology and business.

Technology professionals, software developers, web designers, and business and creative professionals use Safari Books Online as their primary resource for research, problem solving, learning, and certification training.

Safari Books Online offers a range of plans and pricing for enterprise, government, education, and individuals.

Members have access to thousands of books, training videos, and prepublication manuscripts in one fully searchable database from publishers like O'Reilly Media, Prentice Hall Professional, Addison-Wesley Professional, Microsoft Press, Sams, Que, Peachpit Press, Focal Press, Cisco Press, John Wiley & Sons, Syngress, Morgan Kaufmann, IBM Redbooks, Packt, Adobe Press, FT Press, Apress, Manning, New Riders, McGraw-Hill, Jones & Bartlett, Course Technology, and hundreds more. For more information about Safari Books Online, please visit us online.

How to Contact Us

Please address comments and questions concerning this book to the publisher:

O'Reilly Media, Inc.
1005 Gravenstein Highway North
Sebastopol, CA 95472
800-998-9938 (in the United States or Canada)
707-829-0515 (international or local)
707-829-0104 (fax)

We have a web page for this book, where we list errata, examples, and any additional information. You can access this page at *http://oreilly.com/catalog/0636920034124.do*.

To comment or ask technical questions about this book, send email to *bookquestions@oreilly.com*.

For more information about our books, courses, conferences, and news, see our website at *http://www.oreilly.com*.

Find us on Facebook: *http://facebook.com/oreilly*

Follow us on Twitter: *http://twitter.com/oreillymedia*

Watch us on YouTube: *http://www.youtube.com/oreillymedia*

Planning and Architecture

Key topics in this chapter:

- Understanding the transformation from traditional IT
- The evolution of cloud computing
- Definitions and characteristics of cloud computing
- Example cloud service architectures
- Analysis and comparison of cloud deployment models
- Planning and architecture best practices

Before undertaking any transition to cloud computing, it is important to understand its basic fundamentals and how information technology (IT) has evolved up to this point. When cloud computing was just beginning, some of the terms and models were unproven concepts, promising limitless benefits—now, we've had the benefit of time and experience to update those concepts into real-world systems designs, deployment models, and best practices.

Transitioning from Traditional IT

IT is clearly one of the fastest and continuously evolving industries in the world. We all know that the processing power of computers multiplies every few years, storage technology doubles every couple of years, and software applications continuously evolve—usually for the better. Just as the IT industry evolves in general, so too must the IT departments within small, large, commercial, and government organizations.

In the 1960s and 1970s, only large organizations and universities could afford—or more accurately, needed—an IT infrastructure, which often comprised a centralized mainframe computer and remote terminals for access to information and computing resources. Later, organizations began utilizing smaller centralized minicomputers, and then moved toward a system of microcomputers with much larger and distributed processing power to access and manage information everywhere. As you can imagine, this had a significant impact on IT departments.

As we entered the Internet era, outsourcing and staff augmentation exploded so that IT departments could keep up with new technologies and find enough skilled personnel. Today, the IT departments in many organizations are larger than the core business functions the company actually performs or sells to their customers.

With such large and complex internal IT departments, hired consultants and IT outsourcing and augmentation, as well as the actual expense of computer assets (hardware, software, etc.), companies are wondering if they really get a solid return on investment (ROI). Worldwide economic declines are also making organizations reevaluate their business and financial models. One thing that has become clear is that unless an organization is actually in the business of providing IT services, it should focus on its core mission and customers, not on a large internal IT departments or datacenters. Taking this into consideration and comparing the benefits of the cloud, it becomes evident that transitioning to cloud computing can offer both cost savings and corporate IT right-sizing.

A REVOLUTIONARY SHIFT?

Cloud sales and marketing campaigns often use the term revolutionary shift to describe the advancements that cloud computing brings to organizations. The claim is that cloud computing is the most significant change in the industry in more than 10 years. I disagree. This is not a revolutionary shift; rather, it's evolutionary. It is an evolution of information technology enabling a new style of IT services at a faster pace than in the past.

Looking at the IT industry from a broader perspective, the adoption and proliferation of the Internet was a true paradigm shift, and in the more than 15 years since everyone began using it regularly, there has been a steady progression of Internet or web-based technology advancement. We went from static web pages to dynamic content, and then on to hosted applications accessed via the Internet. Then, we expanded the size and domain of traditional IT services to make further use of the Internet and wide area networks (WANs), hosting more servers and applications at third-party Internet service providers (ISPs) and application service providers (ASPs)—essentially the precursor to what we now call public cloud providers.

Cloud computing, as discussed later in this chapter, takes technology and IT concepts from the past and transforms them into a faster delivery model, providing new IT services and business value to customers at a pace we've never before seen. Cloud computing is also somewhat unique in that business value and a focus on the end consumer is now at the forefront of planning and execution. Cloud computing, in general, is not a traditional IT department or service that is often considered a cost factor but is now an accelerator of business innovation, efficiency, and service to customers.

We have all heard the phrase "cheaper, better, and faster." I would easily confirm that cloud computing provides better IT services at a faster development and launch pace; however, there is some debate regarding the "cheaper" part. Although automation, virtualization, and elastic services provide clear cost benefits, the effort and cost to initially deploy the necessary cloud systems does not necessarily provide an immediate cost savings.

Figure 1-1 illustrates how cloud computing is really just an evolution, not necessarily a paradigm shift, contrary to some of the industry marketing hype. Note how application platforms have matured (below the line) versus the computing technology (above the line) as the industry evolved into this cloud computing era.

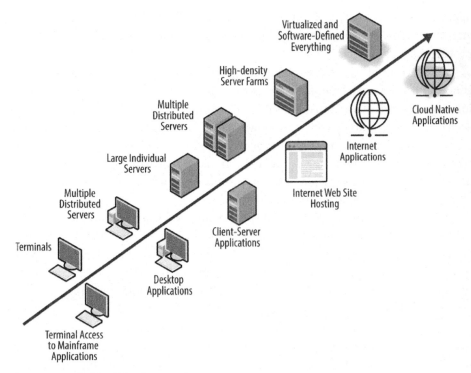

Figure 1-1. Evolution of cloud computing

The Evolution of Cloud Computing

It is important to understand how we arrived at this cloud-centric point in the information technology industry. I won't spend too much time reminiscing about the past, but there is value in understanding the origins of cloud computing. History does tend to repeat itself, and this applies as much to the computer industry as anything else. So, let me take a moment to explain how historical trends put us on this path, how we began using many of these technologies 30 years ago, and how historic IT principles are still valuable today.

Although it did not go by the name "cloud," the concept of cloud computing was predicted in 1961 by Professor John McCarthy of the Massachusetts Institute of technology when he stated:

> *Computing may someday be organized as a public utility just as the telephone system is a public utility ... Each subscriber needs to pay only for the capacity he actually uses, but he has access to all programming languages characteristic of a very large system ... Certain subscribers might offer service to other sub-*

scribers ... The computer utility could become the basis of a new and important industry.[1]

STARTING FROM MAINFRAME CENTRALIZED COMPUTE

In the early days of computer technology, the mainframe computer was a large centralized computing platform with remote dumb terminals used by end users. These terminals could be compared to thin-client devices in today's industry, with the mainframe being the centralized cloud computing platform. This centralized mainframe held all of the computing power (the processing cores), memory, and connected storage, managed by a small operations staff for shared use by a massive number of users.

Sounds a little like cloud computing, doesn't it?

There are further similarities when comparing mainframe-computing environments to today's cloud. Although the mainframe was physically very large, it wasn't all that powerful by modern standards. What the mainframe excelled at was throughput of input/output (I/O) processing—its ability to move data through the system. Ideally, the mainframe systems were managed by a centralized IT staff to maintain security, account management, backup and recovery, system upgrades, and customer support, all of which are components of today's modern datacenters and cloud systems.

Virtualization is another concept that existed more than 30 years ago. Indeed, it was heavily utilized in mainframe computing. Multiple customers and users shared the overall system, but used virtualized segments of the overall operating system, called virtual machines (VMs). This is almost exactly what is done in today's modern cloud computing environments.

Key Take-Away

Virtualization and VMs are not unique to cloud computing; these technologies have existed for more than 30 years.

The basic concepts of cloud computing have been in the IT industry all along; dust off an old mainframe concepts book and you will be surprised by the similarities. Now that we have personal computers and servers with huge amounts of memory, processing power, and storage, virtualization is now even more economical and efficient, and it harnesses excess computing power that

---

1 Source: Simpson Garfinkle, "The Cloud Imperative," *Technology Review*, October 3, 2011, http://bit.ly/ 1cCr5Ux.

otherwise went underutilized. As we move into the next generation of cloud environments, virtualization of servers is commonplace, with the new focus being on virtualizing networks, storage, and the entire datacenter in what is called a *software-defined datacenter* (you can read more about this in Chapter 9).

DISTRIBUTED COMPUTING

Starting in the late 1980s and into the year 2000, the industry began a huge shift from centralized computing to distributed computing. These small distributed servers held more memory, processors, and storage than most mainframes, but the internal server I/O and network were now a challenge. After 20 years of deploying countless new, smaller servers across thousands of datacenters, computer resources (CPU, memory, storage, networking) and management (security, operations, backup/recovery) are now spread out across organizations, and sometimes even across multiple contractors or providers. Many business models have actually shown an increase in the cost of managing the entire systems lifecycle. At least the cost of compute power is a fraction of what it once was due to ever-increasing performance and ever-decreasing prices.

THE MOVE TO CONSOLIDATED COMPUTING

Today's computing environments are highly distributed, but consolidation of server farms and datacenters is in full swing. This consolidation involves deploying higher capacity servers and IT assets into small physical datacenters—providing equal or more computing capability while using smaller, more powerful computers to eliminate inefficient legacy systems. This consolidation will eventually bring down operational and management costs, accomplishing more with fewer IT assets, facilities, and personnel, which are some of the costliest assets.

Consider what to do next with distributed computing platforms. Mobile devices (notebooks, tablets, and smartphones) already outsell desktop workstations throughout the world. Servers are being consolidated at an increasing pace and achieving densities within datacenters never before thought possible. In fact, modern datacenters are packing so many servers into each rack that, often, power and HVAC are the limiting scalability factors rather than physical space.

With smaller and less powerful (compared to a full desktop workstation) end-user devices, we are headed back to a model wherein the compute power is held more in the datacenters than at the edge/user device. This is especially true for thin-client devices and virtual desktop interface (VDI, or in "cloud speak," Workplace or Desktop as a Service). Not that every end-user device will become "dumb" or "thin client," but there is clearly a mix of users who need varying levels of compute power on their edge device.

In a relatively short period of time, we have gone from centralized compute processing with thin end-user/edge devices to a highly distributed compute environment, and now we're headed back toward centralization to a certain degree—this time using clouds and consolidating legacy datacenter IT assets. History is repeating itself. Let's hope we are making some intelligent decisions and doing it better this time. Some could argue that mainframes still play a large role in today's IT industry, and that they were "the best" business model all along.

TRANSITIONING TO A CLOUD ENVIRONMENT

As we consolidate many of the distributed computing platforms, datacenters, and the occasional retiring of a mainframe system, it is important to realize where we are headed and why.

As I look at today's cloud computing environment and our immediate future, we are shifting back to virtualization and multitenancy concepts that were founded in the early days of centralized (mainframe) computing. Though these might be long-standing concepts in the IT industry, cloud computing is pushing ever upward to new heights in the areas of automation, elasticity, on-demand ordering, pay-as-you-go pricing, and self-service management and control systems.

Organizations now understand that they might not benefit from large and costly IT departments that do not directly contribute to your customers and your core mission. Outsourcing IT functions and personnel is nothing new, but cloud computing represents a new form of outsourcing, scalability, and cost control, if managed wisely. With cloud computing, the burden of building, maintaining, upgrading, and operating the compute systems is the responsibility of the provider. This gives the consuming organization ultimate flexibility and choice of providers and eliminates being locked into a single one. This results in faster deployment of services at a lower cost so that the consuming organization can focus on its core business functions and customers, not on an IT department. This is the evolution or new style of IT service delivery that has taken 30 years to achieve.

Key Take-Away

Cloud computing results in faster deployment of services at a lower cost. This means that the consuming organization can focus on its core business functions and customers, not on its IT department.

So how are chief information officers (CIOs) transforming and benefiting from cloud computing? There is clearly a reduction in the use of traditional "managed services" and generic "time and materials" IT contractors providing computer services. Cloud consumers both small and large are able to select the cloud provider, pay for the services utilized, and scale up or scale down if finances or priorities of the business change. Organizations are no longer stuck with unneeded computer systems, server farms, and datacenters, which leads to greater agility in their overall business decisions.

Here are some of the recent trends and updated benefits CIOs can take advantage of by shifting to cloud services:

- Managed service contracts transitioning to cloud service providers with more scalability (up and down) and less risk to consuming organization.

- Ability to slowly shift key applications and traditional IT to the cloud—moving to the cloud does not need to be an all or nothing transition.

- Increased choice and flexibility for the consuming organization by avoiding lock-in to a single provider by using a hybrid cloud deployment model or cloud service brokering.

- Organizations pay for cloud usage, which is carefully monitored and measured. In previous managed services models, it was often difficult to see actual results based on IT costs.

- Centralized and efficiently utilized compute resources managed by fewer personnel with heavy use of automation and consistent processes resulting in lower cost and better quality to the consumers.

- Lifecycle management, upgrade, and replacement of used resources are the responsibility of the cloud provider, resulting in reduced cost, labor, time, and risk for individual IT organizations performing this task in a traditional IT environment.

- Consuming organizations do not need a large number of experienced senior IT personnel, who are expensive, difficult to find, and challenging to keep. The technical staff will be able to better focus on their mission-critical applications of their businesses rather than managing commodity IT.

There are also some challenges that CIOs and business executives need to consider when moving to a cloud service:

- Organizations have significant legacy computing resources (servers, datacenters, and IT personnel) that will need to be transitioned or eliminated in order to achieve the true cost savings and flexibility provided by cloud providers and services. Often these existing computing resources have not yet been fully depreciated, making the adoption of cloud computing challenging to procure. Some organizations do not necessarily see an immediate savings because of the cloud.

- Migrating large mission-critical applications to the cloud can be complicated and somewhat expensive (unlike commodity IT services, which are much easier and less costly to transition). Businesses should evaluate whether their custom and legacy applications are worth the reinvestment, or if an alternative cloud-enabled service exists which might be a better fit in the long term.

- Private cloud deployments do not always have sufficient redundancy in geographically diverse hosting facilities. Using multiple datacenter facilities and/or multiple cloud providers can provide improved service availability and continuity of operations.

- Procurement and budgeting for cloud services is a challenge to some commercial and government organizations. Existing procurement policies might need to be adapted.

- Existing security, operations, and other processes within consuming organizations need to adapt to this new cloud computing model, in which services, applications, and VMs are launched through automation.

Definitions of Cloud Computing and "As a Service"

The first thing to clarify is the use of the term "cloud computing" in general. Throughout this book, I refer to cloud computing as "cloud services"; this is actually a more accurate term. Cloud computing, although the accepted industry nomenclature, originated from the concept of hosting computer (processor, memory, storage) resources in the cloud; hence, the term cloud computing.

Though it is still a relatively new term, cloud computing has already grown in scope and meaning to now encompass applications, virtual desktops, automated deployment, service orchestration, and more—almost anything related to IT that an organization would want hosted and serviced through the cloud. The term used in the industry is as-a-Service which is the "aaS" portion of a number of acronyms that have become ubiquitous in recent years, such as XaaS. This particular acronym refers to any cloud-based application or service provided to consumers. The most common models include Infrastructure as a Servce (IaaS), Platform as a Service (PaaS), Software as a Service (SaaS), all of which you'll see later in this chapter.

DEFINITION OF THE CLOUD

The National Institute for Standards and Technology (NIST) definition of the cloud states the following:

> *Cloud computing is a model for enabling convenient, on-demand network access to a shared pool of configurable computing resources (e.g., networks, servers, storage, applications, and services) that can be rapidly provisioned and released with minimal management effort or service provider interaction.*

Although there are several companies and individuals claiming credit for first using the term "cloud" as pertaining to cloud computing, the real-world meaning of cloud is not truly a rigid definition. Many consider the cloud just another term for the Internet, and, depending on how the term is used, that might be correct; cloud computing frequently includes providing computing resources (processors, memory, storage) over the Internet. The key to remember, however, is that cloud computing doesn't technically require the Internet: you can utilize private communications and network circuits between facilities and essentially form your own private cloud. In many situations, a combination of private WANs, communications circuits, and the Internet is what is actually used for cloud computing services. I fully define and differentiate between public, private, hybrid, and all the cloud computing models later in this chapter.

CHARACTERISTICS OF A CLOUD

Although they began as a pure on-demand compute and storage environment serviced through the Internet, cloud services quickly expanded to include various networking, backup and recovery, platform, application, and hosted data services. There are five key characteristics of cloud services as defined by NIST (note that I have updated the descriptions of each characteristic from NIST's original publication):

On-demand self-service

An organization can order cloud services with automated provisioning of the needed computing, storage, network, and applications from the cloud provider. This includes the ability to expand services or resources as needed automatically or as requested by the organization. This also entails the ability to rapidly scale up or scale down as needs change.

Broad network access

Cloud services are provided over any combination of private network communication circuits or the open Internet, depending on the cloud deployment model and the specifications of the cloud provider's offering. You can make the cloud resources available to or hidden from a wide variety of computers (thick or thin client), laptops, mobile devices, tablets, and smartphones.

Resource pooling

Multiple users share all resources within a specific cloud deployment. The level of sharing or dedicated resources to each user can vary depending on the cloud deployment model. Virtualization of compute, storage, networking, and applications are often utilized to separate one tenant (user) from another. Access controls are in place to maintain separation of user data from all other users. The location of resources is often spread across multiple physical locations or datacenters, and depending on the cloud deployment model, the location of hosted resources might not even be known or specified by the user.

Rapid elasticity

You can scale out services rapidly, with increased capacity or additional compute, memory, storage, and network resources giving the impression of unlimited resource availability. You can also reduce resources when workload utilization decreases. I will define and clarify scale out versus scale up in later chapters.

Measured service

Services are billed on a pay-per-use basis as determined by metering of consumed resources such as compute, storage, network, or applications. You can measure and monitor all resource usage and establish potential limits, or pay-as-used expansion of resources as needed.

Key Take-Away

Even if an organization does not migrate or adopt a true cloud service, the benefits of the cloud are still desirable for on-premises, enterprise customer-owned datacenters and IT departments .

WHERE CLOUD CHARACTERISTICS MEET TRADITIONAL IT GOALS

As organizations move critical compute, storage, and application systems to cloud providers, several additional attributes or characteristics have become more of an emphasis based on recent lessons learned. Many of the characteristics in the following list apply to IT modernization trends in general even if an organization isn't yet shifting to a cloud environment:

Real-time statistics, monitoring, and metering of services (transparency into the cloud environment)

Organizations have transitioned some or all of their data and applications into the cloud, so some form of visibility into the cloud environment is essential for a successful experience. This includes real-time monitoring of service status, metered resource utilization dashboards, and service-level agreement (SLA) reporting scorecards.

Self-service management

As applications are moved to the cloud, organizations want the ability to manage their accounts and application settings without having to submit a helpdesk ticket for routine tasks. This is often an overlooked or underestimated feature of a successful cloud offering. More details on self-service management are provided in Chapters 7 and 9.

Role-based security for multilevel administration

User roles are defined within the cloud management system to allow placing orders, approving orders, or managing service subscriptions. These roles also define the visibility of services between users so multiple organizations or tenants cannot see one another. The roles for each tenant are restricted so they cannot change settings or order services outside of their authorized capacity and account.

24-7-365 support and escalation to a single provider

Users are looking for the provider to fully support all the services and resources hosted in the cloud. Cloud providers typically provide all backend datacenter and server farm management, but the user also needs the ability to escalate real and perceived user and access issues to the provider. Low cost providers might attempt to limit a customer's ability to call into a 24-7–staffed support center.

Little or no capital expenses (funding via operational moneys)

Public cloud services normally provide services to customers with little or no up-front capital expenses, whereas private clouds often require significant capital investment. In a public cloud model, and for some managed private clouds, the provider covers the initial cost of equipment and staging, with each customer paying for usage based on an hourly, daily, weekly, or monthly rate. The provider covers all systems management, patching, and future upgrades of hardware and software. This means that customers can better utilize their money by spreading their costs over multiple years and not having to identify a large amount of funding every so many years for capital equipment and upgrades.

No long-term commitments and the ability to easily scale services up or down as needed or consumed

Customers often desire little or no minimums or term commitments. It is up to the service provider to set the terms and flexibility to customize those terms to meet consumer needs. Although the consumer might desire zero minimums or commitments and the ability to cancel some or all of the services with little or no notice, this represents a significant risk to the public cloud provider or private cloud integrator, which normally results in a higher price per service over a period of time.

Figure 1-2 shows the NIST visual model of cloud computing. Notice how a shared pool of resources is included among the essential characteristics at the top of the diagram. The middle layer represents the cloud service models followed by the cloud deployment types at the bottom.

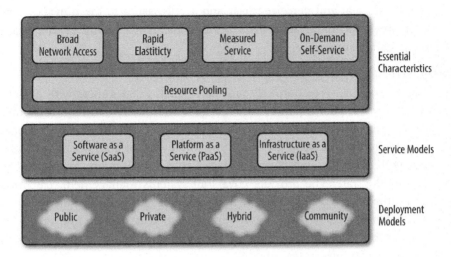

Figure 1-2. NIST model of cloud computing (illustration courtesy of NIST; http://1.usa.gov/ 1GkRKQE)

Cloud Deployment Models

Cloud deployment models proved to be an area of confusion during the initial years of the cloud-computing industry. Table 1-1 provides a summary definition of each cloud deployment model. Later in this section, we will look at each of these in more detail, as we compare them, and review the lessons learned. Although NIST if often referred to for definitions of cloud and cloud models, Table 1-1 represents a more modern breakdown of cloud deployment models.

Table 1-1. Cloud deployment model definitions

Cloud deployment model	Definition
Public cloud	A cloud service offered to the general public. The cloud provider owns, manages, and operates all computing resources located within the provider's facilities. Resources available to users are shared across all customers. Some cloud providers now offer higher, government-compliant security upgrades, which might use physically separate resources within provider datacenters. Customization is limited because the cloud is shared across many customers.

Cloud deployment model	Definition
Private cloud	A cloud infrastructure operated for a single organization. The cloud can be managed by the organization or a third party, and it can be hosted on premises or at a third-party datacenter. Private clouds are typically more customizable than other forms of clouds because they are dedicated to and owned by one customer organization. Many private clouds are deployed within an existing on-premises datacenter.
Virtual private cloud (VPC)	A variation of public cloud wherein a segmented compartment of an otherwise public cloud infrastructure is dedicated to one customer. VPC offerings bring some of the price advantages of a large public cloud provider but with a bit more customization, security, and segmentation of VMs, storage, and networking. Variations of VPC include managed and unmanaged VMs and application services.
Community cloud	A cloud service that provides for a community of users or organizations with shared interests or concerns. The system is managed by one or more of the organizations, by a central provider, or a combination of the two. Organizations utilizing this cloud service have shared missions, governance, security requirements, and policies. Cloud services can be hosted on-premises at the consumer organization, at peer organization facilities, at a provider, or a combination of these. This community cloud term is often used in marketing to explain the target consumers of the service, although the actual cloud might technically be a VPC, private, or hybrid cloud model.
Hybrid cloud	A cloud service that is a combination of two or more of the previously defined deployment models (public, private, VPC, or community). A common example is a private cloud that is connected to one or more third-party public-cloud service providers for certain applications such as email—all integrated by using a common cloud management and automation platform. To manage multiple cloud providers, a cloud management system or cloud-broker system is required (see Chapters 7 and 8 for more details on cloud management and cloud brokering).

Figure 1-3 depicts the relationship of the enterprise (customer) network infrastructure and private (on-premises or off-premises) cloud options. When connected to one or more types of cloud providers, a hybrid cloud is formed. There can be multiple private-or public cloud providers interconnected. Many public cloud providers offer VPC and various other as a service offerings (e.g., IaaS, PaaS, and SaaS) from their public cloud infrastructure.

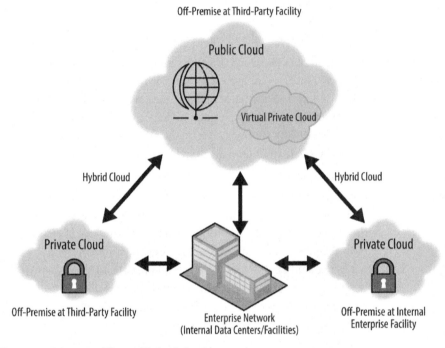

Figure 1-3. Private, public, and hybrid cloud integration

Analysis and Comparison of Cloud Deployment Models

Each cloud deployment model—public, private, VPC, community, and hybrid—offers distinct advantages and disadvantages. It depends upon the customer requirements to determine which model or combination of models is truly the best for a given customer. Understanding these cloud deployment models is essential to begin planning your cloud transition.

Table 1-2 provided a brief definition of each cloud deployment model. Now, I will focus on the unique characteristics of each one as compared to the others.

Ultimately, a full assessment of an organization's requirements is needed in order to pick the best solution.

Although experience and industry trends show that customers have a preference for the economics provided by public clouds, it is private clouds that offer more flexibility with customized features and security. The larger the organization, particularly government entities, the more likely a private cloud will be deployed—conversely, small and medium-sized businesses often cannot afford to purchase or build their own private clouds. Many small businesses also have the advantage of little or no existing investment in infrastructure, so they can more quickly adopt cloud-hosted applications when first forming the organization.

PUBLIC CLOUD

A public cloud service is based on a cloud provider typically offering preconfigured and published offerings. They normally have an online storefront that lists all available products, configurations, options, and pricing. Because the public cloud providers are offering services to the general public and a wide variety of customers, they have implemented their own cloud management platform. The cloud platform and services offered are targeted at the widest group of potential consumers; therefore, customization of the service is normally limited.

The public cloud provider owns, manages, and operates all computing resources located within the provider facilities, and resources available to users are shared across all customers. Customization of a public IaaS application is usually limited to selecting options from a service catalog. Common options include choice of the operating system (OS), the OS version, and the sizing of the VM (processors and storage). Cloud providers often prebundle IaaS VM services into small, medium, large, and extra-large configurations, each with predefined processor, memory, and storage sizes. Customizations to ordering, billing, reporting, or networking might not be accommodated; this is a situation for which a private cloud deployment is more suitable.

Public cloud providers have also entered the virtual private, community, and even private cloud service market—providing more data segregation and customization for each customer rather than the legacy pure public cloud models. Some public cloud service providers are beginning to blur the lines between public, private, and hybrid cloud through integration back to on-premises enterprise datacenter-based identity, authentication, application publishing, and other services.

Industry Trend

A very recent industry trend is public cloud providers launching new hybrid services. These hybrid services focus on integrating traditional enterprise datacenters, typically on a customer's premises, with public cloud services. This hybrid capability makes it possible for customers to federate authentication systems, synchronize data, support both enterprise and cloud applications, and failover enterprise servers to public cloud VMs.

Some cloud providers offer higher government-level security upgrades, which might use physically separated resources deployed in a segmented compartment within the provider's datacenters. A public cloud provider that dedicates infrastructure and services to one customer is essentially offering a VPC, but it might market this under the term "community cloud" or a brand name such as "Federal" or "Gov" cloud. In some cases, a cloud provider might offer completely isolated and dedicated network infrastructures for each of its customers purchasing the government-compliant high-security cloud option; however, technically these dedicated cloud infrastructures would be more accurately defined as private or managed private clouds hosted within the provider's facility.

PRIVATE CLOUD

Private cloud services might begin with the same basic cloud computing services as offered by a public cloud provider, but the service can be hosted at a customer-owned or contracted datacenter. Private clouds offer choices of the cloud services to be deployed, how much integration there is between services, how the management and operations are handled, and the level of security controls and accreditation.

Private cloud is an excellent model for large organizations that have significant existing datacenter and server farm assets, and want to slowly modernize to cloud technologies and processes. The organization can deploy a private cloud within the same datacenter(s) with a longer-term plan to migrate legacy IT systems to the cloud model over time. The customer can then transition applications and data at the discretion of its staff, augmented by IT cloud service integrator or other expertise, as needed.

As I state throughout this book, as soon as you connect a private cloud to another type of cloud (e.g., public), by definition, you now have a hybrid cloud. In addition, if we are going by strict definitions, if you connect existing traditional datacenters, server farms, or applications to the private cloud, you also have formed a hybrid cloud. For this reason, I believe almost all clouds are or will become hybrids and the terms "hybrid," "private," and "public" will disappear over time.

Key Take-Away

Almost all enterprise clouds will become hybrids—using a combination of on-premises IT, private, and public compute and application resources.

PUBLIC AND PRIVATE MODELS COMPARED

Arguably, the first public cloud service provider to achieve wide acceptance and scale was Amazon Web Services (AWS). This is an example of a true public cloud compute offering, with all the key characteristics and benefits of cloud services. Many other providers have built or are building their own public cloud offerings to provide similar capabilities. The key benefits that organizations achieve from using a public cloud are not being questioned here, but there seems to be a misconception about private cloud computing when organizations evaluate and select a provider or deployment model.

Most small and medium-sized businesses (also referred to as SMBs) do not have many choices in selecting their cloud deployment model due to their size, limited budget, internal technical expertise, and needs. Often a public cloud service offering is adequate and cost effective compared to purchasing or deploying a private cloud. For larger organizations that have size, complexity, and unique requirements, a private cloud service is often more suitable. Of course, a private cloud involves deploying the cloud services either within an on-premises datacenter, or hiring a vendor to configure a dedicated private cloud for the organization. This usually costs more money to deploy, but has significant advantages, the most important of which is the ability to customize the private cloud service to meet the organization's security, operational, financial, and other unique requirements—something a public cloud service cannot offer and SMBs often cannot afford.

In my experience, most customers—larger organizations and government entities, in particular—desire the flexibility and scalability of public cloud offerings. Unfortunately, their unique requirements almost always force a private cloud to be considered in the end. These unique requirements, difficult to accomplish using public cloud, include customizations in the procurement, security, operational, reporting, and governance processes. Only private cloud deployments have the ability to highly customize the cloud service to meet customer requirements. Typically, the larger and more complex the customer, the larger and more complex its list of unique requirements will be. For this reason, it is important to discuss early in the planning process all requirements and their level of priority.

Key Take-Away

As new cloud customers see the potential uses and features, there is a tendency to ask for extensive customizations. Private clouds allow for more customization, but is the cost really worth it to manage one-off unique cloud platform configurations in the long run?

Table 1-2 compares private and public cloud capabilities. It does not include community, virtual private, or hybrid, because these are really just variations of private and public.

Table 1-2. Private versus public cloud characteristics

Capability	Private cloud	Public cloud
Service catalog	Customized to customer needs	Established by provider
Billing and reporting	Ability to integrate with corporate billing systems	Preestablished billing and reporting; no integration with corporate billing systems
Service-level agreements (SLAs)	Often customized per customer requirement	Established by provider
Granular resource metering	Granular metering of resources	Established by provider
Infrastructure servers	VMs and physical servers	Normally only VMs offered
Security	Customized enterprise-class security	High but standardized security; rarely customizable per customer
Service offerings	Customized to customer needs	Established by provider
Self-service control panel	Customized to customer needs	Limited
Operations and management	Performed by provider, customer, third party, or a combination	Performed by provider

Capability	Private cloud	Public cloud
Security management, monitoring, and accreditation	Performed by provider, customer, third party, or a combination	Performed by provider
Elasticity and scalability	Unlimited, based within the limits or size of compute resources	Unlimited, service level guaranteed
Time to provision	After initial setup, minutes to hours	Minutes
Support	Dedicated account support	Optional support from provider or reseller/channel
Professional services	Transition, migration, support, and implementation services	Limited customization services; migration and other services available from provider or reseller/channel
Management services	Full application, database, and platform management services	Limited application and database management services

HYBRID CLOUD

A hybrid cloud uses multiple cloud services—any combination of public, private, community, and traditional IT (enterprise) datacenters. A theme throughout this book is the trend for private clouds to be a baseline for many organizations and eventually extended services to one or more public cloud XaaS offerings to form a hybrid cloud. Technically, when you connect one cloud to another cloud, or you connect to legacy datacenters and applications, you then have a hybrid cloud. Industry and early cloud adopters have learned that it is wise to implement a cloud management system with embedded hybrid capabilities to integrate multiple cloud providers and legacy customer IT assets. The cloud management system (this is fully defined and discussed in Chapter 7) is the centralized ordering, automation, and reporting engine that integrates each cloud service, integrated module, or application.

As customers push the limits of what a public cloud is able to offer, or implement a private cloud, the immediate needs often fit within the combined features of both. In the real world, even the newest private cloud customers just starting out can already see potential uses for a hybrid cloud; they just aren't ready for it yet. Although public and private clouds are the dominant models deployed today, expect to see hybrid clouds become the norm. Hybrid clouds will become so commonplace across most organizations and datacenters that the terms private and hybrid cloud might disappear in the future.

Key Take-Away

Many hybrid clouds begin as a private cloud that later extends integration to use one or more public cloud XaaS offerings. There is also a new emerging trend for public cloud providers to do the reverse—using the public cloud platform to integrate back into legacy enterprise datacenters and private clouds. The concepts are the same but the lines between private, public, and legacy datacenters continue to blur as hybrid clouds evolve.

Motivations to implement a hybrid cloud are numerous; primarily, customer organizations might fit within one cloud model (public, private, or community) initially, but future needs to extend their cloud, service, integration, or data sharing with third parties force expansion into a hybrid cloud deployment. Rather than individual management and operations of multiple cloud providers, it is preferable to use a single cloud management system to manage or broker between cloud providers, retaining only one platform to manage all financial, ordering, procurement, automation, workflow, security, governance, and operations in your organization.

After a hybrid cloud service is deployed, the ability to take advantage of the best of breed software applications and XaaS cloud providers is increased, but management of the overall cloud solution is still crucial. Although a customer can purchase cloud services from multiple cloud providers—one hosting a public cloud service, another a private one—purchasing multiple services from different cloud providers requires managing each cloud provider separately. You would use each cloud provider's management portal for ordering, billing, reporting, and so on—multiplied by the total number of cloud providers to which you have subscribed. A hybrid cloud management solution is unique in that all cloud services across any number of cloud providers are all managed through a single management portal. All ordering, billing, reporting, and cloud operations are managed through the centralized hybrid cloud management platform. The level of development and multiprovider integration to create a unified hybrid or cloud broker platform is significant, and it is highly recommended that no individual customer try to develop a system internally.

Key Take-Away

Try to use a single cloud management platform to manage or broker between cloud providers—retaining only one hybrid cloud management system for all financial, ordering, procurement, automation, workflow, security, governance, and operations in your organization.

COMMUNITY CLOUD

A community cloud service provides for a community of users or organizations with shared interests and concerns. Each member organization in a community cloud can host some portion, or application(s), that all departments of the organization can use. Some departments might have the same offering, which can be pooled together for capacity, load balancing, or redundancy reasons. A community cloud can create cooperation between organizations while reducing costs by sharing the infrastructure, operations, and governance.

Organizations utilizing this cloud service would ideally have missions, governance, security requirements, and policies. Cloud services can be hosted on premises at the consumer organization, at peer organization facilities, at a provider, or a combination that allows sharing of the costs and ongoing management. Trends over the past few years indicate limited adoption of this community model—largely because the deployments require an extensive and deep long-term relationship between multiple organizations in order to build, govern, and operate them—this has driven some organizations to consider VPC as an alternative model.

Some cloud providers offer a specialized, community cloud offering. Community cloud is often used as a marketing term to explain a targeted group of customers, such as government public sector organizations, although the actual cloud is technically a VPC, private, or hybrid cloud model.

The primary concern with a community cloud is how the cloud is managed. Standards of communications, cloud management systems, and the services offered need to be agreed upon and upheld across multiple departments or organizations—not just initially, but for many years. This is where business challenges begin to reveal themselves. What happens if, in the future, one of the community cloud departments or organizations changes their business, budget, security standards or other priorities? What if that department was offering critical resources to the community cloud that will no longer be available at the same level as originally agreed upon?

The critical factors to consider in a community cloud are less technical; instead, the focus is on business process, stability, and cooperation-based considerations. Let's take a look at some of these operational and business challenges:

Shared ownership

Is one of the members of the community cloud in charge of the overall management and governance of the system? Decisions by committee are often difficult, so who is the ultimate decision maker if all parties cannot agree on something?

Shared resources

If one member of the community cloud hosts a critical service that everyone else uses, what happens if the service doesn't meet the reliability, operational, or cost factors to which everyone originally agreed? What can one member of the community do to ensure that problems are rectified? What if one member of the community has its budget changed or business realigned and can no longer host that portion of the cloud? Transitioning can be expensive, complicated, and disruptive to ongoing operations.

Cloud management

A successful cloud is a cloud that has a single management system with both provider and end-user control panels. All members of the community cloud will need to either agree on a single management platform—a considerable challenge in and of itself—or agree upon a universal standard for application programming interfaces (APIs) and integration. Even if standards are agreed upon, actually stitching together the final cloud management system to look and function as a truly integrated solution is a huge undertaking.

Procurement and chargeback

Which member of the organization first builds or hires a cloud integrator or provides seed funding? The methods by which one department or organization procures the cloud service might not match other departments. If different organizations host different portions of the cloud service, how are funds exchanged and granular resources (e.g., processor usage, memory, and storage) metered and charged back to each agency, department, and project?

Security

> Will all members of the community cloud be able to agree on the security posture and accreditation of the system? If the information system security officer (ISSO) for an individual department or organization is told in his job description that he is responsible for the systems used and deployed by his organization, is that ISSO going to accept a security accreditation of the community cloud that was done by another agency? If unanimous agreement between all ISSOs across all organizations is the goal, this is even more difficult. What about ongoing security operations and monitoring? Who is responsible and how do information, threats, and mitigation activities get back to the individual department ISSOs? Finally, data privacy standards often change or are dependent on end-user locations or the type of data.

Cloud Service Models

There are several widely accepted "as a service" models in the industry (and as defined by NIST). Each service model is briefly defined in Table 1-3, and then I detail each service model with real-world examples, architectures, trends, and lessons learned.

Table 1-3. Cloud service model definitions

Cloud service model	Definition
Infrastructure as a Service (IaaS)	A service that includes processing, memory, storage, and networking in the form of a VM. Consumers can deploy operating system and applications as they prefer. Cloud providers often supply OS templates as a quick-start to get the system operational quickly. The cloud provider also handles all systems management of backend server farms, networking, storage systems, and virtualization/ hypervisors with the consumer managing the OS, applications, and data. Backup and recovery options and long-term data retention options might be available from the provider. Pricing to the consumer is often based on processor, memory, storage, and network resources ordered, with set limits or the ability to automatically scale up, and thus charges are based on actual utilization of resources.

Cloud service model	Definition
Software as a Service (SaaS)	A service offering that provides one or more applications to the consumer. Applications are hosted and managed by the provider in the cloud with the consumer accessing the application services from various end-computing devices such as PCs, laptops, tablets, smartphones, or web browsers. The consumer does not manage the underlying server farm, applications, or storage. The provider might provide the consumer a web-based self-service control panel to give the consumer some control over certain aspects of the application or user configuration. Pricing to the consumer is often based on a per-seat user license with potential up-charges for additional storage or application features.
Platform as a Service (PaaS)	A service providing a set of applications, tools, and, commonly, multiple VMs to the consumer. The provider manages all underlying VMs, networking, storage, OS, and core applications. PaaS is similar to IaaS but a platform is a more complete "stack" of systems and software rather than individual IaaS VMs. The cloud provider is responsible for not only the VMs, but also the applications, tools, and resources. The provider might supply the consumer with a web-based self-service control panel to give the consumer some control over certain aspects of the application or configuration. Pricing to the consumer is often based on a combination of the compute/ infrastructure cost, licensing costs of a database application, and per-user fees, as well as additional storage or application features.

As the cloud computing industry and customer adoption has progressed, additional "as a service" (what I call XaaS) models have been coined. Most of these new XaaS models actually fit within one of the three aforementioned core definitions. Many cloud service providers started out with clearly defined cloud services such as IaaS. Today, the service lines have blurred with public cloud providers and enterprise private cloud owners now deploying numerous platform and software services.

Table 1-4. Extended cloud service model definitions

Cloud service model	Extended service models	Definition
IaaS or PaaS	Workplace as a Service; Desktop as a Service; virtual desktop interface	Also known as virtual desktop interface (VDI). Some cloud providers categorize this as part of IaaS or PaaS but many utilize a unique name for this service to differentiate this virtual desktop offering from other offerings. This is a cloud service providing a desktop OS —commonly Microsoft Windows or Linux—and applications to consumer end users. The provider manages all server farms, storage, networking, and OS templates with patches/updates. Consumers access the virtual desktop OS and applications via a thick-or thin-client desktop, laptop, tablet, smartphone, and so on. Pricing to the consumer is often based on a combination of the compute cost and licensing of applications.
PaaS	Application as a Service; application publishing	Using the same VDI technology as in Workplace as a Service, application publishing involves starting applications in the cloud with the user interface transmitted to any form of desktop or mobile end-user device. One or more applications appear to run on the end device, instead of a full desktop OS as in a traditional VDI service.
PaaS	Development/ Testing as a Service (Dev/ Test)	This service provides potentially both IaaS VMs with PaaS databases or other applications in a nonproduction network segment. This nonproduction set of VMs, OSs, and applications make it possible for developers to quickly stage new cloud-based servers to perform application development and testing. As part of the application lifecycle, application suites (or sets of VMs), can be promoted from a Dev network to a Test or even Production network. Application lifecycle management (ALM) tools are commonly offered as part of these Dev/ Test tools, including code libraries, collaboration

Cloud service model	Extended service models	Definition
		between developers, compilers, quality testing tools, and so on.
PaaS	Database as a Service	These services provide one or more brands and types of databases as a cloud consumable resource. Database-as-a-Service is actually a PaaS offering with the service consisting of one or more virtual (or physical) servers hosting the databases, search engines, reporting engines, and so on.
SaaS	Email as a Service	This service provides electronic messaging via a cloud delivery model. This service is really a SaaS offering whereby the provider hosts the email system with consumers running a web, PC, or mobile email client application to retrieve, view, and search the data.
SaaS	CRM as a Service	This service provides a customer relationship management (CRM) application via a hosted cloud model. Because many CRM platforms involve multiple application subservices, databases, tiered architecture, and development environments, CRM can also be considered a PaaS offering by definition.
IaaS	Storage as a Service	These services offer more types of cloud-based storage services (object, block, and image) with many of the same elasticity, on-demand provisioning, and pay-as-you-go pricing models as other cloud services.
IaaS	Backup as a Service; online backup	Backup services allow traditional enterprise datacenter servers to use cloud-based storage to keep backup data. Backup software agents running on servers, or SANs, or specialized backup appliances in the enterprise datacenters send the backup data, or a copy of backup jobs, to a cloud provider for off-site data protection.
IaaS	Server failover; server replication to the cloud	This service synchronizes data, in as close to real time as possible, from enterprise datacenters to cloud-based VMs for redundancy and failover. Should the primary

Cloud service model	Extended service models	Definition
		enterprise servers have a planned or unplanned outage, the cloud-based servers can take over temporarily or permanently. This can also be used as a method of operating servers in parallel, in the cloud, in preparation for a permanent migration to solely cloud-based services.
PaaS or SaaS	Data as a Service	These services offer structured or business intelligence data to consumers through the cloud. In a typical scenario, the cloud provider continuously aggregates massive amounts of data from multiple worldwide sources, providing this data to customers in either raw or some form of analyzed, sorted, or formatted configuration to make the data useful to consumers. Technically, these data services have been in the industry for many years, such as LexisNexis and even Wikipedia—the purpose of each is to provide massive searchable data in the cloud. This service fits most closely within the SaaS cloud service model.
XaaS	Anything as a Service (XaaS)	Cloud providers often create their own names for additional cloud-hosted service offerings. These Anything/Everything as a Service" models are now commonly labeled XaaS offerings. XaaS is simply a placeholder term used in this book and in the industry for any cloud-based service that a cloud provider offers or might offer in the future (i.e., yet to be named applications and cloud services launched in the future).

Although I would like to provide you with example cloud service providers for each of the services listed in Table 1-4, there are just too many providers, with a good number of them regularly adding more of these services to their portfolio. This has and will continue to blur the line between public cloud providers because most will claim to provide many of these services; however, the quality and completeness of the services will vary widely. Finally, there are many cloud providers that have decided to offer and focus on only one cloud service, such as

Salesforce.com, which offers CRM. Compare this to public cloud providers Microsoft and Google, which initially launched email-centric cloud services (Hotmail and Gmail, respectively) but have significantly expanded to numerous IaaS, PaaS, and SaaS offerings.

In the following sections, I go into more depth on each service model, provide architecture examples of how the systems work, and present some case scenarios of real-world cloud service offerings available in the market today.

IAAS

Infrastructure services are the most common offering for public cloud providers. Staging IaaS in a private cloud requires a certain amount of initial investment but is often the starting point of the private cloud—adding SaaS and PaaS applications after the basic IaaS compute and storage services are in place. A basic IaaS offering provides VMs with either specific fixed or dynamic and VM sizing options.[2] Cloud providers might offer multiple VM sizes and OSs at fixed prices per hour, day, week, or month. The cost per VM rises as the amount of processor, memory, and storage increases. Note that one provider's definition of a processor unit might not be the same as another provider in terms of performance or speed. In a dynamic resource pricing model (for more information on this, see Chapter 5), the customer is charged a fee per unit of processor, memory, and storage which are more configurable and can afford more scalability than fixed-price IaaS offerings.

Public cloud providers often preconfigure specific offerings, such as VMs; however, the exact processor, memory, and disk space allocated to each VM might not be the same as other providers, so price comparison is not always easy. In fact, some public cloud providers have seemingly intentionally confused their VM configurations, VM size pricing, discount levels, transactions fees, and other metrics to obfuscate their true real-world costs to consumers. The key features you should be looking for are fixed or dynamic sizing, costs for expanding or increasing resources, and the ability to control your VMs through a web-based control panel. High-quality service providers will have an extensive self-service control panel that puts the consumer in control of the VMs, with the ability to

---

2 Some providers also offer physical servers within their IaaS offering. However, these are more expensive, because the provider has less ability to virtualize, load balance, and move workloads; in addition, the provider must have dedicated physical servers idle as excess capacity waiting for customer orders.

reboot, resize, and potentially take a snapshot and restore them. Also, be sure to examine the SLA and any guarantees of system availability.

When it comes to flexibility of options, your public IaaS provider should give you the ability to select your preferred OS, and possibly several versions of each OS to suit your needs. The agreement should clearly specify if backup and restore services are included, or if there are additional charges for those. An advanced feature that might be available is the ability to define your own subnetworks, load balancers, and firewall services.

Although public cloud providers offer a menu of fixed and variable-priced IaaS options, deploying your own private cloud will provide more customization, procurement, and security features unique to your organization. Table 1-5 presents a comparison of features for a typical public cloud service versus what is typical of a private cloud. It is important to note that public cloud providers are constantly enhancing their offerings and self-service capabilities, so the differentiation between public and private clouds pointed out in Table 1-5 does not represent every situation and cloud provider.

Table 1-5. IaaS cloud deployment comparison

Feature	Public	Private
VM-based server	■	■
Selection of OS	■	■
Choice of VM size (CPU, RAM), storage/disk	■	■
Ability to dynamically expand resources (CPU, RAM, disk) as needed	■	■
Ability to configure load balancing, firewalls, and subnetworks	■	■
Ability to define backup schedule and perform self-restores	■	■
Self-service control panel to manage VMs	■	■
Provide OS patches and version upgrades	■	■
Ability to select from multiple backup and restore schedules and retention times	o	■
Ability to select from multiple tiers of storage performance (e.g., high-transaction solid-state disks, slower file-based storage)	o	■

Feature	Public	Private
Ability to manage multiple groups of VMs with separate administrators, operators	o	▪
Ability to customize OS templates	o	▪
Ability to customize metering, billing process, ordering/ approval process	o	▪
Ability to install custom OS versions or customer-defined custom OS	o	▪
Meet consumer-specified security controls	o	▪
Consumer has visibility into security logs, real-time security threats, and activities	o	▪
Consumer has detailed real-time view into cloud operating, statistics, metering, and performance	o	▪
Ability to specify where data is stored (by country or datacenter facility)	o	▪
▪ = Typically available	o = Not typically available	

IaaS applications are defined by the provider in public clouds; the consumer is pretty much limited to the OS templates and versions and standard configuration options the public provider allows. As a part of a larger group of public customers, your ability to customize the offering is limited—applications and settings within the OS that is installed on the VM itself are the only aspects over which you would have complete control. A public cloud provider might allow you to create or import your own VM templates. Private cloud services are essentially a unique instance of the cloud service; you can customize them to a much greater degree.

Architecture of IaaS

The typical architecture of an IaaS application involves the creation of one or more server farms within multiple datacenters. The server farms each contain high-density blade servers in order to fit as many physical servers in a single rack as possible. Racks are installed in numerous rows, each one having at least two redundant power distribution units and cables into the datacenter power plant. The power plant also has various power backup resources, such as uninterruptible power supplies, batteries, and backup generators. Chapter 3 contains details on architecture, design, and deployment of datacenters, server farms, and cloud infrastructure.

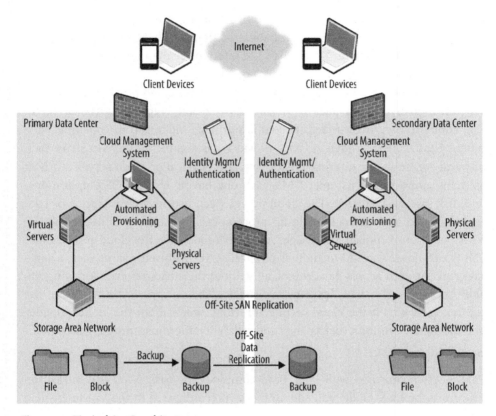

Figure 1-4. Typical IaaS architecture

Multiple pools of servers or server farms are often located in the same data-center both for expansion and local failover due to maintenance or continued operations during a hardware failure. For most large cloud providers, secondary datacenters are also deployed, as a geo-redundant system for both maintenance and facility-level failure protection. The cost of the datacenter facility, heating and cooling, power, and operations personnel are significant enough by themselves that most organizations heavily consolidate or avoid building them entirely—yet one more reason to use a cloud provider, instead.

Shared within the racks, or nearby, are the disk and storage systems—often in the form of a SAN or equivalent storage system. The storage systems are normally scalable independent of the server racks and utilize their own technologies to handle data de-duplication, thin provisioning, backup and recovery, snapshots, and replication to secondary datacenters. I will not spend a lot of time on SAN technologies here (you can see Chapter 3 for that), but these modern storage features afford the cloud provider significant cost savings through technology innovations and the sheer volume and quantity of storage. These savings are passed on to consumers of cloud. These costs are often lower than anything an individual consumer could negotiate and deploy on premises.

Within each physical or blade server in a rack, the cloud provider will have a virtualization hypervisor such as VMware, Microsoft Hyper-V, Citrix, or KVM. The configuration of these hypervisors is normally hidden from consumer visibility by the cloud provider. A cloud provider has significant ways to share each physical server across multiple customers; one physical or blade server can host as many as 20 to 50 customer VMs, each one having its own OS, applications, and disk storage allocation. The cloud provider can use advanced hypervisor configurations to automatically scale up processors and memory as needed to the VMs based on workload and usage. Additional tools give the cloud provider the ability to failover one VM to another physical server within the same rack, a separate rack, or even across datacenters, all without the customer even knowing the shift occurred—this is called *high availability*. This is a perfect example of the technologies within the cloud architecture that benefit both the cloud provider and ultimately, through cost savings and reliability, the consuming organization.

PAAS

PaaS is often confused with IaaS. PaaS combines the basic VMs and infrastructure from the IaaS model and adds software preconfigured in the VM to create a platform.

One example of a PaaS offering is a VM preconfigured with a database management system, all ordered via a single service catalog item. Platforms often consist of multiple VMs that form a multitiered application stack. Using the database example again, a multitiered application might consist of two frontend web servers, two application servers, and a clustered database server—six VMs in total, configured as one application platform or PaaS offering. Note that you can also classify the hosting of web pages—sometimes across numerous datacenters and providers called content delivery networks (CDNs)—as a PaaS offering.

The PaaS cloud service provider has already done the work of properly sizing the VMs and installing the OS, application software, and tools necessary for the customer to begin using the system immediately after provisioning. Technically, a customer could have ordered one or more VMs from the list of IaaS offerings and then installed its own database software, applications, and other tools; however, this requires technical expertise and time on the customer's part. Even more important is that in a PaaS offering, the cloud service provider now manages the entire platform, not just the OS, so all upgrades, patches, and support are handled by the cloud service provider. This is what makes PaaS unique compared to an IaaS offering.

Figure 1-5 demonstrates how the cloud provider has more operational responsibilities for PaaS and SaaS applications compared to IaaS.

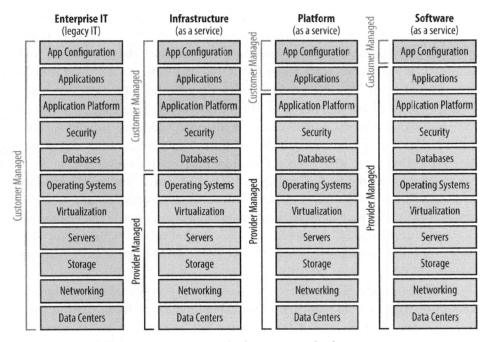

Figure 1-5. Cloud provider versus customer roles for managing cloud services

SAAS

SaaS includes many types of applications such as commercial off-the-shelf (COTS), open source, cloud provider–proprietary, and customer owned or developed. The application along with its required server, storage, and network infrastructure are hosted by the public cloud provider or optionally on a customer or third-party premises. Typical examples of SaaS include email services, collaboration, instant messaging, document libraries, and CRM.

Organizations often have too many applications to list, but it is important to remember that without significant recoding many legacy applications are not suitable for deployment in a cloud service. Many months or years of application transformation (a topic worthy of its own book, but I cover this in Chapter 4) are often necessary. In the meantime, there are techniques used mostly in private, community, and hybrid clouds that make porting of simple legacy applications possible while a full recode of the more complex legacy applications is performed.

Because each application in a SaaS offering is unique in its infrastructure requirements, licensing, cost, and deployment models, there is no single solution that cloud providers use. A smart cloud provider takes advantage of as much of the IaaS architecture described earlier. This means using a shared-storage system or SAN, virtualization of server hardware when possible, and redundancy and load balancing across multiple server farms and datacenters. SaaS cloud providers can implement dedicated server farms and applications for each consumer organization, but this is not nearly as cost effective as sharing a single instance of each application across a multitenant configuration. Additional benefits include the ability to deploy bug fixes quickly and upgrading software to the latest version, precluding the need to support numerous older software revisions.

Depending on the type of software, the manufacturer, the built-in security controls, and login and authentication systems, the cloud provider uses a combination of native software tools and custom-developed programs to maintain separation (or multitenancy) between consumer organizations. This means one consumer cannot see data, user accounts, or even the existence of any other consumer.

Public cloud providers include very economical licenses (after a significant amount of renegotiating with the software vendors) for software used in their SaaS offerings. In some cases, this is no mean feat, because the licensing models of software vendors do not often allow dynamic license expansion and contraction. In an average cloud system, the cloud provider takes on the responsibility of purchasing and maintaining a pool of licenses for all software products, and often across dozens of software manufacturers. This means that consumers do not need to bring their own licenses or purchase traditional software licenses of their own; they simply "rent" a license from the cloud provider. In a private cloud deployment model, you might not have as much leverage with software vendors to negotiate pay-per-user elastic licensing; however, it's possible that you will be able to use existing Enterprise License Agreements (ELAs) that your organization might already own and prefer to maintain.

Table 1-6 shows a comparison of the common capabilities and limitations of public cloud SaaS applications compared to traditional IT or private cloud application hosting. As you can see, a public cloud SaaS offering might not provide the same level of customization or features as a traditional IT or private cloud based-application—this is mostly because the public cloud SaaS application is a shared system, whereas private and traditional is dedicated to one customer.

Table 1-6. SaaS cloud deployment comparison

Feature	Public	Private
Backend infrastructure (server, compute, disk) provided and managed by cloud provider	▪	▪
Licenses furnished by provider, included as part of the per-user fee to consumer	▪	▪
Application updates and patches by provider	▪	▪
Define backup schedule, perform restores	▪	▪
Self-service control panel to manage VMs	▪	▪
Provide OS patches and version upgrades	▪	▪
Selection of additional storage or application options	Limited	▪
Ability to customize application features	Limited	▪
Host legacy customer applications and maintain app operations	○	▪
Ability to select from multiple tiers of storage performance	○	▪
Ability to customize metering as well as billing, ordering, and approval processes	○	▪
Meet consumer-specified security controls	○	▪
Consumer has visibility into security logs, real-time security threats, and activities	○	▪
Consumer has detailed real-time view into operating statistics, metering, and performance	○	▪
Ability to specify where data is stored (by country or datacenter facility)	○	▪

Feature	Public	Private
■ = Typically available	o = Not typically available	

One key aspect of SaaS offerings is that the cloud service provider manages the entire system, including all servers or VMs, the OSs, and all the applications. Technically, a customer could order an IaaS offering (plain VM with an OS loaded) and install its own software applications, but then the customer is responsible for all upgrades, patching, and support. With a true SaaS offering, the cloud service provider handles all management of the system, including all future versions/upgrades. For a diagram of provider responsibilities across IaaS, PaaS, and SaaS offerings, refer back to Figure 1-5, earlier in this chapter. Across all cloud services, the consumer still has the ability to perform some configuration within certain limitations that the provider and application allow.

Other Cloud Service Subcategories

So far, IaaS, PaaS, and SaaS are the primary categories of cloud services that we've explored. Within these primary categories, there are numerous cloud services that have their own "as a service" names; technically, however, they are individual use cases or applications that fit within the definition of IaaS, PaaS, or SaaS.

WORKPLACE AS A SERVICE

To be accurate, Workplace as a Service (WPaaS) fits within the definition of an IaaS or even a PaaS. Similar to IaaS and PaaS, numerous physical servers, each with a hypervisor system, are pooled to offer a multitude of VMs to the consumers. These VMs are very similar to the VMs in an IaaS offering, except that they are normally installed with a desktop OS rather than a server-based OS. Microsoft Windows or Linux are common desktop OSs. Citrix is one of the most popular hypervisor technologies for WPaaS. Desktop as a Service or virtual desktop interface (VDI) are other names that cloud providers use for these hosted virtual-desktop platforms.

The VMs in a WPaaS solution also include application software for users such as Microsoft Office. Users log on to the VMs through the Internet or other WAN communications circuit and essentially "take control" of the virtual desktop. All processing (compute, memory, and storage) is actually running within the cloud service provider's datacenter with only display, keyboard, and mouse activity transmitted over the network. The end user functions as a thin client using a desktop, notebook, tablet, or other thin-client terminal.

The applications that are shown for one consumer organization, or subset of users within an organization, might be different from other users. This is done through the configuration of roles and profiles in the OS and application software. Based on the user's logon credentials, certain applications are available and preinstalled on the virtual desktop. There might be several levels or types of users that each consumer organization defines, such as Executive User, Knowledge User, or Task User. In this example, an Executive virtual desktop would have all available software installed, and maybe a higher level of storage and compute or memory, compared to that of a mid-level Knowledge user. A Task user might be a specific role for end users who only access a single program rather than an entire virtual desktop with a suite of applications. Of course, the cost that the cloud provider charges will depend on the definition of the users, the size of the VMs, and the cost of the software licenses for the apps.

In a public cloud service model, the cloud provider is responsible for all management and upgrades to the OS and all applications. In a private cloud model, the organization that owns/operates the cloud could take on full OS and application upgrade responsibility or allow participation from end-user departments to manage portions of the application stack or user profiles. The consuming users need only load the thin-client or remote desktop software tool that enables the connection through the cloud to the virtual desktop server farm.

You can also integrate custom applications into the virtual desktop solution, but this usually requires the cloud provider to host the application itself and assume full responsibility for the application lifecycle, including all management and future upgrades. Because the customer already owns the application, cloud service providers might not charge a license fee for these homegrown applications, but they will normally charge fees to manage them (e.g., backup and restore, upgrades, and patches).

Use-Case Scenario: WPaaS

A good example scenario for WPaaS is to replace traditional end-user desktop computers with smaller, cheaper, and less complex thin-client or edge devices—even a mobile tablet. These edge devices have a monitor or display with a keyboard and mouse but very little in terms of processing power, memory, and storage. In this WPaaS scenario, end users log on to their thin-client or edge devices as if they were a normal personal computer; however, all of the computing power, memory, data, OS, and applications are actually run on a more powerful server within a datacenter. A pool of servers (typically with a virtualization or hypervisor) is configured to provide these virtual desktop services to end users as they log on to their virtual desktops. Hardware and software is easier to manage in this centralized computing environment because data and applications are not stored on each end-user edge device.

The benefits of this WPaaS scenario are lower cost for end-user computer operations, maintenance, and ongoing support. The end user is, in theory, not aware that she is using a thin-client edge device because the operating system and application software function the same as if she were running on a full desktop personal computer. WPaaS also makes it possible for end users to log on to their virtual desktops via a mobile device such as a tablet—getting the same user interface and applications on that device as if they were using a full PC. Users can even leave an application open on their virtual desktop and go to another office, home, or airport and log back on to their virtual desktop on another edge device—bringing up the applications and data right where they left it.

Microsoft Virtual Desktop Infrastructure, Citrix XenDesktop, and Vmware Horizon View are some of the top desktop virtualization software platforms used by cloud providers or organizations with private clouds. Each of these software vendors has multiple product differentiators both at the server and end-user level. There are many other desktop virtualization systems that public cloud providers utilize behind the scenes, and they do not always publish which software platform they use.

APPLICATION PUBLISHING

Application publishing uses similar technology as the aforementioned WPaaS. This service has one or more individual applications available to end users instead of the entire OS desktop interface. This is ideal for several types of situations, including the following:

- Task workers who only need to run one application that they use all day long (there's no point in presenting a full virtual desktop OS for these users).

- Application publishing for very large or legacy applications that need to be available to a large number of end users but are easier to manage when in the cloud rather than installing them on every end user's computer. By publishing an application, end users can click an icon on their full desktop OS and run the application from the cloud. The application technically runs in the cloud with display, keyboard, and mouse activity transferring over the Internet. The application is never installed on the end user's desktop computer, so whenever the application is updated, the user gets the latest version immediately; there's no need to upgrade it on every end-user desktop.

- Mobile devices (e.g., tablets and smartphones) are now very common and also greatly benefit from application publishing. This app publishing is particularly important for mobile computing because end users rarely turn their devices over to an IT department to install or routinely update software, especially when the mobile devices might be owned by the end user, not the company.

Application publishing is quickly gaining popularity with some public cloud providers such as Microsoft Azure. Azure, as described in Chapter 5, has recently added a new service called RemoteApp. With RemoteApp, administrators can select any cloud-hosted applications that users are allowed to use. End users can run the RemoteApp application on a Windows, Macintosh, Android, iOS, and Windows Mobile device—running full Microsoft Office applications, for example, on their desktop or mobile devices. Behind the scenes, these applications are fully run on the cloud servers within Azure with only the user interface transmitted to the end user's desktop or mobile device. This RemoteApp service is a good example of a cost-effective way to manage a wide variety of end-user devices and enterprise applications at a very low cost. Because RemoteApp is a cloud-based service, organizations pay only for the actual services used, and Azure automatically scales servers up and down to keep up with utilization.

Use-Case Scenario: Application Publishing

A good example case scenario for application publishing is very similar to WPaaS or virtual desktops. Instead of the end user seeing and using a full desktop OS such as Microsoft Windows, application publishing involves just one or more individual applications visible and usable by the end users rather than the full Windows desktop in this scenario. The organization's IT administrator configures which application(s) are available to each end user. From the end-user perspective, he sees a typical icon for an application, just as if it were the normal Windows desktop. The application is run in the usual way from the end user's mobile or desktop thin-client edge device, but it is technically running "in the cloud" at the datacenter. Just as with WPaaS, users can leave an application running and move to another location (home, another office, etc.) and log on to a different end-user device, such as a mobile tablet, and resume their application where they left off.

The benefits of this application publishing scenario are lower cost for the organization's IT department to deploy and upgrade software because there is no need to install the software onto each end user's personal computer. Organizations might also experience improved data security because the IT department has more control of software access and data storage as a result of there being nothing stored or maintained on the end user's edge device.

The future of application publishing holds huge promise. There is only one major downside to using it: users must be connected to the Internet or connected to the cloud in some way to use their applications; there is no offline use. There is some newer application publishing software that incorporates an offline capability. These applications will still run over the cloud and require access via the Internet, but it will save a copy of itself on the local desktop or mobile device the first time it is run. After this background copy is finished, the next time the end user runs the application, it will still try to run the application online, but if there is no connection to the Internet, the application will run locally. When the user next runs the application while connected to the cloud, if the application has been updated to a newer version, it will still run remotely while quietly updating the stored version for offline use.

DEVELOPMENT AND TEST AS A SERVICE

A Development and Test as a Service (also called Dev/Test) offering technically fits within the definition of PaaS with several unique features that facilitate application development, testing, and automated release management efforts.

Customers benefit from a Dev/Test by being able to quickly launch new VMs within minutes, perform testing of an application, and turn off the Dev/Test service when it is no longer needed. Because all the servers are hosted with VMs in the cloud, the consuming organization does not need to prepurchase and deploy a dedicated server farm, sitting idly when an application development team has finished their work, or between application releases. Dev/Test teams often utilize numerous VMs residing in on-premises private cloud facilities or in a public cloud. Then, there are multiple work streams, multiple development teams, testing and quality assurance teams, and multiple versions of each application being developed simultaneously—all of this benefiting from the elasticity and pay-as-you-go features of a private or public cloud.

Use-Case Scenario: Dev/Test

A good example scenario is when the application development team needs a new 10-computer environment deployed. With one purchase via the cloud management portal, 10 new VMs are provisioned with two clustered SQL servers, two frontend web servers, two middleware application servers, and four QA workstations (to be used by the development team for testing). Upon launch, the application team can load its custom application code and begin further programming or testing. It can add or remove additional VMs as needed or take a "snapshot" of the environment, test the system, and roll back the entire 10-system environment to the snapshot state, retrying its test each time based on the snapshot image.

There are often many versions of the environment held on the storage system so the development team can roll backward or forward to various software versions. The development team can also operate multiple sets of the 10-system environment so that the operations team can do routine testing or troubleshooting against a copy of the production code while the development team works to develop the next release. This requires multiple sets of the 10-VM environment, but this is economical because everything is based on VMs that can be brought up and down, paying only for actual usage to the cloud provider.

Specific features of a Dev/Test environment are detailed in the list that follows (the basic offering and systems architecture is the same as IaaS, which means there is a pool of physical servers, each running a hypervisor system providing capacity for hundreds of thousands of VMs on-demand):

Isolated Dev/Test network

Many organizations have strict policies and procedures that must be followed whenever a new VM or application is installed in the production network. In a Dev/Test environment, the application developers need to have the ability to quickly bring VMs up, reconfigure them, install application code, test the code, and then shut the systems down. All of this is performed regularly during the time a development team is creating its application for production release, and can last for months. For the developers to have this freedom without being restrained by paperwork, isolating the Dev/Test network from the production network using a firewall is a common technique.

Even if both the production and Dev/Test networks are hosted by a cloud provider, organizations want to protect their production network from untested or new application code. Some Dev/Test systems provide a separate subnetwork for each application project, so that one application development team cannot interfere with others. This protects other development teams from such possibilities as an untested, "run-away" application clogging the network with traffic.

Multiple versions, snapshot, and rollback

The ability of the application development team to make a backup or snapshot of a VM—or the entire environment—was briefly touched on earlier. This snapshot saves a copy to disk and makes it possible for the development team to run numerous copies of its system. It can perform testing against a copy of its environment rather than on a single instance, and avoid potentially messing it up. If testing is successful, a rollback of the environment is not necessary, and this set of VMs would become the new baseline release. This feature is a very significant benefit of using VM/hypervisor technology, and by paying only for the usage of VMs and storage, the consuming organization truly benefits from on-demand just-in-time provisioning and shutdown in developing its application projects. Creating numerous copies of VMs with many different versions can consume a great deal of storage space; thus a great deal of storage space can be required by the system. To keep costs low, delete older copies that are no longer needed.

ALM tools

Many application development teams use ALM tools to help coordinate and facilitate the development process. You can install these tools on one or more VMs within the cloud, alongside the application VMs and database systems. The application development team uses the ALM tools to track its project milestones, maintain a code repository, perform QA checks, perform load testing, and promote application revisions from Dev/Test into production. Popular ALM suites in the industry include offerings from Microsoft, IBM, and Hewlett-Packard. There are also smaller tools, and even open source tools, that an application team can use. Additionally, some cloud service providers that offer Dev/Test will offer the ALM suites as an option—this is a nice benefit, because the ALM suite will already be configured and ready for use upon ordering, and the licensing costs the cloud provider charges might be less than a single customer would pay for its own copy.

Promotion into staging and production

Some Dev/Test offerings provide the application development team with the ability to promote individual or multiple VMs to the next phase of the application lifecycle. For example, when all testing of an application release is completed in the Dev/Test environment, clicking a "promote" button would automatically copy or move the VMs to a staging or production network within the cloud provider's datacenter, facilitating an Agile software delivery and continuous application delivery automation (for more information about this, refer to Chapter 4). An additional benefit to the customer is the ability to launch a new release of its application into production while maintaining the availability of its Dev/Test environment for the next release. If the Dev/Test VMs are no longer needed, they can be de-provisioned and the customer stops paying for them. Figure 1-6 shows a Dev/Test network with multiple isolated network segments for development, testing, and production.

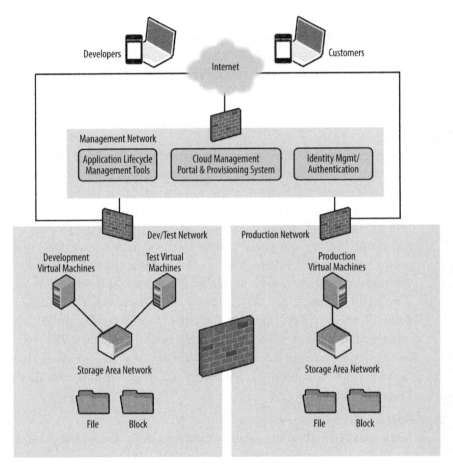

Figure 1-6. Sample Dev/Test architecture

Pricing for Dev/Test offerings is typically in the same range as multiple VMs within an IaaS—any ALM tools you purchase will of course incur additional charges. You pay either a fixed fee and/or variable fees each day, week, or month for using the VMs and storage. You can pick your VM sizes, OS templates, and storage amount just as you would in production. You often don't need as large a VM in Dev/Test as you do in production, because you are usually not running simultaneous production users (unless you are using your Dev/Test service for load testing and quality assurance). This can result in savings by ordering smaller, less powerful VMs in Dev/Test.

Figure 1-6 shows a Dev/Test network with multiple isolated network segments for development and testing and production. In theory, there could be even further network segmentation for the Dev/Test and production portions of this notional architecture and for each unique application or development team. Also, Figure 1-6 intentionally does not indicate whether this is a private or public cloud. Many organizations utilize public cloud for its significant elasticity and no initial investment in IT assets that a private cloud requires. Some organizations use a combination of public and private clouds to do their development testing and hosting of production applications using ALM tools to replicate, synchronize, or promote development code between environments.

STORAGE AS A SERVICE

Storage as a Service is an essential part of the IaaS and PaaS offerings because VMs need storage in order to run. Storage as a Service provides various forms of data storage, as described in the list that follows, via the cloud, which makes it possible for end users to access their data from any location, personal computer, tablet, or other device connected to the cloud or Internet. Storage as a Service provides low-cost elastic storage that expands and shrinks based on utilization. Deployment and operational best practices for storage is detailed in Chapters 2 and 3.

Storage as a Service is distinct from requesting additional storage as an option for an IaaS VM: Storage as a Service is storage sold as a standalone product. Because this storage is not connected to a specific server or VM, it can be sold and configured in several forms.

It is important to understand that cloud storage is often sold and described in terms of the type of storage being offered, such as object storage. The underlying storage method (e.g., SAN, network-attached storage [NAS], and direct-attached storage [DAS]) is not disclosed to cloud consumers. Refer to Chapter 3 for details on how to build a private-enterprise cloud and use this cloud storage hardware, along with software, to create a cloud storage service offering.

These are the forms of data storage provided by Storage as a Service via the cloud:

Object-based storage

Object-based storage is the most common form of cloud storage. It can be sold and configured as a standalone service offering without a VM. Object storage uses a specialized technique of writing data and metadata used for long-term data storage, archiving, and unique applications that benefit from this technology. Public cloud providers sell this, under various marketing brand names, for customers that want backup, archiving, and file storage services. Many popular desktop and server backup and storage applications sold to consumers are actually just frontend interfaces to object-based storage systems hosted by a cloud provider.

Object-based storage is not a particularly high-performance storage system, but it can handle very large files (or objects) and related metadata, which is actually why it is ideal for a cloud environment. It is optimized for data that is stored once and held indefinitely. It is ideal for use cases and applications for which the network latency is unknown or might be high depending on the end user's location, device, or network bandwidth. Object storage is capable of maintaining the connection and reliability across these nonpermanent, usually Internet-based connections.

The cloud provider uses specialized software to present object-based storage features to the cloud consumer, utilizing the underlying SAN, NAS, DAS, or similar form of storage.

Block storage

Block storage requires a host server or VM and is similar to a local hard drive or the default storage included with every VM ordered. You can add the storage to existing VMs or you can add it as independent volumes that the VM OS formats and manages.

Block storage is typically capable of higher performance and is more sensitive to latency. It is typical to use block storage as the primary volume for VMs and applications within a datacenter and within the cloud provider. Block storage is also ideal for heavy read/write functionality versus object storage, which is more adept with write once/read many use cases. It is less ideal to map a block-storage volume across the Internet or slower, higher latency network connection.

Pricing for storage is usually by the gigabyte (GB) or terabyte (TB) depending on the cloud service provider and the quantity of storage purchased. Because this is a cloud-based offering, providers normally charge only for the amount of data you have utilized rather than preallocated amounts. This pay-as-you-use storage model is one of the fundamental characteristics of cloud computing.

Daily backups should be a standard feature of Storage as a Service pricing. The cloud service provider needs to maintain their SLAs as much as you need them to protect your data, so a base level of backup is normally standard and included in the price. The provider might also offer more frequent backups (including real-time data replication) and long-term data retention options.

BACKUP AS A SERVICE

Backup and Recovery as a Service (Backup as a Service) is a category of service that replicates data to multiple IT systems and datacenters with the purpose of recovery should the primary data be lost or becomes corrupt. Backup and recovery of servers, applications, and data is nothing new to a datacenter or IT department. In a cloud environment, there are changes in the backup/recovery hardware and processes that are needed to backup and protect a cloud environment. Chapter 3 details operational best practices for cloud backup and restore.

Backup as a Service is often sold and configured in two variations described here (in both variations, the underlying service is usually object-based cloud storage; however, public cloud providers charge less for these backup services as the data is normally written once, seldom accessed/read, and stored on slow relatively disk media):

Upgraded backup and restore options

IaaS, PaaS, and SaaS applications normally include some default level of backup and restore capability and SLA defined by the cloud provider. Customers who need more data retention or faster recovery options might want to order upgrades to the base level of IaaS/PaaS backup.

Depending on the service offering, platforms, or software applications, these backup and recovery options can vary widely. For example, a normal backup of a PaaS system might be performed daily by the cloud provider; however, a customer might want to have database snapshots performed every four hours. This way, during a restoration request, the data is more up to date (this is referred to as *recovery point objective* or *RPO*). There might also be a need for daily mailbox backups of the email system, rather than the entire database. This accommodates more granular restoration of data, but the cloud provider might charge more for this level of backup.

Depending on your need, it is important to consider the cost for X years of data retention, whether the data is stored offsite from the primary datacenter(s), and how long it will take for the cloud provider to actually restore the data upon your request (this is referred to as *recovery time objective* or *RTO*). Most modern cloud providers and datacenters are moving away from tape-based backup systems, opting instead to use SANs (or equivalent NAS, object, or storage network systems), snapshot techniques, de-duplication, and disk-based backup hardware to improve the RTO (for definitions and details on these technologies, see Chapter 3). If there are regulatory or legal requirements for ensuring that the backup data is held within the United States, you will need to confirm the cloud provider offers sovereign data options or consider a private cloud deployment model which offers more flexibility.

Online backup and archiving

This variation of Backup as a Service is unique in that the source data is usually located at an existing or legacy customer datacenter. Backup soft-ware agents or a backup hardware appliance device would be installed at each legacy enterprise datacenter. All backup software agents within the datacenter are usually already in place, but the target tape or disk system for backups is shifted to the new backup hardware appliance. This local backup appliance holds the initial backup data and then automatically repli-cates it to the cloud provider's datacenter(s) over the Internet or another WAN circuit. This means that the data is backed up both locally at the orig-inal datacenter and offsite for maximum protection. The local backup appli-ance is usually only large enough to hold the most recent one to four weeks' worth of data. The cloud provider hosts a massive amount of stor-age capacity and can retain all of the backup data for many years, depend-ing on the customer's needs.

The online backup service is both very cost effective compared to a legacy datacenter maintaining large tape drive libraries and sending tapes offsite regularly. This online backup offering is also ideal for migrating data from a legacy datacenter to a new cloud provider.

Figure 1-7 shows an example of an online backup architecture in which data is backed up locally within the primary datacenter but also replicated, in near-real time or via snapshots, to a secondary datacenter or datacenters. In this example, the data is transferred via the Internet but this could also be performed via high-speed private data circuits.

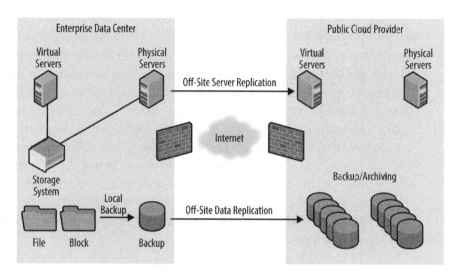

Figure 1-7. Typical online backup service architecture

OTHER "AS A SERVICE" OFFERINGS

Cloud providers often market additional "as a service" offerings to customers. Most cloud offerings technically fit within the definitions of the IaaS, PaaS, or SaaS models. There is a tendency for cloud providers to market and advertise their services by using newly invented terminology—something called Anything as a Service or *X* as a Service (XaaS).

The following list describes some of the unique XaaS offerings that have been coined (however, note that this is an ever-growing list, as cloud providers are constantly inventing new names for their services):

Data as a Service

Data as a Service is normally offered as part of a public or community deployment model, where the cloud service provider hosts a large centralized repository of information. Consumer organizations pay a fee to search for and access all of this information in the cloud. This data can be gathered and maintained by the cloud service provider, or it can be customer-specific information that just needs to be hosted in the cloud for distributed users across the world to access. Often, the cloud service provider hosting the Data as a Service operates a behind-the-scenes hybrid network that collects the data from multiple sources and provides the result to consumers for a fee.

From a technical point of view, Data as a Service is a form of SaaS that has existed for years over the Internet, long before cloud computing became a popular term. Good examples are the LexisNexis service for legal information, or pre-Wikipedia online encyclopedias. As long as the data is useful and valuable to customers who are willing to pay for it, it can be hosted in a Data as a Service model. Data services also specialize in gathering or collecting massive amounts of data from numerous sources, formatting or indexing the data to be more useful to consumers. One difference between this data service and a website hosting massive data is that the data service offering will usually have API or database-level access rather than solely rely upon a web-based frontend. This makes it possible for data in the Data as a Service model to interact with on-premises-hosted options or other cloud service offerings.

Customer Relationship Management as a Service (CRMaaS)

This service is technically a SaaS offering (and in some cases, PaaS), providing clients with a customer relationship management system. These are used to track customer sales, contacts, orders, issue tracking/ticketing, and a complete history of customer transactions. CRMaaS offerings are very popular in both public- and private-cloud methods—before the term became heavily utilized. Salesforce.com is an excellent example of this type of SaaS-based CRMaaS.

Email as a Service

Email as a Service is usually a SaaS offering providing customers with cloud-hosted email, calendar, and collaboration tools. Being a SaaS offering, the cloud provider is responsible for the management, operations, and upgrades of the entire software application, OS, and VMs that comprise the Email as a Service offering. Email as a Service offerings are popular in both public and private cloud models. Public email providers include Microsoft Office 365, Google's Gmail, and Yahoo! Mail, whereas private clouds might use Microsoft Exchange, IBM Lotus Notes, or Novell GroupWise.

Planning and Architecture Best Practices

Based on lessons learned and experience from across the cloud industry, you should consider the following best practices for your organization's planning.

PLANNING FOR CLOUD

Planning for the transition to the cloud is the most critical factor for success. Organizations often have a significant number of legacy computing resources such as servers and datacenters that will need to be transitioned or eliminated in order to achieve the true cost savings and flexibility provided by a cloud. Organizations can chose to modernize existing IT systems with cloud-like features such as virtualization and automation, or make a plan to completely transition some or all IT applications and infrastructure to a public, private, or hybrid cloud. Planning involves technical, financial, operational, and business process changes for your IT department and possibly your entire organization:

Business planning
 Evaluate the business needs and how IT services those needs:

- Consider what applications, server farms, storage, or entire datacenters might not be critical to the mission of your organization and your customers.

- Identify and prioritize by application of business function—not necessarily by technology—IT services and applications that are commodity functions and not unique to your company (i.e., would shifting to a cloud provider or service relieve your IT operation from this burden with equal or better services and costs?).

- What could your existing, or restructured IT department better focus on if some or all commodity IT services were outsourced or migrated to the cloud? Focus on applications that are unique to your business and your customers that could benefit from increased support, enhancements, resources, operations, security, and so on.

- Evaluate current contractors, temporary employees, and resource levels. Nobody is saying that a cloud service should automatically include staff reductions, but would realigning current staffing (permanent or contracted) benefit your organization as a whole?

- Evaluate how the existing IT department interacts with and provides services to the overall organization. Is IT a trusted advisor and facilitator of services to the business and your customers or is IT perceived as an obstacle (for whatever reasons) to the business needs? This is a good time to reconsider how IT provides IT services, how IT might centralize (i.e., broker) IT services from multiple departments, possibly removing some legacy silos or unnecessary tiers or structures.

Financial planning

Evaluate the financial aspect of your current IT organization and business operations:

- Analyze the cost of all current IT infrastructure systems, datacenters, applications licensing, data storage, and ongoing operational costs.

- Analyze the cost of existing IT personnel, contractors, and any supporting vendors or service contracts.

- Begin identifying any particular applications or legacy systems that you know or suspect are outdated, cost more to support than they are worth, and could be retired or replaced.

- Include financial calculations for datacenter, network, server, storage, and application lifecycle replacements, depending on the useful service period (usually three to five years). Consider infrastructure costs for items for which warranties have expired, are about to expire, or are such a significant ongoing cost that an alternative might be considered.

- Remember to include indirect costs such as power, cooling, building facilities, leased assets, or other costs that the business incurs but might not have been directly budgeted from an IT perspective (until now).

- Attempt to break down all costs to a per-user and per-application basis so that you can truly understand the cost per user per month (or year) for your IT operations. This is often the most difficult and underestimated aspect of financial planning—most organizations underestimate or simply have never calculated all of the direct and indirect financial costs.

- Calculate where your major IT assets are in terms of their depreciation schedule, because this will affect your financial plans, return on investment strategy, and possibly the entire idea of transitioning to the cloud.

Technical planning

Decide your current technical infrastructure, operational processes, facilities, equipment and software lifecycles, current staff skillsets, and effectiveness of your current IT department:

- Evaluate which applications, data, or workloads are mission critical for performance, availability, and security and whether hosting on premises (enterprise IT or private cloud) is required.

- Determine a draft list of candidate workloads that might be commodities and outsourced to a cloud provider (or not).

- Evaluate current personnel skillsets and whether services hosted in a cloud might be more beneficial (the cloud provider likely has more specialized and skilled personnel).

- Assess and document which data might be required by policy, preference, or regulation to be hosted in a particular country or region.

- Which of the business's mission-critical applications (that your customers use) can most benefit from a dynamically scalable, elastic environment to handle spikes in the workloads or regularly expanding and contracting workloads.

- Determine the security protections and risk profiles for each application or dataset.

CLOUD DEPLOYMENT MODELS

Consider which applications, data, and workloads are best suited to be hosted in a low-cost public cloud and which might require a more customizable private cloud (possibly one hosted on premises):

- Decide which workloads and data could be hosted in a public cloud and any concerns or risks with hosting in a public cloud environment (regardless of provider at this point). Then, consider which applications and data are too sensitive, too specialized, or otherwise would be best hosted in a private cloud (hosted on premises or in a managed private cloud hosted by a provider).

- Determine whether your existing IT organization and staff should or could manage (continue to manage?) all of the applications, server farms, networks, and storage. and which workloads could be moved to the cloud. It is recommended that the internal IT department focus on applications that are critical to your business customers and that are unique (not a common commodity IT service that anyone can host). This consideration of who will host, manage, and operate any future clouds or modernized IT services combines technical, financial, and business planning.

- If there are significant requirements for a private cloud, consider whether your organization can use a managed private cloud hosted by a provider or if deploying an on-premises private cloud is required. I recommend leaving out the financial and operational considerations of this decision initially when making this assessment.

- Industry trends as organizations choose cloud deployment models:

  — Although experience and industry trends show that customers have a preference for the economics provided by public cloud, it is private clouds that offer more flexibility with customized features and security.

  — Small businesses often have little existing internal IT assets and are more likely to use public cloud SaaS models to meet their needs. Many of these small businesses start out using a SaaS offering rather than building something on premises and migrating to a cloud-based SaaS.

  — Larger businesses and public sector organizations often have a significant number of applications and data that they determine is best hosted on premises using a private cloud. If some workloads can benefit from a public cloud, the private cloud is enhanced with hybrid cloud management capabilities so that some workloads are provisioned to one or more public cloud services.

  — Trends over the past few years show little adoption of this community model. The primary concern with a community cloud is how the cloud is managed. Standards of communications, cloud management systems, and the services offered need to be agreed upon and upheld across multiple departments or organizations—not just initially, but for many years. This is where business challenges begin to reveal themselves. What happens if, in the future, one of the community cloud departments or organizations changes its business, budget, security standards, or other priorities? What if that department was offering critical resources to the community cloud that will no longer be available at the same level as originally agreed upon?

— A recent industry trend is public cloud providers launching new hybrid services. These hybrid services focus on integrating traditional enterprise datacenters, typically on a customer's premises, with public cloud services. With this hybrid capability, customers can federate authentication systems, synchronize data, support both enterprise and cloud applications, and failover enterprise servers to public cloud VMs. Consider this type of hybrid cloud (public cloud reaching back into internal enterprise IT) as a technique for early adoption, bursting, or long-term migration to a public cloud.

DEVELOPMENT AND TESTING

- Often the easiest workloads to shift to a cloud computing environment are software development and testing tasks. Considering the immediate on-demand elasticity and low cost of basic VMs in a public cloud, it is often difficult to justify the legacy method of staging and hosting your own internal servers for Dev/Test purposes.

- Consider what security level, if any, that the Dev/Test environment must meet. Dev/Test environments don't usually host production data that might have security or privacy concerns. Because of this, development, coding, quality testing, and user testing utilizing a public cloud provider is a very attractive service offering.

- Remember that a basic IaaS application that offers VMs is not necessarily suitable for a complete Dev/Test environment. The more robust Dev/Test environments often have ALM tools for developers to store programming code, testing tools, and the ability to promote development code to testing or production. When evaluating public cloud providers or building your own private cloud for Dev/Test purposes, consider what tools and operating systems are supported by the cloud platform.

- Consider what ALM tools your company or developers utilize and whether the cloud provider will make these tools available, at potentially lower cost in a shared model, or how you can install your own copies of the ALM tools into the cloud service.

- Consider implementing multiple virtual networks or subnetworks within your Dev/Test environment to simulate development and production networks. You might also want the ability to promote your Dev/Test applications into production subnetworks using ALM tools, as mentioned earlier.

- Consider how you will save your Dev/Test cloud systems when there is a pause in the project. Will the cloud provider still charge for idle Dev/Test systems that continue to take up storage in the cloud? How long will the cloud provider maintain the idle (turned off) Dev/Test systems   before deleting them?

WORKPLACE AS A SERVICE, REMOTE DESKTOPS, AND APPLICATION PUBLISHING

- When considering hosting virtual desktops in the cloud, assess the users and their applications and whether they are suitable for hosting in the cloud.

- Consider that most virtual desktop services do not work in an offline mode (when disconnected from the Internet or corporate network); this might require data replication back to local laptops or tablets so that users can work offline while traveling, for example.

- Consider where the data will be located for your normal desktop users and applications versus those who might use virtual desktops from the cloud. How will these users interact or share the same experience if there is data held in the cloud and also data back on the internal network?

- Carefully test the cloud-based virtual desktop and applications for printing capability back to a local printer wherever the end user might be located (e.g., a hotel, at home, or at a remote office location).

- Consider application publishing of one or more applications for those that a large number of users need to access from any office, location, or Internet/

cloud accessible device. This is often more agile and easier to accept (by end users) than a full virtual desktop environment.

- Consider the IT skills and effort required to manage a full remote desktop or application publishing environment. The creation of OS images, applications, profiles, and permissions is significant—not necessarily more than would be required on an internal traditional desktop environment.

Operational Transformation

Key topics in this chapter:

- Transforming managed services into cloud services
- Virtualization of servers, network, and storage
- The relentless pursuit of automation
- Adding customer visibility and transparency into cloud operations, monitoring, and reports
- Accessing cloud services
- Data sovereignty and on-shore support operations
- New backup and recovery techniques
- Cloud operational changes in an Information Technology Infrastructure Library model (ITIL)
- Operational transformation best practices

This chapter focuses on the operational lessons learned during the initial years of the cloud services industry. Based on customer cloud deployments and industry leader experience, it became apparent that the transition to the cloud is much more than just implementing new technology. The day-to-day aspects of how an organization operates also need to evolve, whether you're following a public cloud consumption model or especially if you're deploying an enterprise private cloud for your organization.

Whether you have started your cloud transition or are still considering it, this chapter will help you on your way. We will discuss topics valuable to any organization looking to gain the benefits of cloud computing or just modernize a traditional IT department. I will cover the changes relating to IT and datacenter operations, changes in staffing skills, processes, and recommended organizational changes to carry out a successful transition to the cloud—in other words, how to transform to this new style of IT service delivery.

Transforming Managed Services

Many organizations have a significant amount of existing network, computer, and application infrastructure hosted on one or more datacenters. Modernizing these existing datacenters involves deploying new technology and processes that are also critical to a cloud environment. In this section, I will cover specific people, process, and technology topics to transform from a traditional managed service within existing enterprise datacenters to a cloud environment.

An area in which organizations fail is underestimating the transformation from a managed service to a cloud service. One common mistake made by even the most experienced IT managers is to take a traditional server farm or datacenter used over the past 10+ years, implement some form of virtualization, and then declare that you now have a cloud service. Although many are successful in staging some individual cloud-like capabilities and processes within traditional enterprise datacenters, it is the traditional managed services model that must be replaced with a service-oriented cloud model. You can begin the transition to a cloud service model within an existing enterprise datacenter by first adopting new procedures and technologies, improving IT personnel skillsets, and then deploying an initial private cloud infrastructure within the existing datacenter. Here are some high-level guidelines for modernizing an enterprise datacenter, and managed services mode, that will start your journey to cloud services:

Automation

A key aspect of cloud computing is the automated provisioning of compute and application services. To truly meet the cloud characteristics of elasticity and on-demand resource ordering, allocation, and provisioning, you cannot rely on human beings or manual processes. Your cloud service must be able to provision new services on the fly, anytime, 24-7-365, without delay or human intervention. If you are still relying heavily on manual processes and personnel, you are still in the *managed services* model, not a cloud model. To host cloud services at an appropriately low price, you must implement automation in as many places as possible, or you will not achieve the proper financial business model to support a cloud service offering. Automation isn't just about cost efficiency: it's also about providing consistent quality, rapid provisioning and scale up/scale down, continuous software updates and patching, and auditable processes for security and compliance.

Key Take-Away

If you still rely on manual processes and extensive operational staff, you are still in a managed services model—not a cloud model.

Security

Although you are automating the provisioning of new servers or virtual machines (VMs), you should not remove the process for a security accreditation or security officer's approval. The cloud provider, along with the customer in private cloud scenarios, must adapt legacy security processes to fit within this automated cloud provisioning environment. This usually means preapproving or certifying the templates by which all new VMs are launched. If the template is approved, so too should be any VM that is an exact replica of that template. All manual security approvals or pausing within the automated ordering and provisioning workflow should be avoided.

Key Take-Away

Security operations need to adapt to support the automated deployment of new servers, applications, and software-defined datacenter resources (e.g. storage, networking, monitoring). Security operations are often one of the most difficult legacy processes that must adapt to the new style of IT.

Operations and monitoring

Due to the level of automation, the cloud system should also automatically update asset and configuration management databases within the cloud datacenter. This means updating server, network, application, and security monitoring systems at all hours of the day or night. When you bring new cloud services (e.g., VMs) online, you should immediately add them to the security and operational systems so that proper management and monitoring can begin. If a manual process by a human being is involved, there will be delays in the system going online and becoming part of the monitored ecosystem, which will result in less guaranteed consistency and build quality.

Attempting to use existing IT or datacenter staffing and processes can lead to failure. Many legacy pre-cloud IT operational team structures and skill-sets are aligned by technology such as servers, operating system (OS) type, storage, networking, and security. Consider implementing staff and structure in a more service-oriented model such as automation, infrastructure, and applications, with a focus on the end-customer application and use case. I discuss this in depth later in this chapter.

Key Take-Away

Legacy enterprise operational staff and processes should be evaluated and possibly restructured with a new cloud service-oriented model.

Cloud management

The cloud management system usually begins with a web-based portal that gives customers visibility into their cloud services, billing, reporting, and self-service management of their applications and user accounts. A cloud management platform, which is detailed in Chapter 7, performs all IT systems management, provisioning, and automation. If you do not have this self-service control panel, and customers must place a support ticket for a manual administration task, you have a managed service, and not a cloud service.

Cloud management systems are by far the most underestimated and over-looked area in the transformation to cloud services. This is especially true when a large organization deploys a private cloud without a well-designed and carefully configured cloud management platform. The cloud management system forms the basis for the customer's user interface and user experience, automation, provisioning, billing and financial tracking, and system operations.

Key Take-Away

The cloud management system is by far the most underestimated and over-looked area in using or deploying a cloud service. Without the automated provisioning, resource tracking, elasticity, and on-demand service ordering provided by the cloud management system, you do not have a cloud service.

Cloud security

Security is often pointed to as the number one concern of organizations planning their cloud transition. The first thing to understand is that clouds are not automatically less secure than an internal enterprise network—this is a common misconception. As a basic starting point, take all of the traditional IT security best practices and then combine them with security risks that are specific to a cloud environment, as I detail in Chapter 6. Also evaluate all of your applications and data to determine which are more sensitive workloads that should have special protections in a cloud environment, or if they should remain an on-premises mission-critical application not deployed in a cloud environment. Lastly, reevaluate all security processes and update them to support the elasticity, automation, and on-demand nature inherent to a cloud environment. As discussed in Chapter 6, with proper planning, technology, processes, and governance, cloud environments can be even more secure than a typical on-premises enterprise cloud.

Beginning the Cloud Transition

Most successful organizations begin to use cloud services for rather simple applications or use cases and then steadily migrate more and more applications and data to the cloud over time. Organizations cannot adopt and move to the cloud instantaneously. Migrating applications and data to the cloud takes significant time and planning. Organizations can begin with the services easiest to migrate, such as public website hosting and email services, and then move on to databases, development and testing, multitier platforms, and custom enterprise application transformation.

Figure 2-1 illustrates how organizations often move to cloud-based services in phases—because this is a complex process, moving too quickly can result in spiraling costs, delayed schedules, and other negative impacts to the organization's mission.

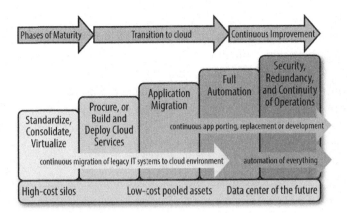

Figure 2-1. Phases of the cloud transition

The transition to cloud-based services is represented in five phases, which are described in the following list (note that some of these phases are more applicable to the transition to an enterprise private cloud—a core focus of this book—and less applicable to consumption of a public cloud service):

Phase 1: *Standardized, consolidate, virtualize*
> To begin the transition, organizations often begin (even in their legacy datacenters) to standardize technologies and consolidate their server farms and datacenters—this is part of any datacenter modernization project, even if the cloud is not the end goal. This often includes implementing virtualization instead of physical servers as well as the implementation of centralized or virtualized storage using storage area networks (SANs) or similar storage systems. This phase is also where you should begin automating all existing server, OS, and applications using a combination of scripting and automated software installation tools (achieving full automation is phase 4).

Phase 2: *Procure or build and deploy cloud services*
> A second phase of cloud deployment and transition is the deployment of a private cloud management platform (this is discussed further in Chapter 7), often within an existing enterprise datacenter. Building a private cloud requires careful planning, design, and implementation, so hiring an experienced cloud systems integrator is often the best way to ensure success. You might also begin procuring and using some public cloud services

in this phase, such as one or more SaaS applications, Dev/Test services, or cloud storage.

Phase 3: Application migration

After the basic infrastructure and services of the cloud are deployed, you need to consolidate and modernize legacy applications. As detailed earlier, you can port some applications to a cloud service model rather easily, whereas some will require significant software development and transformation. Some large organizations have so many internal software products that this phase can take many years. At a minimum, you should target all new application development projects for cloud deployment while legacy applications are carefully evaluated on their return on investment (ROI) and feasibility for migration.

Phase 4: Full automation

Use the cloud management platform to configure automated ordering, approvals, provisioning, upgrades and patching, and monitoring. It is important to continuously evaluate and transform all legacy IT processes into automated ones. As much as possible, you should automate every process, from online ordering to provisioning of VMs and applications, to shorten deployment time, reduce personnel labor costs, and improve the accuracy and consistency of systems configuration. Although you should have begun basic automation in phase 1, this phase is where you bring the numerous individual scripts, application installers, and automation tools into an overall orchestration system in which you create service designs and workflows using the cloud management platform.

Phase 5: Security, redundancy, continuity of operations

You should evaluate legacy operational and security processes, because many will need to change before the cloud services are completed and online. Automated provisioning requires some precertification or blessing from IT security personnel of the VM templates, software-defined networks, storage mapping, OSs, and application platforms. This phase also includes building redundancy and resiliency, including the ability to continue operations of server farms, VMs, applications, and the cloud management platform in the event of localized or complete datacenter failure. Security operations and governance will be fully defined and matured in this phase—eventually transitioning to a fully operational state at the end of this five-phase cloud transition plan.

Virtualization

There are several types of virtualization technologies ranging from servers to networks and storage. Virtualization is an essential tool in setting up cloud computing, automated service provisioning, distributed computing, and portability of cloud services. Virtualization is part of modernizing a datacenter, but deploying virtualization in a legacy datacenter is not the same as a fully automated, on-demand, elastic cloud environment.

Figure 2-2 depicts the evolution from traditional on-premises datacenters to enterprise cloud computing. Similar to Figure 2-1, this illustration shows the maturity and evolution of capabilities, such as virtualization and automation, that a traditional IT service goes through during the journey to a cloud—whether it's a private on-premises option or hosted with a third-party or public cloud.

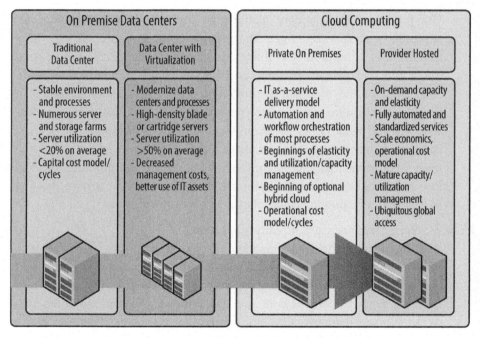

Figure 2-2. Modernizing datacenters with virtualization and the evolution to the cloud

SERVER VIRTUALIZATION

Virtualization of servers is often the first thing everyone envisions when you talk about cloud computing. This technology makes possible the virtualization of physical servers into multiple VMs using hypervisor software systems such as

VMware or Microsoft Hyper-V. Server virtualization means that instead of loading one OS onto a physical server, you split that server into multiple logical or virtual servers, each of the virtual sessions being a VM. There are numerous software applications that load on the physical server to create multiple VMs—these are usually called *hypervisors*. Microsoft Hyper-V, VMware, Kernel-based Virtual Machine (KVM), Citrix Xen, and Parallels are the five most common virtualization products on the market. Although VMware is arguably the most mature product in this category, I will not compare these products in this book—there are benefits to each, and cloud providers often use multiple hypervisors.

Key Take-Away

Virtualization is a tool often used to modernize datacenters and is a critical technology for cloud environments; however, implementing virtualization does not mean you now have a cloud environment.

There is a certain amount of overhead resources (compute, memory, and storage) used by the hypervisor itself that affects both the number and size of VMs that can fit onto a single physical server. Using numerous physical servers —whether they are rack mounted or blade based—you have access to a pool of servers, each running the selected hypervisor. This gives you significant capacity to start multiple VMs as needed, with each capable of being a different sized VM, based on how much processor power, memory, and storage is needed. By splitting the physical servers into many VMs, you gain efficiencies that you would not normally have using strictly physical servers. This is one of the primary techniques that cloud providers use, as well as within traditional datacenters, to make better use of hardware assets.

Virtualization of servers brings several unique advantages to a cloud-computing environment:

Better CPU utilization

Most physical servers with a single OS suffer a significant amount of underutilization. A properly sized physical server is deployed to handle the normal workload expected for its business purpose, but often these workloads have spikes in utilization, such as when users first log on each morning or during large batch jobs or processes that run every evening. During the lesser-used period of time, all of the excess CPU cycles are idle. A hypervisor virtualization system will take all spare CPU cycles from across all VMs and use them on the VMs that need and can benefit most from the additional processing power. This dynamic allocation of CPU resources is handled by the underlying hypervisor product and is completely transparent to both the consuming organization and usually the OS and applications running on the VMs. Note that hypervisors and VMs can be configured (by the cloud provider) so that they guarantee a minimum level of performance at all times, but it is also possible for the system to be "oversubscribed," and VMs could compete for available CPU cycles. Consumers of VMs should understand their hypervisor and VM configurations and the minimum guaranteed VM CPU service level.

Memory allocation

Each VM and the operating system running within it must be allocated a certain amount of memory in order to run. Because of the limitations of most OSs, it is difficult or impossible to dynamically allocate additional memory on the fly without an OS reboot. A common but mistaken belief is that you can dynamically allocate memory on all running OSs—this is only possible in some situations, but it will become increasingly common in future OS versions from some software vendors. The solution is to install a lot of memory into each physical server and continue using static memory allocations for each VM. This is made realistic due to the relatively low cost of memory.

VM portability

In a properly configured cloud environment, each VM can be booted from any available physical server node in the server farm, datacenter, or across multiple datacenters. This provides a level of continuity of operations and redundancy, with the OS and applications within the VM being unaware of this capability. This portability, or moving a VM to any available node, also affords infinite expansion of the server farm for more capacity as well as flexibility in operations and maintenance. You can shut down physical servers easily for maintenance purposes, with all VMs moving to another hardware node with zero customer impact.

HYPERVISOR VIRTUALIZATION TYPES

The exact method that each hypervisor utilizes to virtualize the OS into VMs is proprietary to each software vendor. Most hypervisors are capable of running different types and versions of the most popular Windows and Linux OSs. Where hypervisors differ is in the way they handle processor, memory, and network isolation within each physical server and in the way large quantities of VMs are managed. There are essentially two types of hypervisor architectures, which were originally defined back in the mid-1970s but are still valid today: Type 1 and Type 2. Both of these are defined and described here:

Type 1

A *Type 1* hypervisor runs on "bare-metal" computer hardware as the system kernel or base OS and then manages multiple VMs—each VM running its own OS and applications. This is the most commonly used form of hypervisor for IaaS virtual machines.

Figure 2-3 shows an example of a Type 1 hypervisor architecture in which one physical server is divided into multiple VMs, using software (the hypervisor) to create individual OS and application stacks. This notional example in Figure 2-3 presents only 3 VM "stacks," but physical servers can often host 20 or more VMs depending on its installed processor and memory.

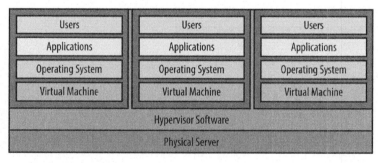

Figure 2-3. Type 1 hypervisor architecture

Type 2

A *Type 2* hypervisor runs a single OS and virtually provides multiple users with their own applications and/or desktop sessions—technically, there is only one instance of the OS with virtual sessions (simulating a VM) allocated to each user. Figure 2-4 shows a Type 2 hypervisor architecture. Notice that there is one instance of the OS running on the physical machine and, technically, there are no VMs—the hypervisor isolates applications and user sessions from one another rather than creating actual VMs as in a Type 1 architecture.

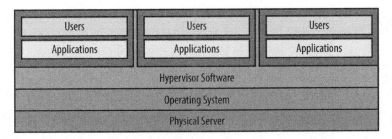

Figure 2-4. Type 2 hypervisor architecture

Throughout this book I use the term *hypervisor*, but I do not specify which type; however, commercial cloud providers most often utilize Type 1 hypervisors because they provide more separation and isolation of VMs and user sessions. Type 2 hypervisors are most often used for virtual desktop sessions such as remote desktop protocol (RDP) access into Microsoft Windows Server operating systems. Table 2-1 lists examples of each hypervisor type.

Table 2-1. Examples of hypervisor types

Type	Hypervisor
1	• VMware ESX/ESXi • Microsoft Hyper-V • Kernel-based VM (KVM) • Citrix XenServer • Parallels Server Bare Metal
2	• Microsoft Terminal Services—RDP • VMware Workstation • VirtualBox • Parallels Virtuozzo • Oracle VM Server

Although not a specific type of hypervisor, there is significant new movement in the industry for application container technology. This involves an application engine running on each VM with multiple application containers, each container running a separate isolated application in its own memory space. You can load and run application containers on multiple VMs as a scale-out, redundancy, and resiliency technique. This technology is further discussed in Chapters 7 and 9, but I mention it here because this application container technology is often incorrectly defined as a form of hypervisor. Although application containers are similar to Type 2 hypervisors, they are actually just an individual application platform running on top of an OS that happens to support multiple application containers and handles allocation of memory.

Figure 2-5 demonstrates this application container architecture. In this example, the application engine is run on top of a Type 1 hypervisor architecture (i.e., within VMs); however, these application engines could be run on a dedicated physical server without a hypervisor. Also note that this example shows only three VMs and only two application containers, but in a real-world production scenario, there could likely be 20 or more VMs and application containers in each, depending on the amount of available memory and processor capacity in the physical server.

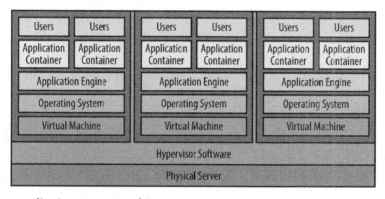

Figure 2-5. Application container architecture

VM TEMPLATES

One of the critical time-savers and benefits of using VM or hypervisor technology is the ability to define one or more VM images. These machine images, also called *VM templates*, are preconfigured images of the OS, updates and patches, and any software applications. When a cloud customer orders a new VM, it can select from one or more VM templates, with each one offering a unique configuration, OS version, or preinstalled applications. Upon the automated provisioning of each VM, the hypervisor copies the template and the OS is booted—all within seconds. The cloud system can normally boot dozens, if not hundreds, of new VMs within minutes of being ordered, which is a capability provided by automation within the cloud management system.

It is best to avoid having so many templates that their management becomes a burden. For every template you have, you must also manage that template going forward so that the latest OS version, patches, and applications are preloaded. If you have too many variations of the templates because every customer claims they are "unique," you end up paying for the management of all these templates, either directly or through the cost of the hosted cloud service provider. Also understand that when you take on responsibility for each VM template, you own all future updates and new OS revisions for that VM until that OS is retired many years from now.

Another consideration is the use of templates and "recipe-based" application installation packages. Templates are fully configured images of a disk preconfigured with an OS and applications. An installation package approach means that you stick with a very basic template that contains the base OS to launch the VM, followed by a scripted installation process that installs all of the latest updates and most of the application software. Using this installation approach, you can have fewer templates, and whenever you want to change or update your cloud service offering, you simply change the scripts and application installation packages.

NETWORK INTERFACE VIRTUALIZATION

Within each VM are virtual network interface cards (NICs). These virtual cards emulate physical NICs found in a physical server. The flexibility is tremendous in a VM environment, because you can have numerous virtual networks per VM, creating subnetworks for VMs to communicate with one another, all within the same physical server. You can create multilayer networks for frontend web application servers, middleware application servers, and backend database servers, each with their own network subnet and each using virtualized NICs. Of course, some of the virtual NICs will need an external network address and connection to the real production network. The key here is that you do not need to use physical network switches, routers, and load balancers to set up all of the networking, VLANs, and subnets you need. The virtual networking tools within the hypervisor can handle much of the work and be launched and configured in an automated fashion when a customer orders and starts a new VM. You can configure this level of automation on physical network hardware, but it is often risky and against traditional IT security policies.

The preceding is solely a description of virtualized network interfaces within a VM configuration. The overall topics of network virtualization, software-defined networking, and software-defined datacenters are covered in Chapter 9.

STORAGE VIRTUALIZATION

Virtualization of storage is typically implemented by using a SAN or other hardware and software devices that present massive pools of storage through a unified storage management interface. When you configure and start a VM, the needed amount of storage is allocated from the existing pool of available storage logical unit numbers (LUNs) on the SAN. Storage is mapped to VMs over a SAN or network fabric or switch in most cases.

You can also utilize local storage installed within each physical server when configuring hypervisors and VMs, but it is not recommended, because you lose significant capabilities. This is a somewhat controversial topic, given that some modern clouds and storage systems now recommend numerous scaled-out storage nodes with direct-attached storage rather than deploying a SAN. I will explain here and in Chapter 3 why SANs are arguably still superior for traditional IT data centers and enterprise cloud environments. For example, if you have a VM mapped to a storage LUN (not an internal hard drive), you can then relocate the VM to another physical server anywhere in your server farm, or even another datacenter, and still have it map back to the correct storage LUN. If the storage on the local physical server were used, the only way to have the VM "move" to another physical server would be to replicate all of the data to the other physical server. However, in a true cloud computing environment, you don't know which other physical server the VM will be moved to, and therefore you don't know where to precopy the data. This virtualization of storage is a key technology used in cloud computing and most modern datacenters, because it utilizes both the flexibility of VMs with the flexibility of virtual storage mapping.

Storage needs, whether structured or unstructured, increase massively each year. To handle this data, there are two possible solutions: either store less data for less time, or keep increasing the storage. Many organizations are finally starting to realize that they cannot keep up with the amount of new data being created and are thus setting limits on what should be stored—and more important, evaluating whether we really need to keep aging data forever. For those organizations that cannot delete older data, due perhaps to compliance or legal reasons, storage technologies such as compression and de-duplication come into play.

The relationship between storage and cloud compute is clear. You cannot have cloud computing without storage, and currently, disk-based storage (or hard drives) is the primary method. Advancements in solid-state drives (SSDs) and memory-based storage will ultimately bring about the end of disk platters within storage systems. We will also see technologies such as memory resistors (or *memristors*, for short) potentially replace all existing storage devices. This storage technology is important both in terms of capacity and performance, but it would take an entire book to cover this development in great detail.

As for the importance of storage as it relates to cloud computing, the back-end storage system for a cloud service requires unique characteristics that might not normally be required of traditional server farms:

- Ability to provide multiple types of cloud storage (e.g., object, block, application-specific), regardless of actual physical storage hardware

- Ability to quickly replicate data or synchronize across datacenters.

- Ability to take a snapshot of data while the system still operational. These are used for backup or restoration to a point in time.

- Ability to de-duplicate data across entire enterprise/storage system.

- Ability to thin-provision storage volumes.

- Ability to back up data offline from production networks, and back up huge data online without system outage.

- Ability to expand storage volumes on the fly while the service is online.

- Ability to maintain storage performance levels, even as data changes and load increases. It also must have the ability to automatically groom data across multiple disk types and technologies in order to maintain maximum performance levels.

- Ability to recover now-unused storage blocks when VMs are shut down (auto-reclamation).

- Ability to virtualize all storage systems, new and legacy, so that all storage is represented as a single storage system.

- Ability to provide multiple tiers of storage to give customers a variety of performance levels, each at a price per gigabyte or terabyte, depending on need.

Figure 2-6 depicts how server virtualization combined with key cloud attributes is the foundation for cloud computing. That being said, these same virtualization and cloud characteristics (e.g., automation, scalability, and self-service) can easily be part of any datacenter modernization project, even if cloud computing is not the goal.

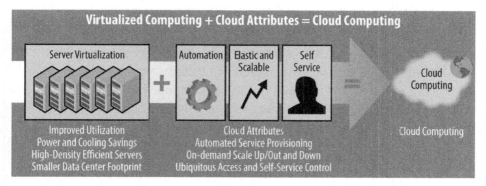

Figure 2-6. Virtualization + cloud attributes = cloud computing

Automation

The automation of provisioning and launching of new services has been mentioned throughout this chapter. Cloud management systems are covered in depth in Chapter 7, but the important point to note at this juncture is the importance of automation in cloud computing environments. Without automation, many of the benefits and characteristics of cloud computing could not be achieved at a price point and service level that makes cloud services attractive to customers while still allowing the business to be viable. Failure to automate as many processes as possible results in higher personnel labor costs, slower time to deliver the new service to customers, and ultimately higher cost with less reliability.

What is meant by automation? This can best be described by going through a typical case scenario of a customer placing an order within their cloud service portal, and following the steps necessary to bring the service online.

Use-Case Scenario: Automation Within Cloud Management Software

1. A staff member of a small business that works with a cloud services provider logs on to a web-based cloud portal and views a catalog of available services.

2. She selects a cloud service: a medium-sized VM running the Linux OS. The service catalog shows this VM size comes with two CPUs, four GB of memory, and 50 GB of disk storage at a price of $250 per

month. She choses two of these packages and then goes to the checkout section of the cloud provider's website.

3. In a public cloud, customers normally pays for services using a credit card or an existing financial account or purchase order agreement that is on file with the cloud provider. Private cloud customers often use a chargeback method of accruing fees that are billed back to one or more departments at the end of each billing period. The customer's employee completes the checkout process.

4. The customer has an approval process in place (especially for a private cloud deployment) that requires the organization's procurement team to sign off on the order before it is finalized. So, the cloud management system sends an email to the designated approver of this order. The procurement team's designee receives the email, clicks the URL link, logs on to the cloud portal, and approves the order.

5. The cloud management system sees the order was approved and immediately begins the process of building the requested VMs. The system knows which server farms and pools of available resources it has, and automatically selects which physical server node will host the VMs initially. Storage is allocated and assigned to the new VMs and a template is used to create them.

6. The VMs are booted for the first time and any needed patches or updates are automatically installed. The cloud management system detects that the VMs have launched and are ready for the customer. It charges the customer's credit card or deducts funds from the customer's online account with the provider.

7. The cloud management system automatically updates internal assets and configurations, and operational and security systems about the newly created and booted VMs. This triggers other internal IT operational systems for performance, capacity, configuration, and security monitoring of the new VMs—there is no manual process or delay bringing these new VMs under full management and operational control within the datacenter.

8. The cloud management system sends a welcome email to the customer's employee indicating the network address along with logon instructions for how to use her new VMs. The email also contains

information on where to obtain documentation and who to call for support.

9. The customer's employee logs on to the VMs and performs any further application installations, configurations, and loading of production data. The cloud provider manages all future system updates and ensures that systems are operational at all times, while the customer's employee manages her organization's applications and custom configurations. Many cloud providers offer optional fully managed services for OS and application patching and updates.

10. The cloud management system automatically renews and bills the customer every month (or whatever the billing cycle is). Depending on the type of service offered, there also might be variable expenses; for example, if she wants the VMs to automatically increase memory, processors, or storage upon increased load. The cloud management system will provide the metered resource information to the customer, and charge her organization accordingly.

Key Take-Away

Without automation, most of the characteristics and benefits of cloud could not be achieved at an economical price.

The preceding scenario demonstrates that there does not need to be a human involved with the cloud service provider anywhere in this process. In a real public cloud scenario, this process takes place repeatedly at all hours, thousands of times each day. This is where the cloud provider gains such scales of economy that the customer is paying less for their cloud service than it would have if it built and hosted the service itself. Without automated processes and cloud management systems, none of these economies of scale are possible and the cloud provider's costs would be anticompetitive. For an enterprise private cloud, automation provides cost savings and efficiency, but other benefits are just as important, such as rapid time to market and provisioning, consistent quality, improved compliance and security, elasticity, and so on.

There are many other aspects of automation, provisioning, and self-service control panels, which you can read about in Chapter 7. This is an incredibly important topic—arguably a top-five reason why a cloud provider or on-premises cloud system will succeed or fail in the long run.

Providing Customers Transparency to the Cloud

An important yet often overlooked feature of a successful cloud is the ability for the consuming organization to have visibility into its service status, security, costs, and utilization statistics. When an organization moves its services to the cloud, it depends on the cloud service provider to perform the organization's mission-critical business functions or service its customers. A major obstacle for new cloud customers to overcome is the feared loss of visibility and control.

In a cloud that is owned and operated by a cloud provider, there is normally a centralized staff and an array of deployed tools to handle cloud management, monitoring, assets, alerts, security, and network operations. The goal is to minimize staffing labor costs and best service the customers; the problem is that all the centralized data and the aforementioned software tools are not often designed to allow numerous customers to see these activities. The best tools that a cloud provider might utilize are not necessarily the best tools for multitenant access and separation of dashboards, statistics, and reports for each customer. This leaves the customers essentially blind when using cloud services as compared to legacy IT environments, in which the customer might have hosted server farms and applications themselves and had a complete view or access to their system.

Implicit trust in the cloud provider only goes so far; customers who cannot see their service status, performance statistics, security, and event logs might not be able to satisfy the needs of their customers, their internal employees, and their executive management. Imagine that you have no way to track the usage of your cellular phone minutes, history, or missed calls. Now, imagine you needed this data for your compliance requirements, chargeback to specific departments, or to just confirm that your service plan isn't so large that you are overpaying for the actual amount of services you use. This cell phone example is simplistic, but it effectively illustrates the idea.

Customers looking to procure services from a cloud provider—or implement their own private or community cloud—must evaluate providers and services. The cloud service must be able to share needed metrics, reports, system status, logs, and other data in real-time; less ideal is receiving a monthly report that is already a week or two old when you receive it.

Key Take-Away

Customers shifting to cloud computing want visibility into all of their systems, including status, utilization, and event logs, just as they had (or even better than what they had) with their internally hosted IT systems.

CLOUD PROVIDER MANAGEMENT TOOLS AND CUSTOMER VISIBILITY

It is important to note that cloud providers are not intentionally concealing all of this data from customers. The base software systems for network, security, and operations management within datacenters and server farms are usually the weak link. Major customer organizations and cloud providers often deploy software tools that provide robust features to monitor and manage the hypervisors, applications, and network infrastructure. However, these software tools are often not "cloud aware," or cloud friendly; they often have no concept of multitenancy, so events, statistics, and logs across all server farms and applications end up in one giant database for the centralized support team to utilize. In fact, these software tools were designed to consolidate utilization and system events from thousands of IT systems for a centralized IT team to view, manage, and remediate problems. These tools have no awareness of which VMs, for example, are being used by a certain customer—each physical IT asset and VM is identified only by IP address or some other nomenclature that is not personally identifiable to a customer. The bottom line is that some of the best compute and network management tools available in the industry are not necessarily the best for multitenant cloud environments.

To tackle these issues, leading cloud providers either create their own infrastructure monitoring tools that integrate with their cloud management systems or heavily adapt multiple commercial off-the-shelf (COTS) products. This is an enormous and expensive undertaking and the reason why there is a significant gap in capabilities between one cloud provider/cloud management system and another when you compare them carefully.

The most flexibility and customization of infrastructure management tools and the cloud management platform is in a private cloud deployment, whereby a public cloud will have significantly less configuration flexibility. This is not intended to excuse cloud providers; rather, it's to help you better understand why they will often have significant issues providing the visibility their customers desire at the expected low cloud computing prices.

MULTIPLE TENANTS/CUSTOMERS

A key feature of a public cloud—and even some private clouds—is the ability to host services for multiple customers, departments, and users. When a cloud is sold to multiple organizations or departments, all customers benefit from the shared environment in the form of reduced costs and increased capabilities that no single organization could afford or have the skills necessary to deploy and manage. Multitenant is the term used when referring to hosting multiple customers—or tenants—in a shared environment. Critical to offering services to multiple tenants is the isolation and security of data, portals, workflows, and reporting such that no customer would otherwise be aware that other customers even exist. This separation of functions and security of data is done through a combination of security roles, policies, permissions, access control lists, and, in some cloud models, physical separation of servers, storage, networks, or applications.

Shared customer management

Some customers want to share the work of managing the cloud or its applications; a common solution is for the cloud system to have a customer-accessible, web-based control panel. From this portal, the provider defines roles for each customer, giving its administrators and support personnel a limited view of the services and applications. The customer might be allowed to configure the applications or manage user accounts. This self-service control panel also hides the complexity of the behind-the-scenes computing and applications, providing customers with consistent user-friendly administration across many applications. This concept is very common in public cloud services, but more flexibility and control is possible in a private cloud model.

Chapter 7 is dedicated to cloud management and addresses this issue and what customers can expect—and should demand—from a cloud provider or an enterprise private cloud management platform.

Accessing Cloud Services

Another often-overlooked area is how your organization will access its cloud services. By definition, cloud services are available via the Internet, or a wide area network (WAN) communications circuit between an organization and cloud provider. The concerns to be discussed involve bandwidth, network or Internet latency between end users and the cloud provider, and physical or virtual network circuits.

Many organizations that have traditionally hosted their own server farms have now moved their systems to a cloud provider, so the servers and applications they access might lie somewhere very distant. Because this distance might entail network hops and bandwidth limitations, your end users might no longer experience the same level of performance to which they had become accustomed. You must carefully plan a combination of application architecture, cloud infrastructure, and communication paths.

APPLICATION PERFORMANCE

Applications hosted by a cloud provider can both benefit and suffer from the cloud transition. The applications themselves will likely run faster and, of course, be more scalable because the cloud offers more compute, memory, and storage capacity as needed. All cloud compute and storage systems reside with each other in the same datacenters, so performance is often improved. Also, other applications, VMs, and hosted virtual desktops all being located in the same facility can improve performance. End users might now access these services via Internet connections with greater bandwidth than a single customer datacenter would possess.

The potential downside of cloud applications is encountered with *chatty* (also called *thick*) client-server applications. These programs are characterized by running the server portion on the cloud, with a locally installed application on desktop workstations. Many legacy applications are considered chatty (*noisy* is yet another term), meaning they have a significant amount of network traffic between the user's workstation and the backend server-side application. If these legacy applications exist, they are good candidates for being rewritten, or customers might consider using Workplace as a Service, which deploys virtual desktops in the cloud, located in the same datacenter as the server-side application. Another approach is to use similar Workplace as a Service technology to implement *application publishing* rather than full virtual desktop. This is described at greater length in Chapter 4.

Key Take-Away

Large legacy applications can sometimes use virtual desktop or application publishing techniques—allowing legacy applications to be hosted in the cloud without rewriting them. These legacy applications might not fully benefit from cloud elasticity and scalability, but you can use application publishing as a temporary bridge while apps are redesigned as a cloud-enabled system.

CLOUD COMPUTE VMS

Accessing VMs hosted in the cloud, as in Infrastructure as a Servce (IaaS) and Development/Testing as a Service (Dev/Test), is normally accomplished in two ways. The first is for customer IT staff or administrators to log on to the cloud management portal, from which there is normally a self-service control panel with which customers can start, stop, reboot, or check the status of their VMs. Also through this control panel, the customer might be able to remotely control the VM, similar to a virtual desktop sending display, keyboard, and mouse activity back to the end user. However, the actual VM and OS are hosted and running in the cloud.

Accessing the cloud-based VMs through self-service cloud management is sometimes cumbersome. Often, the customer only wants to grant higher-level managers access to the cloud management portal. How does an average network administrator log on to his VM to install software or change the configurations of the OS? You can do this through remote control software such as the Microsoft Remote Display Protocol (RDP) client application, which is a part of the base Windows OS. Another popular alternative is Virtual Network Connect (VNC), which is native on some OSs, or the customer can install it on top of an OS. The cloud provider will need to have its firewalls configured to allow such remote control sessions.

When assessing VM services and various public cloud providers or cloud management platforms for private cloud, there are key features that you should compare. Not all VMs or IaaS applications are the same when you really take an in-depth look. The following are some important features to compare:

OS availability
> Do you have choice of OSs and versions?

Size of VMs
> Do the VMs scale large enough for your current and future needs?

High availability
> Look for redundancy, disaster recovery, availability groups, and the ability to easily configure additional continuously replicated clones of each VM within same datacenter or secondary datacenters/regions.

Scale up and scale out

> The ability to increase the size of VMs (scale up) or increase the quantity of VMs (scale out) automatically based on workload or peak usage, and then scale down automatically when workloads return to normal.

Updates and patching

> Does the cloud provider continuously update and patch the OS and applications, or is this the customer's (i.e., your) responsibility? Cloud providers might charge more for this optional service.

System events and visibility

> As the customer, what real-time visibility do you have into utilization statistics, and event monitoring (e.g., security or system status events)?

WORKPLACE AS A SERVICE

Workplace as a Service (WPaaS) is dependent on connecting end-user thin-client devices with a virtual desktop, hosted at the cloud provider's datacenter. This requires more bandwidth than was needed when the desktop OS was running locally on a physical workstation. The cloud provider or systems integrator can assist with the planning, testing, and upgrades to network circuits to meet the increased bandwidth needs. Sometimes, you can use network acceleration appliances, but they cannot perform miracles if the available bandwidth is too low.

WPaaS offerings also have other network-related considerations that you should discuss with the cloud provider or IT systems integrator. This includes network access from virtual desktops hosted at the cloud provider facility, and the ability to print or access shared data located at the end user's home network.

Use-Case Scenario: Printing via Virtual Desktop

Imagine a situation in which a virtual desktop user wants to send a file to a network printer located in his office. Because he is accessing the virtual desktop via a thin-client laptop or tablet, all of the computing is actually occurring in the cloud with just the display, keyboard, and mouse activity transmitted over the Internet.

When he prints his document, if the printer is hardwired to his thin-client device, the virtual desktop software knows how to send the print job to the printer via his laptop. However, if the printer is not locally attached just down the hall, this is a different problem entirely. Now, the virtual desktop running in the cloud needs to send the print job over the Internet and then into the company's internal network to that printer located down the hall. How does the cloud provider know from which office the end user is logging on? Although today he is logging on from the company's main office, tomorrow he might be doing so from a hotel room across the country. In most cases, the virtual desktop does not have the ability to detect this.

Assuming that the necessary firewall ports are open and configured for this, the print job frequently involves a large amount of data. So, in this scenario, not only is it difficult to determine which printer is the closest device, but due to the size of the print job, the user experience is often very poor—the amount of data being sent over the network is so large that the printing is slow or it times-out with an error before the printer completes the job.

For the network firewalls to allow a remotely running virtual desktop to send a print job back into the corporate network, the IT staff at the user's office will most likely need to know the IP addresses of the remote virtual desktops. This is a problem because the cloud provider is hosting thousands or tens of thousands of virtual desktop users, and the IP addresses are dynamically assigned as each one logs on; IP addresses are often not in a fixed range.

Another area to be considered for WPaaS is personal and shared files. When users migrate from traditional workstations to virtual cloud-hosted desktops, there is no ability to store files locally. This means that the virtual desktop has both personal and corporate file shares hosted in the cloud, where users can access their files. Part of the WPaaS transition means moving this data to the cloud; but what if not all users are migrating to virtual desktops? Where are the shared data files for the corporation held? What if, on some days, a user logs on via a workstation with local storage, but on other days she logs on to virtual desktops? How then does the user edit a document that she doesn't have on her virtual desktop, which she might be accessing via tablet or smartphone?

WPaaS is not a new technology; there was a huge push for this thin-client service in the IT industry more than 10 years ago, but the challenges that existed back then still exist today. These challenges are not insurmountable, but they do require more than just purchasing WPaaS from the cloud provider; this particular service needs significant planning to be successful.

SOFTWARE AS A SERVICE

Software as a Service (SaaS) provided and hosted by a cloud provider does not normally include any ability for a customer to log on to the backend servers or OSs. These SaaS offerings are fully managed services, and only the provider's IT staff are permitted such access to upgrade or manage the applications. To allow customers the capability to configure routine aspects of the software, they create web-based cloud management or self-service control panels. Through these typically web-based portals, the cloud provider grants some level of management of the SaaS applications. This is convenient when a customer has multiple SaaS applications, because this simple user-friendly control panel provides a consistent interface across all applications hosted by the cloud provider, hiding the complexity of numerous individual software consoles that the provider has to deal with on a daily basis. For more details on cloud management systems and self-service control panels for SaaS applications, refer to Chapter 7.

When assessing a SaaS application or service provider, consider the following in your planning and comparison:

- Which traditional applications running in my organization can be replaced by a SaaS tool? What gaps in functionality would there be?

- What level of customization is available through a web-based self-service control panel from the SaaS provider?

- Can any existing software licenses you might have for the traditional application be tranferred to the SaaS application?

- Are there any minimal contract duration terms or commitments? What steps will you need to take if you decide to stop the SaaS application? Are there early termination fees? How would you export any hosted/online data?

- Does my cloud management platform have preintegrated support for this SaaS provider and is there a published API by the SaaS provider so that integration and automation can be created?

- SaaS applications are provided and hosted for multiple customers; they are often less customizable than a traditional IT application run inside the firewall of an enterprise IT organization—this is part of the cost-benefit trade-off.

- What are the SaaS provider's standard backup, recovery, and disaster recovery procedures? What about recovery time objectives (RTO) and recovery point objectives (RPO)? What are the service-level agreement (SLA) terms and any limitations on liability to protect data availability and integrity?

Data Sovereignty and On-Shore Support Operations

Data sovereignty refers to the actual geographic location at which the data is stored in the cloud, whether that data is stored in one or more datacenters hosted by your own organization or by a public cloud provider. Due to differing laws in each country, the data can be legally subpoenaed, potentially forcing the cloud provider, or any organization, to turn over the requested data. There is an increasing trend for customers to require that data never be hosted or stored outside of a specific country—meeting mandatory regulations or simply satisfying customer preferences. Further government monitoring, or snooping, on behalf of law enforcement agencies has also become a concern.

Data sovereignty and *data residency* has become a more significant challenge and decision point than most organizations—and cloud service providers—originally anticipated. Initially, a cloud service provider would state that "you, the customer, shouldn't care or be bothered with where and how the cloud provider stores your information: we provide service-level guarantees to protect you." Experience now informs us to ask or contractually force your cloud provider to store your data in the countries or datacenter locations that satisfy your data sovereignty requirements. Customers can also ask that all operational support personnel at the cloud provider be located within your desired country and be local citizens (potentially with background checks performed regularly)—this in combination with data sovereignty will help to ensure that your data remains private and is not unnecessarily exposed to foreign governments or other parties with whom you did not intend to share it.

Key Take-Away

In addition to data sovereignty and residency, customers can ask that all operational support personnel at the cloud provider be located within your desired country and be local citizens (potentially with background checks performed regularly).

Other security regulations and industry standards for data privacy, financial and credit card transactions (e.g., Payment Card Industry Data Security Standard [PCI DSS]), data retention, and archiving might also apply to customer organizations. The more customized and unique the requirement, the more often a private cloud is needed to meet the requirements—public clouds usually service a large number of customers and are less likely to provide individual customization.

The Information Technology Infrastructure Library (ITIL) and Operational Process Changes

When you migrate or add a cloud service to a traditional datacenter or managed service, there are numerous recommended changes in operational procedures. Many of these are based on lessons learned in transitioning from traditional managed service datacenters to cloud-enabled service environments. Some organizations use the term Concept of Operations (ConOps) to introduce these new operational procedures to existing staff. This doesn't relate as much to a public cloud service, because the provider handles most of these functions for you; the ConOps changes are really for private cloud models, in which the customer is involved with all operations. The operational topics that follow are arranged in Information Technology Infrastructure Library (ITIL) format and nomenclature, to match the many organizations that have adopted ITIL as their service management model.

> Most of these ITIL-based process changes are specific to a private or hybrid-cloud models in which the customer or contracted support vendor is performing the daily management and operations of the system. In a public cloud, the cloud provider has most of these responsibilities that must be met to achieve the promised SLA.

REQUEST MANAGEMENT

Ordering of cloud services will be done through the cloud management system, usually a web-based portal. This portal includes a service catalog of all available offerings and options. All orders, cancellation orders, and usage tracking for billing purposes will be handled within this system. Legacy methods for consumers to order services will normally be retired, with this service catalog becoming the new method for ordering services—even if money does not change hands, as in some private or communication clouds.

There can be a link from the cloud management portal to a traditional support ticketing system to allow customers to request assistance. These will be handled in the same manner as any other legacy user request or support ticket.

INCIDENT MANAGEMENT

A common change to incident management will be the monitoring of additional event logs within the cloud services. Because the majority of cloud compute provisioning will be performed in an automated fashion, careful tracking of the event logs and creation of alerts will be essential to detect any failures in the automated processes. For example, you could run out of available memory or storage space—something which you should be proactively monitoring—and therefore all new orders for VMs would fail. As the cloud manager, you will have two areas to monitor and manage incidents:

Cloud infrastructure
> You must manage the cloud infrastructure itself, meaning the datacenter facilities, server farms, storage, networks, security, and applications.

Customer services
> You will also need to detect when a new VM or other resource is automatically provisioned so that you can begin monitoring it immediately. Because customers will use these services, you might be managing virtual instances of a server or monitoring how many resources a customer is using for billing purposes.

Another area of change in a cloud environment is the integration with any existing helpdesk, incident, or ticketing systems. It is common that the cloud service provider is not the same contracting company that provides the helpdesk or user support ticketing system—often, the ticket system is an internally hosted function of the organization. Integration between cloud-based services, applications, and internal or externally hosted ticketing systems is not a difficult technical task, but it will require support process and operational changes.

Key Take-Away

Organizations often underestimate the changes to traditional IT operations and support when transitioning to a cloud environment. Although there is cost-savings potential in moving to the cloud, it is often the organization's culture, procurement, security, and political challenges that prevent or delay realized cost reductions.

CHANGE MANAGEMENT

Due to online customer ordering, approval workflow, and automated provisioning systems within the cloud service, change control will be significantly affected, and will need to adapt existing processes.

New VMs

When a customer places an order, the VM(s) will be automatically provisioned. Each VM will be based on preapproved and security-certified OS images, applications, and patch levels. The cloud service portal should be programmed to automatically generate a change control request, with a completed status, upon every successfully automated provisioning event. Any exceptions or errors in the automated provisioning process will be handled through alerts and generate a "completed" change ticket when the VM is online.

Changes to servers and hosts

Customer-requested changes would follow normal change control procedures already in place. Routine maintenance, updates, security patches, and new software revisions will also follow existing change control procedures. A typical exclusion is the Dev/Test service, because these are often VMs provisioned behind a firewall to keep noncertified development applications isolated from production networks. With this service, VMs do not require a change control to allow the developers to do their job without unnecessary delays.

Updates to the Common Operating Environment (COE)

Cloud services automatically deploy templates or build-images of standard configurations. These COE templates will be created by the cloud provider or customer with all updates, patches, and security certifications included. These COE images can be automatically deployed within the cloud environment without going through the typical manual accreditation process for each server. The cloud provider is usually required to update COEs at least every six months to keep the catalog of available OSs and applications up to date. All updated COEs will again go through the manual security approval process, and then they can be ordered and deployed using the cloud's automated systems.

Key Take-Away

Creating and managing too many common operating environments or VM templates can quickly become costly and unmanageable. Transitioning to the cloud should be accompanied by better discipline and standardization for COEs and templates.

Adding a server (VM) to a network and domain

As each VM is automatically provisioned, it will automatically be added to the network domain. This will be an automated process, but the specific steps required as well as legacy change and security control policies involved need to be adjusted to facilitate this; in the past, this process of joining the domain typically required manual security approval.

User and administrator permissions to new servers and hosts

Similar to the preceding process, as new machines are automatically added to the network, permission to log on to the new OS will be granted to the cloud management system, usually by using a service account. Specific steps to automate this process and adjustments to the existing security processes will need to be made to accommodate this automated process.

Network configuration requests

Every VM-based server has a preconfigured network configuration. In the case of an individual machine—physical or VM—standard OS and applications are installed that require outbound initiation of traffic within the production network, and possibly to the Internet.

All network configuration, load balancing, or firewall change requests follow existing procedures. When possible, the cloud management self-service control panel will allow customers to configure some of this by themselves, although advanced network changes will need to go through normal change control and possibly security approval.

In some VM templates or COEs, there might be multiple servers deployed as part of a COE. For example, a complex COE might include one or more database servers, middleware application servers, and possibly frontend web servers; this collection of VMs is called a *platform*. In these situations, the VMs have already been configured (as part of the overall platform package) to communicate with one another via the virtual networking built into the VM hypervisor. In the given example, only the frontend web servers would have a production network address, whereas all other servers are essentially "hidden" within the VM network enclave.

Cloud consumers may submit requests to have production firewalls, load balancers, or other network systems custom configured for their needs. When evaluating these requests, the cloud provider should always default to making the changes within the hypervisor virtual network environment.

If that is not sufficient, he might consider changing physical datacenter switches, routers, and firewalls; many of the requests can be handled using virtual networking settings within the hypervisor tool.

VM configuration changes

Customers may have the ability to upgrade or downgrade their VM CPU, memory, or disk space within the cloud management portal. Changing this configuration requires a reboot of the customer's VMs, but no loss of data.

If a customer requests a manual change through a support ticket, the cloud provider will make this change using the cloud management software so that billing and new VM configurations are automatically updated. Do not make changes to the backend hypervisor directly, or the cloud management system will have no knowledge of that change.

> ### Key Take-Away
>
> Manually changing the VM configurations is *not* the appropriate process; billing and configuration management will not be aware of the new settings, and the downstream asset and change control databases will not be updated. Never make a manual change to a configuration that the cloud management system cannot track.

Release management

All VM templates, COEs, and software will be fully tested in an offline lab or staging network. It will then be quality checked and security approved before any changes to production cloud service is scheduled. Due to the level of automation and precertification of VM compliance and security, software, updates, and so on, release management will be an ongoing effort with increased impact. If new releases go into production with errors or inadequate planning and testing, automation and the cloud will multiply the impact compared to traditional IT.

CONFIGURATION MANAGEMENT

The cloud management system will automatically populate the configuration management database of all VMs as part of the automated provisioning process. Because cloud compute services can be ordered, approved, and automatically deployed at any time and on any day the customer desires, this automated update to configuration management is critical. Following are changes to configuration management that you should consider in a cloud environment:

- Changes to the actual VM servers and hypervisor software should be treated differently than customer-owned (also called guest) VMs. Normally, the cloud provider upgrades its server farm. Then, in a different maintenance window, it schedules any necessary customer upgrades.

- Customers expect near-zero downtime in a cloud environment, so traditional maintenance windows or outages should be replaced, when possible, with rolling-over production systems to secondary hosts, performing upgrades on the offline systems, and then transitioning back to the primary hosts—preferably without customers experiencing any downtime.

- VMs running within isolated Dev/Test subnetworks may not require the same level of configuration management as production VMs because they are sandboxes in which developers can work. There is little point in enforcing strict change and configuration management, which only slows down development efforts. Only when the VMs are deployed into production must the developers begin to follow all change, security, and configuration management policies.

- Updates to the Common Operation Environment (COE) must also be considered. Cloud compute services automatically deploy templates or build-images of standard operating environments. These COE templates will be created by the cloud provider or customer with all updates, patches, and security certifications completed. These COE images can be automatically deployed within the cloud environment without going through the typical manual security process for each server. The cloud provider is usually required to update COEs at least every six months to keep the catalog of available OSs and applications up to date. All updated or new COEs will again go through the manual security approval process before they can be ordered and deployed using the cloud's automated systems.

- Finally, update notifications must be considered. Users or consumers of the cloud must be provided with advanced notice—10 days, for example—before any changes or updates are made to already deployed customer VMs. Customers may "opt out" of any planned upgrade within this window if they believe it will have a negative impact on their project, timeline, or code stability. It is the cloud provider's goal to keep all new and existing VMs up to date; therefore, the cloud provider should adequately document the need, importance, testing results, and impact of each upgrade to encourage customer adoption of the new updates.

IT ASSET MANAGEMENT

All existing procedures for asset management should be followed; however, the automation within the cloud management platform will automatically update asset databases. This automatic real-time update is often part of many government IT security requirements.

As the number of customer orders increases, additional physical blade servers and storage will be required; capacity planning and monitoring is critical to success. As new servers or storage is added, the asset management system will be updated as per normal procedures.

VMs running within Dev/Test (preproduction) and IaaS/PaaS (production) networks must have all assets tracked, including the VM itself and potentially applications contained within VMs.

Cloud environments are normally based on shared infrastructure equipment within datacenters. Assets are usually not owned or dedicated to any one customer. It might be difficult or impossible to assign physical equipment to individuals, departments, or subagencies in an asset database.

SERVICE DESK FUNCTION

Most cloud providers—certainly public cloud providers—do not provide tier-1 end-user support; customers normally provide this function or contract a third party. The cloud provider manages all devices and software within its cloud service, and customer IT staff typically manage only their applications or VMs. However, issues can be escalated to the cloud provider through the management portal, email, or telephone, depending on the offering, terms, and conditions.

It should be noted that Dev/Test customers might attempt to submit tickets relating to software development programs or problems found in their custom applications; each of these are development issues that should be handled by the customer's development staff, not the cloud provider. As a private cloud operator, you might have a software developer support provider or internal team that would be able to assist these Dev/Test consumers.

Key Take-Away

A traditional service management ticketing system is usually not suitable for use as a cloud management system. You can use service management systems as portals for requesting cloud services, but legacy service management systems lack the backend architecture, automation, IT orchestration workflows, and preintegration with various Anything as a Service (XaaS) systems and providers.

As described earlier, the integration with an existing helpdesk, incident, or ticketing systems and the cloud services is necessary. It is common that the cloud service provider is not the same contracting company that provides the helpdesk or user support ticketing system—often the ticket system is an internally hosted function of the organization. Integration between cloud-based services, applications, and internal or externally hosted ticketing systems is not a difficult technical task, but it will require support process and operational changes.

SERVICE-LEVEL MANAGEMENT

Service-level management (SLM) has increased importance in a cloud environment. Cloud services are ultimately based on service availability rather than a detailed scope of work or contract terms between a provider and consumers. This applies to public and enterprise-private clouds. In a cloud environment, the theory is that the cloud provider offers one or more services and a guaranteed level of availability. As long as this is met, the service is considered delivered as promised. This service-oriented approach is more simplistic for a cloud provider to sell its services, but there are many areas a consumer of cloud services, even an on-premises private cloud consumer, should consider.

Although the cloud provider normally establishes service levels, customers might request additional or more enhanced SLAs. Accepting the modified terms is ultimately up to the cloud provider—normally public providers do not change their SLAs; this benefit is available mainly to private deployments. The provider should offer customers some form of reporting mechanisms, such as the following:

- Online dashboards as well as monthly manual reports (typically included with invoices).

- SLA performance dashboards showing current and historical SLA adherence and alerts.

- Utilization metrics shown on dashboards, showing VM CPU utilization levels, memory, disk, network and disk throughput, and uptime. These are all examples of what is normally measured and reported.

- Billing history as well as all reports and metering should be shown per customer and department.

In a multivendor cloud broker environment, the aggregation of SLA data gathered from all XaaS providers is critical. The cloud broker management system normally performs this aggregation and reporting, providing customers with a single view of the entire hybrid/broker cloud ecosystem. Chapter 8 covers cloud brokering roles, technology, and definitions in more detail.

AVAILABILITY MANAGEMENT

Cloud providers will utilize numerous technologies such as autoscaling and bursting, redundancy, failover, disaster recovery, data replication, and multiple datacenters to ensure system availability. Inclusion of availability statistics should be included in the cloud management portal for customer visibility.

Other than the cloud service provider(s) meeting the contracted SLAs, availability management and dynamic allocation of resources are functions performed by the cloud provider. Details regarding how the cloud provider performs these functions as well as event logs on activities might not be available to customers or consumers of the cloud service; in this service-level-driven business, the cloud provider's ability to maintain system availability is built into its SLA calculations and guaranteed availability level.

It is important to remember that, although not specifically part of the definition of the cloud, cloud consumers and the industry have an expectation of near 100% system availability. Public and private cloud operators should not plan or expect to use weekly or monthly maintenance windows or other declared service outages. The technologies used in a modern datacenter and in cloud facilitate failing-over active servers, VMs, and applications to secondary systems to accommodate maintenance and upgrades. The expectation is that a cloud provider should never intentionally or accidentally have all systems offline and unavailable to its customers.

CAPACITY MANAGEMENT

Constant monitoring of the cloud compute servers and storage systems is required. Because ordering and provisioning is done automatically, 24-7, it is easy for the system to run out of available physical servers or storage, thus caus-ing a failure in future provisioning of new orders. There is lead time required to purchase, install, configure, and certify any new equipment, so monitoring and establishing alert thresholds is critical; the cloud provider needs sufficient time to add capacity. The cloud provider *could* purchase too much capacity that remains idle until utilized, but this costs money to procure, power, and cool—costs which are eventually passed on to customers. It is far preferable to have a reasonable amount of extra capacity but also put into place rapid replenishment plans.

Note that capacity management needs to consider that the following technol-ogies are deployed in the cloud environment, affecting methods and calculations for capacity planning:

- All cloud compute physical servers normally run a hypervisor product such as VMware or Hyper-V. These servers and VMs boot from a shared storage and may have no local hard drives.

- Thin provisioning is commonly used throughout the SAN, thus you need to carefully calculate actual disk usage versus what has been sold and what is remaining in capacity.

- Thin provisioning free-space reclamation might be a scheduled process to run, not an automatic one. Automatic is preferable, but not all SAN system support it.

- If over subscription of processors or memory was calculated within the hypervisor configuration, monitoring of system performance and capacity is even more critical.

- Usable capacity on the SAN does not include additional space to hold any daily backups or snapshots, so actual usable capacity will be 25%-50% higher.

- Consider having the SAN supplier provide a *utility storage* agreement, whereby it stages additional SAN capacity at the cloud provider's datacenters but does not charge the cloud provider until it is utilized. This shares the costs and risk of managing extra storage capacity between the cloud provider and its SAN vendor.

Key Take-Away

Note that several VM sizes are normally available to the customer; as such, the more that an "extra-large" VM is ordered, the more processors, memory, and disk space must be allocated. This means fewer VMs will fit on each physical server, so additional capacity might be needed sooner than expected.

The most important thing to remember with capacity management in a cloud environment is the impact of failure. In a traditional IT environment, running out of capacity might cause a minor inconvenience, a delay in staging a new service or application, or even a short outage while you free up some disk space. In an automated, highly elastic, rapid-provisioning, multitenant cloud environment, failure to monitor, anticipate, and keep up with capacity needs will effect a significant number of customers, costing the organization significant money, reputation, loss of future business, and more. The bottom line is that capacity management has gone from a relatively low-importance item to an extremely high-importance role in a cloud environment.

IT SERVICE CONTINUITY

Cloud providers utilize numerous technologies such as data replication, failover, and multiple datacenters to ensure system availability and continuity of service and operations. Details into how the cloud provider performs these functions as well as event logs on activities might not be available to consumers of the cloud service—the SLA is the key reporting mechanism and standard of performance.

It's important to understand that continuity is not necessarily just a technology issue. Although not unique to the cloud, your continuity plans might include procedures for how your employees access the company network and applications in the event of natural disasters, datacenter outages, and so on. The only cloud-specific consideration is that the use of a public cloud might give you more options and availability of applications and data because they are hosted in the cloud by a third party as opposed to hosted in a traditional on-premises datacenter.

As a private cloud operator, you are now responsible for both your internal organization and user continuity and any external consumers of your service. There are numerous technologies and products that can facilitate the load balancing, failover, and continuity functions. For details on how to plan and deploy a cloud service (for on-premises use or to become a cloud provider), refer to Chapter 3.

Remember that the redundant systems for high availability or disaster recovery must include the cloud management platform and the actual consumable XaaS servers, storage, and networking. The system will be severely limited and possibly unmanageable if all the XaaS VMs were to failover while the command and control (the cloud management) system remains offline.

FINANCIAL MANAGEMENT

Depending on the cloud provider and how billing occurs, customers might need to modify the way they procure the services, amortize IT assets, and manage their budgets. Customers might be able to use ongoing operational funding instead of capital funding to procure cloud services, as was discussed earlier.

Customers might want to establish pools of funding, or purchase orders, so that individual cloud service orders (called *subscriptions*) are charged against this pool of money. To avoid the finance or procurement department being involved in every microtransaction and subscription, these pools of money have proven to be a more acceptable financial management technique.

Given the ability to place orders through the cloud service provider's portal, cloud owners must establish policies and governance to delegate authority to managers within the organization who are allowed to place new orders. Purchase orders and contracts would already be in place prior to online ordering but authorization to selected managers also means these managers are allowed to commit the funding of the services. Most service catalogs offer a customizable approval workflow that can be used by the organization to notify and/or seek active approvals from multiple persons to approve each new cloud service subscription.

Remember the key tenets of cloud computing: specifically, pay-as-you-go, shared infrastructure, and scalability. This means the chief information officer (CIO) has better control over utilization and has the ability to scale down as well as scale up as workload and projects require. By analyzing utilization statistics, CIOs can better identify trends in cost and resource usage to scale systems up or down depending on needs and budgets. This detailed level of statistical data is often difficult to collect and analyze for legacy IT systems, but it is a huge benefit to the cloud computing model. The ability to view this data across multiple departments, subagencies, and the organization as a whole will require changes in process, auditing, and oversight.

SECURITY MANAGEMENT

Security management will be significantly involved in the certification of a private cloud offering. VM templates or COEs will need to be precertified by security teams so that users can order services at any time and have the automated cloud management launch everything immediately.

Key Take-Away

Precertification of COEs is often the most significant change to the way organizations run today, but this is critical to the automation of a cloud, and it saves time and money for the customer.

Security will also be involved with any networking change controls or custom COEs created or requested. Internal network changes between VMs in the cloud environment also need to be approved by security, unless the network settings are part of a preapproved COE, in which case security has already approved.

Monitoring and scanning of all physical servers and customer VMs must be continuously performed; data scanning of all new VMs to safeguard against sensitive data loss might also be necessary. The key to success here is to use the cloud management system to automatically add new compute devices to the monitoring systems, so security personnel are immediately aware of new systems, and the monitoring can begin immediately.

In a multivendor hybrid or cloud broker environment, the initial accreditation of each cloud service, provider, and process can be complex and time consuming. U.S. government organizations have recently adopted standards (refer to FedRAMP in Chapter 6) to reduce repetitive accreditation processes by individual agencies, providing a certification for each cloud provider, instead, that each consuming organization will accept.

Security event management and response is another area that often requires changes for cloud environments. The public cloud provider will certainly have its own IT security systems and experts monitoring and responding to potential issues; however, the provider might not share all of this detailed information to its customers. Depending on SLAs and contract terms, the provider might only provide a summary of system and security events every month, for example. Organizations that traditionally have in-depth involvement in every security incident, event, or threat, might not have this level of visibility or involvement when services are hosted and managed by a contracted cloud provider.

TECHNICAL SUPPORT

The public cloud provider will normally provide technical support to a set, specifically named group of customer personnel. End-user support is often not provided by cloud providers, which forces customers to escalate prevetted issues through select designees to the cloud provider.

The private cloud technical support staff, or developers within a Dev/Test environment, will need to become familiar with hypervisor and cloud management systems to conduct normal operations, troubleshooting, patching, and upgrades.

Key Take-Away

Most public cloud and Dev/Test cloud services do not include software development support for programmers. The public cloud provider is normally only responsible for keeping the IaaS or PaaS infrastructure available, not to respond to questions from software development teams, unless the customer is willing to purchase a higher-priced support option.

Figure 2-7 is a repeat of Figure 1-5, which I'm showing here again to emphasize the roles that the cloud provider handles versus those handled by the customer. Only the SaaS applications are fully managed by the cloud provider, so organizations using cloud services will need to contract for or maintain specific skills in house.

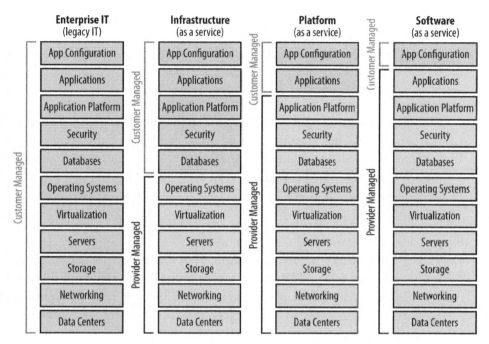

Figure 2-7. Cloud provider versus customer roles for managing cloud services and legacy/enterprise IT

Using Existing Operational Staff

Traditional datacenter or IT operations personnel have specific skills and experience with stable environments and applications, often managing day-to-day systems through runbooks, checklists, and standardized processes for any given event. Operational personnel are often not suited to build and deploy the newest systems and applications. The operational staffs are trained and accustomed to existing IT systems and applications; thus, there is a significant gap in skills when compared to experienced highly skilled cloud network, storage, server, and applications specialists.

Changes in staffing levels and skillsets to support the new cloud environment is a given. As the legacy IT systems are migrated to cloud-centric technologies or providers, the existing IT staff must also evolve. IT staff with new cloud-centric skillsets should be added to legacy IT staffs who are designated to morph into cloud roles. The truth is that the cloud does make it possible for an organization to support more users and applications with the same staff (assuming a growing consumer or customer base) or to reduce staff (for organizations with a fixed or stable consumer or customer base).

There are two recommended operational themes that you can promote and adopt:

Relentless pursuit of automation
All processes—from ordering to approvals and from provisioning to allocated storage and networking—should be automated by using the cloud management platform. Continuously improve the processes and remove manual processes. Use continuous monitoring and alerts to track anomalies and provisioning problems and catch problems before your customers call you.

Continuous migration to the cloud
It takes time and a continuous long-term effort to assess, plan, and migrate legacy data, servers, applications, storage, and the like to cloud-based services. Legacy systems were likely deployed with a three- to five-year technology refresh plan in mind, so this is a good time to roll applications and data to the cloud when the current lifecycle and depreciation has been completed. Mission-critical enterprise applications often require the most amount of planning and potential reengineering to shift to the cloud.

STAFFING EXPECTATIONS FOR THE PUBLIC CLOUD

Organizations utilizing public cloud services should evaluate which applications and IT services can shift to cloud-based services. Based on how much and which workloads are shifted to the cloud, legacy IT staff are often refocused to other purposes critical to the mission of your organization. It is really a myth or extremely rare that an entire organization moves so wholly and quickly to the cloud that IT staff needs to be displaced. The existing staff does need to adapt to the fact that commodity servers, VMs, storage, and applications can now be more quickly staged in the public cloud than through traditional procurement, equipment installation, and configuration—what I call the new style of IT. Applications and server workloads that are shifted to the cloud are typically managed and operated by using a combination of the public cloud's web-based management portal and remote control/remote desktop logon to the cloud-based server hosts.

STAFFING EXPECTATIONS FOR THE PRIVATE CLOUD

When deployingand planning to operate your own private cloud, using and adapting current datacenter operations staff is more complex. There are many skillsets and legacy processes that need to evolve when managing cloud-based services; virtualized servers, networking, and storage; backup and recovery; software updates and patching; and application installation and maintenance. Experience has shown that many organizations encounter resistance or pushback from existing operational personnel who are now being asked to adapt to new processes and techniques. Usually the legacy staff have every good intention to do well at their job but might have difficulty accepting that their legacy skills and experience are not appropriate or no longer a "best practice" in this new style of IT.

Transforming legacy skillsets and team silos

Many legacy datacenters and operations teams are organized by technology or skillset. Often, teams are organized into silos with a department manager, based on technologies such as servers, OSs, storage, backup and recovery, networking, monitoring, operations, and patching and updates. Because a private cloud involves new processes and best practices that span all of these areas, this is a good time to consider redistributing personnel into different team structures more in line with a service-oriented architecture.

Table 2-2 shows some operational staffing recommendations to consider.

Table 2-2. New operational team structure recommendations

TEAM/ ROLE	DESCRIPTION	TECHNICAL SKILLSET
Service/ offering manager (applicable mostly for organizations that provide cloud services to other departments or clients)	This is usually a small team, or even a single staff member, that manages what services are offered and future roadmap of feature releases. Responsibilities include the following: Consider having one unique offering manager for every major XaaS offering, depending on customer demand and adoption.	The person(s) in this role have a unique combination of business, consultative sales, and technical knowledge. Specific skills include the following: • Consulting expertise • Requirements analysis • Managing customer expectations and requests for new features (and determining financial,

TEAM/ ROLE	DESCRIPTION	TECHNICAL SKILLSET
	This is not a pure sales position; rather, it is an advisor to the customer but with enough technical knowledge to document customer feature requests and know how those requirements translate into new XaaS or cloud portal changes. Individual works closely with new contracted customers to smooth the initial onboarding process and ensure initial orders and needs are met. • Describing the solution, developing corresponding service offerings, and defining the necessary releases. • Working with the internal/ external clients to articulate the cloud solution capabilities. • Coordinating with the deployment manager to direct project teams. • Acting as the escalation point from customers to cloud management and technical staff. • Demonstrating and promoting cloud solution to other departments, potential tenants, and customers within the greater (or peer) organizations.	technical, and support impacts of potentially adding those features). • Ability to demonstrate all customer-facing portals, online ordering, and customization features to customers and end users • Ability to translate customer requests and issue escalation to internal sales, engineering, and support staff
Cloud management platform and	This team focuses on configuring, monitoring, and continuously improving the private cloud	These are the senior-most technical engineers in the operations team requiring

TEAM/ ROLE	DESCRIPTION	TECHNICAL SKILLSET
automation team	management platform. Responsibilities include the following: • Implementing updates and additions to the consumer-facing cloud portal, the service catalog, XaaS specifications and pricing, and automated provisioning tools and scripts. • During initial cloud launch, this team will be heavily focused on monitoring all new orders, ensuring that they provision successfully, and immediately correcting both the failed provisioning but also the automation/scripts so that future customer orders process correctly. • It is highly recommended that the manager or director of this team also be the manager over server, storage, patch and update, and backup and recovery teams to eliminate individual manager silos and delays in decision making.	knowledge across all network, server, storage, virtualization, OSs, and applications. Specific skills include the following: • Expertise in the cloud management platform, automation tools and scripts, virtualization tools, and APIs • Ability to continuously create and enhance automation processes and tools across all hardware and software components • Expert knowledge of network virtualization, VLANs, virtual private networks (VPNs), and software-defined networks • Expert knowledge of high-density server farms, storage systems, and datacenters spanning multiple datacenters • Expert knowledge of high availability at network, storage, server, and application levels • Expert knowledge of continuity of services across multiple datacenters and facilities or providers • Expert knowledge of service-oriented systems design and automated provisioning

TEAM/ ROLE	DESCRIPTION	TECHNICAL SKILLSET
		• Expert knowledge of multitenant security, operations, and user support
Server infrastructure team	This team focuses on all physical and virtualized servers, regardless of OS. Responsibilities include the following: This team of engineers is often taken from legacy server OS installation and configuration teams. • Handling the creation, testing, and management of existing and new VM templates, automated server provisioning and deployment, connectivity to storage, networking, and backup and recovery systems. • Planning and performing, on a continuous basis, migration from legacy datacenters and servers to the new cloud-based services. • Coordinating with the update and patching team that handles automated deployments of OS and application updates.	The server infrastructure team should have the following skills: • Expert knowledge of server virtualization and hypervisors, Infrastructure as a Service • Expert knowledge of high-density cartridge or blade server systems, including virtual network/storage connections within shared server chassis • Expert knowledge of multiple OSs, current and legacy revisions of each OS, gold VM image creation, evaluation, and management • Proficiency with traditional and software-defined networking and storage to be able to understand and coordinate with storage and networking teams
Storage team	This team focuses on SANs or equivalent virtualized storage networks, and virtualization of multiple legacy storage systems to be managed in a consolidated	The storage team should have the following skills: • Expertise in all legacy storage and modern SAN technologies, disk striping and RAID (best

TEAM/ ROLE	DESCRIPTION	TECHNICAL SKILLSET
	environment. Responsibilities include the following: Most storage teams are small or an individual person in legacy environment. It is often not best practice to hire an all-new staff just for cloud-based storage systems, so training and shift in processes is recommended for existing staff. • Ensuring automation and server teams have preconfigured and readily available storage for new customer orders. • Managing capacity and keeping up with new and future storage demands as new customers onboard 24-7. Maintaining a relationship with hardware manufacturer for quick deployment of new storage as needed. • Configuring cloud storage services (based on object and block-storage technologies) and application frontends used by customers to access object storage.	performance and configuration practices vary per SAN hardware manufacturer) • Understanding and expertise using thin provisioning, de-duplication, encryption, compression, snapshot, and SAN-based replication • Expertise in best practices for mapping storage volumes to VMs—may vary depending on hypervisor(s) in use • Familiarity with new capacity management techniques to ensure there is always excess storage available for new orders • Knowledge of storage virtualization appliances, software platforms, and software-defined storage mappings to virtual servers over converged network fabrics • Understanding of network-attached storage (NAS) • Understanding of object and block-storage services and how to configure hardware and software to provide a cloud-based storage service

TEAM/ ROLE	DESCRIPTION	TECHNICAL SKILLSET
Backup and recovery team	This team focuses on the cloud-based backup and recovery systems. Responsibilities include the following: Legacy backup/recovery personnel can be used for this new team but sometimes these people have difficulty understanding new techniques and processes. • Maintaining backup systems for new private cloud platforms (this often requires new tapeless/VTL technologies with little or no traditional backup windows). • Enabling redundant/continuous replication to a secondary datacenter for DR purposes using compression, and de-duplication. • Working closely with storage and server/virtualization teams to adopt and best utilize new cloud technologies.	The backup and recovery team should have the following skills: • Experience with high-speed, preferably tapeless, backup and recovery systems, data de-duplication, SAN replication, agentless backup software of mass-quantity VMs • Expertise on continuous backup technologies, SAN-based snapshots of data and VMs rather than legacy backup software agents on each server/OS • Knowledge of rapid data restoration from disk-based VTL into virtualized servers is different from many legacy environments

Operational Transformation Best Practices

Based on lessons learned and experience from across the cloud industry, the following best practices should be considered for your organization's planning.

TRANSITIONING TO THE CLOUD

Very few organizations can migrate all of their legacy infrastructure and applications to the cloud immediately—nor should they. Here are some considerations:

- Evaluate what applications are critical to your business customers and which applications most benefit by moving to the cloud.

- Depending on the applications to be migrated, the decision to use a public cloud provider or build your own private cloud should be discussed. Sometimes, organizations will build their own private cloud as well as integrate some services from a public cloud provider.

- Infrastructure services, VMs, and storage hosted in the cloud (IaaS) are widely available from numerous public cloud providers. You can also deploy IaaS techniques in a legacy datacenter as part of a modernization program that might lead to a future full of private or hybrid clouds.

- It is all about the applications. Moving IaaS storage and VMs to a private or public cloud is relatively easy—it is the custom-built legacy applications that take time to evaluate, sometimes reprogram, and transition to the cloud.

AUTOMATION OF EVERYTHING

The automation of the service ordering, provisioning, billing, and management of all infrastructure and software is critical to an efficient cloud environment. Here are some considerations:

- Avoid the temptation to implement or continue manual provisioning processes with the intention of automating later. Experience shows that implementing automation after core IaaS, PaaS, or SaaS applications are launched is very difficult and disruptive to the cloud environment.

- Automation means efficient and fast ordering and constituent provisioning (configuration management) with the lowest operational costs.

- Automation requires careful monitoring of status, errors, and capacity. Continuously improving the automation tools and scripts is essential.

- Automation applies to everything in the datacenter, not just cloud-based services. Automation is just one characteristic of a cloud service, but you can automate most technologies and processes within a datacenter to reduce costs, improve delivery times, and improve configuration consistency.

SECURITY PREAPPROVALS

Changes to security policies and procedures are necessary to accommodate the automated configuration and deployment of servers (physical or virtual), storage, network segments, and applications. Here are some considerations:

- OS and server/virtual server configurations should be scanned, vetted, and preapproved by security teams so that they can be deployed in an automated manner, 24-7, whenever a cloud service is ordered.

- Try to avoid having security involved in the approval process for every cloud order. Cloud service orders should be fully automated with almost immediate provisioning of services. Avoid adopting any manual processes, including security accreditation, in the actual provisioning workflow.

- Build any security features, tools, and network configurations into prebuilt and precertified services that appear in the cloud portal service catalog.

- Some organization, particularly in the public sector, might require that the overall cloud system, management tools, infrastructure, network, and applications be assessed and certified by the government or a third-party entity before the cloud can be officially brought online. One example of this certification is FedRAMP for public cloud providers servicing U.S. government customers.

CONTINUOUS MONITORING

Monitoring of the automation provisioning, customer orders, system capacity, system performance, and security are all critical in a 24-7, on-demand cloud system. Here are some considerations:

- All new applications, servers and virtual servers, network segments, and the like should be automatically registered to a universal configuration database and trigger immediate scans and monitoring. Avoid manually adding new applications or servers to the security, capacity, or monitoring tools to ensure continuous monitoring begins immediately when services are brought online.

- Monitoring of automated provisioning and customer orders is critical in an on-demand cloud environment. Particularly during the initial months of a new private cloud launch, there will be constant tweaks and improvements needed to the automation tools and scripts to continuously remove manual processes, error handling, and efficient resource allocation across multiple server farms, storage, and networks that make up the overall cloud environment.

- Clouds often support multiple tenants or consuming organizations. Monitoring and security tools often consolidate or aggregate statistics and system events to a centralized console, database, and support staff. When tracking, resolving, and reporting events and statistics, the data must be segmented and reported back to each tenant so that they only see their information—often the COTS tools used by the cloud provider have limitations in maintaining sovereignty of customer reports to multiple tenants.

SYNTHETIC TRANSACTION MONITORING

Monitoring of the network, servers, and applications is commonplace in any cloud or datacenter. Improvements in operations and monitoring should include the following:

- Utilize a system or third-party provider that can continuously process synthetic transactions to your websites and applications. These scripted transactions actually confirm that your customers are actually able to access and utilize your applications—not just simple ping test monitoring that only confirms the server is online.

- Also utilize these synthetic transactions to send alerts when an application has a problem and to measure performance treading.

CAPACITY MANAGEMENT

Capacity management in a cloud environment is even more critical than traditional IT as the number of impacted users and applications is much greater. Recommendations for capacity management include:

- An on-demand elastic cloud requires a new emphasis on capacity management and monitoring.

- Avoid initially overbuilding the capacity of server, virtual server, storage, and
  application licenses, or your initial costs will far exceed revenues and destroy
  an ROI model.

- Constant monitoring, alerts, and usage trending is necessary to ensure that
  the cloud infrastructure always has sufficient compute (CPU, memory, storage, network) resources for new customer orders.

- Negotiate on-demand, preferably pay-as-you-go, contracts with hardware and
  software vendors to quickly add new capacity as needed. A cloud should
  never run out of available system capacity or resources.

- Software manufacturers and vendors might initially demand up-front payment for a quantity of application licenses. The cloud model dictates that software licenses are prepurchased and then left unused until they are sold. A
  more preferable software agreement is to negotiate a pay-as-you-go license
  agreement with little or no up-front purchase and a true-up or end-of-month
  accounting (and payment to vendor) for all used software licenses.

- It is becoming more common for hardware vendors, especially storage vendors, to support the concept of on-demand rapid delivery of new resources or
  prestaging of excess capacity that the cloud provider doesn't pay for until
  actually utilized (and then more excess capacity is back-filled to maintain the
  level of available resources for future orders).

- Include some terms in the cloud provider SLA that indicate how large spikes
  or periods of resource utilization are handled. For example, having excessive
  resources idle and available costs too much money for the cloud provider to
  be profitable. So, what is the right amount of excess capacity that should be
  maintained to allow for future customers orders without over-purchasing
  additional capacity? Experience has shown that 25%-50% excess capacity on-

hand is a reasonable number with an SLA to customers requiring advanced notice of unusually large cloud purchases.

LEGACY MIGRATION AND SYSTEM-LIFECYCLES

Few organizations can move every legacy datacenter, server farm, network, and application to the cloud immediately. Soon after new cloud services are established, a long-term and ongoing process should begin to assess when and which of the existing legacy infrastructure and applications should be migrated to the cloud. Here are some considerations:

- Cloud customers often have not fully utilized or depreciated existing IT assets, and therefore moving to cloud in mid-lifecycle might destroy existing ROI models.

- Organizations or cloud providers that host a cloud service might actually cannibalize customers of legacy datacenter infrastructure and services if everyone suddenly demands the new, often cheaper, cloud service and pay-as-you-go pricing models. Have a migration strategy and plan in place to accommodate migrations and timing to avoid this cannibalization.

- Consider moving legacy infrastructure (servers, storage, network) to the cloud only when the three to five-year systems lifecycle is about to expire. Instead of replacing legacy hardware or software, transition the system to the cloud. This plan can help reduce or prevent cannibalization of your existing datacenter services and customers moving to the cheaper cloud model too soon.

PATCHING AND UPGRADES

Although not technically unique to a cloud environment, the patching and upgrading of firmware, OSs, and application software is critical. Here are some considerations:

- You should use automation tools for patching and software distribution wherever possible. Newly provisioned cloud services, such as IaaS VMs, are often deployed using a predefined VM template, but the patching and upgrade tools should immediately run against all new VMs to ensure stand-ards and compliance.

- Eventually, the number of patches and updates to an OS can become so extensive and take so much time to apply for new VMs that it might be better to update the master VM template(s) so that most of the patches and updates are included in the base VM image.

- Some customers, particularly in a Dev/Test service, might not want to have updates and patches automatically applied because it can break or disrupt applications in development. Have a process for consumers to opt out of sys-tem updates, but then also include SLA terms that protect the cloud provider from liability when a customer declines these automatic updates.

- Utilize monitoring software to scan for missing or removed software updates. Remember that customers sometimes remove or add software updates acci-dentally or on purpose and later claim the cloud provider is at fault.

BACKUP AND RECOVERY

Backup and recovery processes change significantly in a cloud environment. New backup hardware using VTL/disk-based (nontape) storage is recommended. These modern backup storage systems include technology such as de-duplication, snapshots, encryption, and efficient replication to secondary datacen-ters. Legacy datacenter backup systems are not normally efficient or effective for use in a modern on-demand higher SLA cloud environment. Here are some con-siderations:

- Backing up numerous VMs is best done through hypervisor and SAN-facilitated snapshots and replication with no backup software agents on each VM. Assuming that the cloud usage grows, there will be too many individual VMs to complete backups each day or night in the traditional manner. The more advanced cloud services are configured to take multiple snapshots per day for maximum data protection, lowest recovery point objective, and roll-back if needed.

- Maintenance windows each week or each month are decreasing industry wide. Customer expectations, particularly cloud customers, are 24-7-365 or 99.95% and higher availability. The days of declaring 4- to 8-hour system maintenance and outage windows, excluded from the SLA, are almost over.

This means that all backup systems should be designed with little or no planned service outages in mind. You can do this easily with modern SAN-based storage systems, new disk-based backup hardware, hypervisor and SAN-facilitated snapshots, and the latest VM-aware backup software platforms.

- Just as in cloud provisioning, automation is the key to a successful backup program. Everything should be automated with little or no manual processes remaining. Monitoring and alerts of successful or unsuccessful backups is critical, as is continuous improvements in automation tools and scripts. As capacity increases, so will backup windows, so diligence in managing the backup timing and processes is also important. Using SAN-based replication and snapshot technologies are recommended to greatly reduce backup windows.

- Restoring entire VMs—replacing or in addition to a functioning VM—is a unique process in an automated cloud environment. New techniques and software to restore data from SAN or VTL are necessary to ensure that the automated patching and upgrading, provisioning/de-provisioning, and other monitoring systems function properly.

DISASTER RECOVERY AND REDUNDANCY

Most major public cloud providers will already have some degree of redundancy, fault tolerance, and possibly redundant datacenters to ensure the guaranteed availability levels. When planning a private cloud to own and operate, disaster recovery and redundancy requires some initial design decisions, even if full continuity or recovery services are not part of the initial cloud deployment. Here are some considerations:

- VM hypervisors are particularly complex when you are planning to enable high availability, redundancy, and continuity within a datacenter or across multiple facilities. If you plan to enable disaster recovery, VM replication, and spanning across multiple datacenters, ensure that your initial cloud design and selection of hypervisor and SAN platforms support your ultimate goals, even if you are not deploying multiple datacenters initially.

- Automated provisioning when you also have high availability, replication, and multiple datacenters can be extremely complex to configure. The cloud management platform and the actual hypervisors, VMs, storage, and networks require specialized configurations. Different applications will use one or more techniques such as multiple mirroring, data replication, snapshots, or other forms of parallel processing to achieve high availability and redundancy across datacenters.

- Some cloud services or applications are much easier to configure for multiple datacenters, load balancers, and redundancy (or elastic capacity expansion). Examples of easier use cases include websites, static data, and applications developed with multithreaded, multiprovider cloud in the original design. To obtain true multi-VM and multi-datacenter scalability, reliability, and performance, legacy enterprise applications often need significant redesign and redeployment.

VIRTUALIZATION

Virtualization within an existing datacenter or cloud implementation is critical to achieving efficiencies, reliability, quality, and manageability of the infrastructure and applications. Here are some considerations:

- Server virtualization using one or more hypervisor software products is often a first step toward modernizing a legacy server farm. Virtualization itself does not mean that you have a cloud, but server virtualization and VMs are critical technologies used in a cloud environment.

- Virtualization of storage is a modern way of managing numerous existing and future storage systems through a common storage management platform. After a "master" storage virtualization platform is deployed, the brand, quantity, and configuration of the many disk systems and manufacturers become transparent—the virtualized storage platform performs all of the integration and management of disparate storage systems throughout the datacenter. An important feature of virtualized storage is its use of dynamic mappings between server farms, VMs/hypervisors, and the actual storage systems. It is no longer efficient to connect physical cables from each server to each storage system; instead, connect high-density cartridge or blade-server farms to a SAN fabric and use software to map storage volumes to hypervisors and VMs.

- Virtualization of the network—also called software-defined networking—is also critical to cloud environments because it facilitates a dynamic mapping of multiple network segments, VLANs, or software-defined network zones to VMs and applications. By removing static and manually configured hardware routes and configurations, VMs and applications can be more easily scaled, stretched across datacenters or ported from one cloud provider to another.

CHANGE CONTROL

Legacy change control processes need to evolve in an automated cloud environment. When each new cloud service is ordered and automated provisioning is completed, an automated process should also be utilized to track change controls. Here are some considerations:

- Avoid all manual processes that might slow down or inhibit the automated ordering and provisioning capabilities of the cloud platform.

- When new IaaS VMs are brought online, for example, configure the cloud management platform to automatically enter an entry into the organization's change control system as an "automatic approval." You can use this immediate addition to the change database to trigger further notifications to appropriate operational staff or trigger automatic security or inventory scanning tools.

- Utilize preapproved VM templates, applications, and network configurations for all automatically provisioned cloud services—avoid manual change control processes and approvals in the cloud ordering process.

- Remember to record all VMs, OS, and application patching, updates, and restores in the change control database. Finally, also remember that you should immediately update the change control and inventory databases when a cloud service is stopped or a subscription canceled.

Deploying Your Cloud

Key topics in this chapter:

- The consume-versus-build decision
- Building your own cloud—lessons learned, including architecture examples and guidance
- Managing scope, releases, and customer expectations
- Redundancy, continuity, and disaster recovery
- Using existing operational staff during deployment
- Deployment best practices

Deciding Whether to Consume or Build

A critical decision for any organization planning to use or build a cloud is whether to consume services from an existing cloud service provider or to build your own cloud. Every customer is unique in their goals and requirements as well as their existing legacy datacenter environment, so the consume-versus-build decision is not always easy to make. Cloud systems integrators and leading cloud providers have learned that there is often customer confusion with regard to the terms *public cloud, virtual private cloud, managed cloud, private cloud,* and *hybrid cloud.*

Figure 3-1 presents a simplified decision tree (from the perspective of you as the cloud customer or client) that explains different consume-versus-build options and how they map to public, private, and virtual private clouds. For definitions and comparisons of each cloud deployment model, refer to Chapter 1.

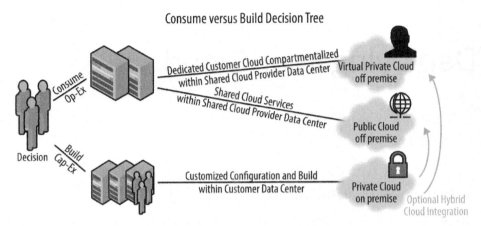

Figure 3-1. The consume-versus-build decision tree

To better understand the consume-versus-build options that are presented in the following sections, read "Capital versus Operating Expenses" on page 220 in Chapter 5.

CONSUMPTION

Consumption of cloud services refers to an organization purchasing services from a cloud service provider, normally a public cloud. In this consumption model, there are little or no up-front capital expenses; customers incur service fees on a daily, weekly, monthly, or yearly basis, which cover subscribed services and resource usage. This model requires no on-premises computing infrastructure be installed at the customer's facility or added to its network.

Also understand that a consumption model also can apply to a virtual private cloud or managed cloud that is fully hosted at a cloud provider's facility. This is just like a public cloud subscription model but with some level of customization and usually a private network compartment. Cloud providers might require some level of minimum quantity or term commitment and possibly some initial capital investment to configure this virtual private or managed cloud on behalf of the customer organization.

BUILD

Building a cloud service is usually for a private cloud deployment that can be located in a customer's datacenter or chosen third-party datacenter. In this private cloud deployment model, the customer would normally take on the burden of most or all of the capital expenses to deploy and manage the cloud service. The customer organization can chose to use a systems integrator that has expertise in deploying private clouds, or the organization can design and procure all of the hardware and software components to build its own cloud. Experience demonstrates that hiring a systems integrator that specializes in private cloud deployment results in a faster deployment, lower risk, and a more feature-rich cloud environment—more important, this allows your organization to focus on your core business and customers rather than trying to also become a cloud integration and deployment expert.

There are numerous business decisions to be made in the planning process when building your own cloud for internal, peer, or suborganizational consumption. You will need to determine who your target consumers or organizations are, which cloud deployment model to start with, how you will sell (or chargeback) to end consumers or users, and how you will govern and support your customers. The technical decisions, size of your initial cloud infrastructure and your cloud management system will also vary depending on your business decisions.

CLOUD DEPLOYMENT MODELS

The first thing to decide is what cloud deployment type best fits your target end consumers (your own organization or customers/consumers of your cloud service for which you might host IT services). These are the choices you'll need to decide among (for complete descriptions and comparison of each cloud model, refer to Chapter 1).

Public cloud
    If you truly want to become a public cloud provider, you need to build your infrastructure, offerings, and pricing with the goal of establishing a single set of products standardized across all of your customers. These cloud services would typically be available via the Internet—hence the term public—for a wide number and array of target customers. You would normally not offer customized or professional services; instead, you would focus on automation and as little human intervention in the management of your system as possible, keeping your costs low and putting you in a competitive position.

Virtual private cloud
    Another offering gaining popularity is called the virtual private cloud, which is essentially a public cloud provider offering a unique (i.e. private) compartment and subnetwork environment per customer or tenant. This

smaller private subcloud—or cloud within the larger cloud—can have higher security and some customization, but not to the level possible with a pure private cloud.

Private cloud

If you plan to offer your internal enterprise organization or customers a personalized or custom cloud solution, a private cloud deployment model is likely your best choice. You can deploy and host the private cloud within any customer or third-party datacenter. One of the most important technologies that must be evaluated, procured, and installed is a cloud management platform that will provide a customer ordering and subscription management portal, automated provisioning of Anything as a Service (XaaS), billing, and reporting.

Community cloud

Community clouds are essentially a variation of private clouds. They are normally designed and built to the unique needs of a group of organizations that want to share cloud infrastructure and applications. Some portions of the organization host and manage some cloud services, whereas other portions of the organization host a different array of services. There are countless possible variations with respect to who hosts what, who manages services, how procurement and funding is handled, and how the end users are managed. The infrastructure, network, and applications deployed for a community cloud will depend upon the customer requirements.

Hybrid cloud

Most organizations using a private cloud are likely to evolve into a hybrid model. As soon as you connect one cloud to another, particularly when you have a mix of public and private cloud services, you have, by definition, a hybrid cloud. Hybrid clouds connect multiple types of clouds and potentially multiple cloud service providers; connecting to a legacy on-premises enterprise cloud is also part of a hybrid cloud. You can deploy a hybrid cloud management system to coordinate all automation, provisioning, reporting, and billing across all connected cloud service providers. Hybrid cloud management systems, sometimes call *cloud broker platforms*, are available from several major systems integrators and cloud software vendors for deployment within an enterprise datacenter or private cloud. After you deploy one, you can configure these hybrid cloud management systems to integrate with one or more external cloud providers or legacy data-center IT systems.

Cloud Infrastructure

There are significant consume-versus-build decisions to be made when you're determining the design and deployment of the cloud infrastructure. The cloud infrastructure includes everything from the physical datacenters to the network, servers, storage, and applications.

The cost of building and operating the datacenter is extremely expensive, and sometimes not within the expertise of non-technology-oriented organizations. Professional cloud service providers, systems integrators, or large organizations with significant IT skills are better suited to managing an enterprise private cloud infrastructure.

DATACENTERS

Most cloud service providers will have at least two geographically diverse datacenters; thus, loss of either does not interrupt all services. Cloud providers (or organizations building their own enterprise private cloud) can either build their own datacenters or lease space within existing datacenters. Within each datacenter is a significant amount of cooling and power systems to accommodate housing thousands of servers, storage devices, and network equipment.

Modern datacenters have redundancy built in to everything so that any failures in a single component will not harm the equipment hosted within. Redundant power systems, battery backup, and generators are deployed to maintain power in the event of an outage. Datacenters have a certain amount of diesel fuel housed in outdoor or underground tanks to run the generators for some period of time (24 to 48 hours is typical) with multiple vendors prearranged to provide additional fuel if generator power is needed for a longer period of time.

Similar to the redundancy of the power systems, the cooling systems within a datacenter are also redundant. Given the vast number of servers and other equipment running within the facility, maintaining the interior at an ideal temperature requires a significant amount of HVAC equipment. This is of paramount concern because prolonged high temperatures will harm the network and computer infrastructure.

The power required by a datacenter is so significant that often, a datacenter can become "full" because of the lack of available power even if there is available physical space within the building. This problem is exacerbated by high-density servers that can fit into a smaller space but still require significant power.

Physical security is also a key component. Datacenters are often housed in unmarked buildings, with a significant amount of cameras, security guards, biometric identity systems, as well as interior cages, racks, and locks separating sections of the floor plan. Datacenters use these tools to ensure that unauthorized personnel cannot access the computer systems, which prevents tampering, unscheduled outages, and theft.

Figure 3-2 presents a simplified view of a typical datacenter. The three lightly shaded devices with the black tops, shown on the back and front walls of the floor plan, represent the cooling systems. The dark-gray devices are the power distribution systems. The medium-shaded racks contain servers, and the remaining four components are storage and data backup systems. Notice that I don't show any network or power cables: those are often run in hanging trays near the ceiling, above all the equipment. These depictions are for explanatory purposes only; actual equipment within a datacenter varies greatly in size and placement on the floor.

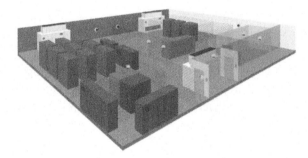

Figure 3-2. A simplified view of a datacenter's interior components

Datacenters sometimes contain pods (cargo type containers preconfigured with servers, network, and storage infrastructure), caged areas, or rooms, each with similar equipment to that shown in Figure 3-2. Cloud providers or customers often lease out entire pods until they are full and then begin filling additional pods as necessary.

NETWORK INFRASTRUCTURE

The "vascular" system of a cloud service provider is the network infrastructure. The network begins at the *edge*, which is where the Internet communication circuits connect to the internal network within the datacenter. Network routers and firewalls are typically used to separate, route, and filter traffic to and from the Internet and the internal network. The network infrastructure consists of everything from the edge and firewall to all of the datacenter core routers and switches, and finally to each top-of-rack (ToR) switch.

INTERNET SERVICES

For customers to use the cloud services, the cloud provider needs to implement a fairly large and expandable connection to the Internet. This connection often includes purchasing bandwidth from multiple Internet providers for load balancing and redundancy; as a cloud service provider, you cannot afford to have Internet connectivity lost. Because the amount of customers and traffic are likely going to rise over time, ensure that the agreement with your Internet providers allows for increasing bandwidth dynamically or upon request.

INTERNAL NETWORK

Within the datacenter, the cloud provider's network typically begins with routers and firewalls at the edge of the network connected to the Internet communication circuits. Inside the firewalls are additional routers and core network switching equipment with lower-level access switches cascading throughout the datacenter. The manufacturer or brand of equipment deployed varies based on the cloud provider's preference or skillset of the network engineers. Like computers, network equipment is often replaced every three, five, or seven years to keep everything under warranty and modern enough to keep up with increasing traffic, features, and security management.

Today's internal networks are not only for traditional Internet Protocol (IP) communications between servers, applications, and the Internet; there are numerous other network protocols that might need to be supported, and various other forms of networks such as *iSCSI* and *Fibre Channel* that are common to storage area networks (SANs). Cloud providers might decide to use networking equipment that handles IP, SAN, and other forms of networking communications within the same physical network switches. This is called *converged networking* or *multiprotocol/fabric switches*.

Because networking technologies, protocols, and speeds continue to evolve, it is recommended that you select a manufacturer that continuously provides new and improved firmware and software. Newer versions of firmware or software include bug fixes, newer features, and possibly newer network protocols. Some networking equipment is also very modular, adding small modules or *blades* into a shared chassis, with each module adding more network capacity, or handling special functions such as routing, firewalls, or security management.

The diagram shown in Figure 3-3 is a simplified view of a sample network infrastructure. The top of the network begins where the Internet connects to redundant *edge routers* that then connect to multiple lower-layer distribution and access switches cascaded below the core. The final end points are the servers, storage devices, or other computing devices. What is not shown, but is typical, are multiple network circuits connected to each end-point server to provide load-balanced, redundant, or *out-of-band network* paths. These out-of-band network paths are still technically part of the network, but are dedicated communications paths used for data backups or management purposes. By keeping this network traffic off of the production network, data backup and management traffic never slows down the production network.

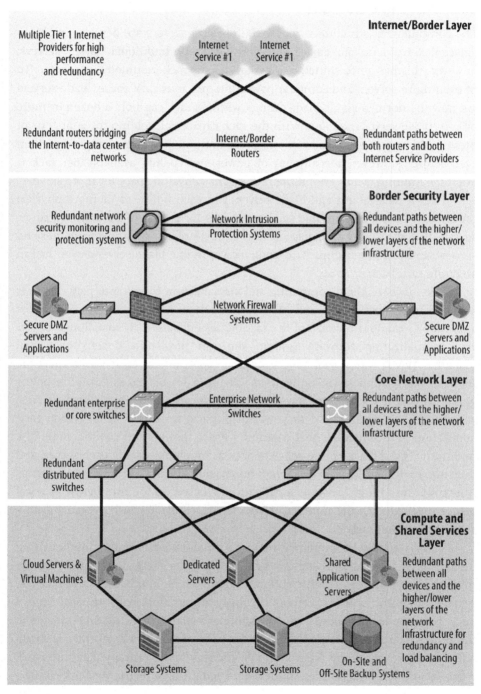

Figure 3-3. Network infrastructure layers

COMPUTE INFRASTRUCTURE

The compute infrastructure is where the physical servers are deployed within a datacenter. Not long ago, datacenters were filled with traditional "tower" servers; however, this has since shifted to a higher-density rack-mounted form factor. To fit even more servers and compute power into precious rack space, blade servers are now the norm; a single blade cabinet within a rack can hold a dozen or more plug-in blade-server modules. With the rack capable of holding three or four of these cabinets, you can achieve more server compute power in a single rack than ever before. However, the amount of power and cooling available per rack is often the limiting factor, even if the rack still has physical space for more servers.

Modern rack-mount and blade servers can each house 10 or more physical processors, each with multiple processor cores for a total of 40 or more cores. Add to this the ability to house up to a terabyte of memory in the higher-end servers, and you have as much compute power in one blade server as you had in an entire rack back in 2009.

Here is where cloud computing and virtualization comes into play. There is so much processor power and memory in today's modern servers, that most applications cannot utilize all of the capabilities efficiently. By installing a hypervisor virtualization software system, you can now host dozens of virtual machines (VMs) within each physical server. You can size each VM to meet the needs of each application, rather than having a lot of excess compute power going unused if you were to have just one application per physical server. Yes, you could simply purchase less powerful physical servers to better match each application, but remember that datacenter space, power, and cooling come at a premium cost; it makes more sense to pack as much power into each server, and thus into each rack, as possible. When purchasing and scaling your server farms, it is now common to measure server capacity based on the number of physical blades multiplied by the number of VMs that each blade can host—all within a single equipment rack.

Figure 3-4 shows a simplified view of a small two-datacenter cloud environment. This example shows both physical and virtual servers along with the cloud management platform, identity authentication system, and backup and recovery systems spanning both datacenters. In this configuration, both physical servers and virtual servers are shown, all connecting to a shared SAN. All SAN storage in the primary datacenter is replicated across to the secondary datacenter to facilitate disaster recovery and failover should services at the primary datacenter fail. Notice that the firewall located in the center indicating a secure network connection between datacenters that allows traffic to be redirected. This also facilitates failover of both cloud management nodes and guest/customer VMs if necessary. In the event of a total outage at the primary datacenter, the secondary datacenter could assume all cloud services.

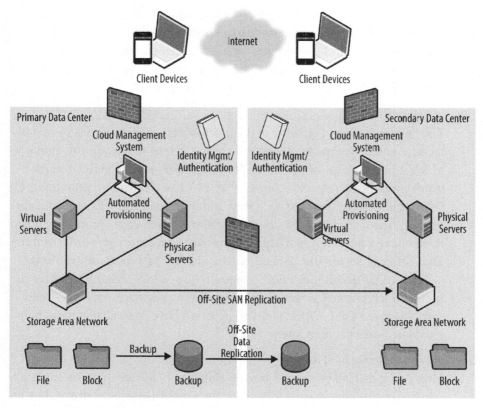

Figure 3-4. Typical network and server infrastructure (logical depiction)

Here are some factors you should consider when selecting and deploying the compute infrastructure:

Server hardware

A typical cloud infrastructure would start with one or more server-blade chassis populated with multiple high-density blade servers (see Figure 3-5). You should consider standardizing on a single vendor so that your support staff can focus on one skillset, one brand of spare parts, and one server management system. Most servers in this category have built-in management capabilities to remotely monitor and configure firmware, BIOS, and many other settings. You can also remotely reboot and receive alerts on problems from these built-in management capabilities. Forwarding these alerts, or combining the manufacturer's management system with a larger enterprise operations system, is ideal for completely integrated management. In a cloud environment, servers and blade chassis that have advanced virtualization and software-defined mappings between chassis, blades, storage, and networking present a significant advantage—so a "cloud enabled" server farm is not just marketing hype, but a real set of technologies that cloud providers can take advantage of.

CPU and memory

The performance and quantity of the processors in a server varies by manufacturer and server model. If you were trying to host the maximum amount of VMs per physical server or blade, you would want to select the maximum amount of processor power that you can get within your budget. Often, purchasing "last year's" newest and best processor will save you significant money, compared to buying the leading-edge processor, just released, at a premium markup. The amount of memory you order within each physical server will depend on the amount of processors you order. Overall, try to match processor to memory to see how many VMs you can host on each physical server. Popular hypervisor software vendors—Microsoft, VMware, KVM, Citrix, and Parallels—all have free calculators to help size your servers appropriately.

Internal versus external hard drives

Most rack or blade servers have the ability to hold one or more internal hard drives; the question is less about the size of these hard drives, but if you really want any at all inside each server. I highly recommend not installing local hard drives; instead, use shared storage devices that are connected to the blade server chassis via a SAN technology such as Fibre Channel, iSCSI, or Fibre Channel over Ethernet (FCOE), as depicted in the logical view in Figure 3-4. (A physical view of the SAN storage system is shown in Figure 3-5.) The servers boot their operating system (OS) from a logical unit numbers (LUN) on the SAN, rather than from local hard drives. The benefit is that you can install a new server or replace a blade server with another one for maintenance or repair purposes, and the new server boots up using the same LUN volume on the SAN. Remember, in a vast server farm, you will be adding or replacing servers regularly; you don't want to take on the burden of managing the files on every individual hard drive on every physical server. Also, holding all of the OS, applications, and data on the SAN allows for much faster and centralized backup and recovery. Best of all, the performance of the SAN is several times better than that of any local hard drive; in an enterprise or cloud datacenter, you absolutely need the performance that a SAN provides.

It should be noted that SANs are significantly more expensive than direct-attached storage (DAS) within each physical server; however, the performance, scalability, reliability, and flexibility of configuration usually outweigh the cost considerations. This is especially true in a cloud environment in which virtualization of everything (servers, storage, networking) is critical. There are storage systems that take advantage of inexpensive DAS and software installed across numerous low-cost servers to form a virtual storage array. This approach uses a large quantity of slower-speed storage devices as an alternative to a high-speed SAN. There are too many features, costs and benefits, performance, and operational considerations between storage approaches to cover in this book.

Server redundancy

Just as with the network infrastructure described earlier in this chapter, redundancy also applies to servers:

Power and cooling

Each server you implement should have multiple power supplies to keep it running even if one fails. In a blade-server system, the cabinet that holds all the server blade modules has two, three, four or more power supplies. The cabinet can sustain one or two power failures and still operate all of the server blades in the chassis using the surviving power modules. Fans to cool the servers and blade cabinet also need to be redundant; similarly, the cabinet itself houses most of the fans and has extra fans for redundancy purposes.

Network

Each server should have multiple network interface cards (NICs) installed or embedded on the motherboard. Multiple NICs are used for balancing traffic to achieve more performance as well as for redundancy should one NIC fail. You can use additional NICs to create supplementary subnetworks to keep backup and recovery or management traffic off of the production network segments. In some systems, the NICs are actually installed within the shared server cabinet rather than on each individual server blade; this affords virtual mapping flexibility and redundancy, which are both highly recommended.

Storage

If you plan to use internal hard drives in your servers, ensure that you are using a Redundant Array of Independent Disks (RAID) controller to both *stripe* data across multiple drives (I'll explain what this is shortly), or mirror your drives for redundancy purposes. If you boot from SAN-based storage volumes (recommended), have multiple Host BUS Adapters (HBAs) or virtual HBA channels (in a shared-server chassis) so that you have redundant connections to the SAN with greater performance. Be wary of using any local server hard drives, for data or for boot volumes, because they do not provide the performance, virtual mapping, redundancy, and scalability of shared or SAN-based disk systems. Again, as stated earlier, there are alternative storage systems that use large numbers of replicated, inexpensive disk systems, without a true RAID controller, to achieve similar redundancy capabilities but the cost-benefit, features, and a full comparison of storage systems is beyond the scope of this book.

Scalability and replacement

In a cloud environment, as the service provider you must continually add additional servers to provide more capacity, and also replace servers for repair or maintenance purposes. The key to doing this without interrupting your online running services is to never install an application onto a single physical server (and preferably not onto local hard drives). If that server were to fail or require replacing, the application or data would be lost, leaving you responsible for building another server, restoring data from backup, and likely providing your customers with a credit for the inconvenience.

Key Take-Away

Using a SAN for OS boot volumes, applications, and data is recommended. Not only is the SAN significantly faster than local hard drives, but SAN systems are built for massive scalability, survivability, backup and recovery, and data replication between datacenters. This also makes it possible for the new blade servers to automatically inherit all of its storage and network mappings. With no configuration of the new or replacement server needed, the blade automatically maps to the appropriate SAN and NICs and immediately boots up the hypervisor (which then manages new VMs or shifts current VMs to spread workloads).

Server virtualization

Installing a hypervisor onto each physical server provides for the best utilization of the hardware through multiple VMs. As the cloud provider, you need to determine which hypervisor software best meets your needs and cost model. Some hypervisors are more mature than others, having more APIs and extensibility to integrate with other systems such as the SAN or server hardware management systems. The key to virtualization, beyond squeezing more VMs into each physical server, is the ability to have VMs failover or quickly reboot on any other available physical server in the farm. Depending on the situation and hypervisor's capability, you can do this without a customer even noticing an outage. With this capability, you can move all online VMs from one server to any other servers in the farm, facilitating easy maintenance or repair. When you replace a failed server blade or add new servers for capacity, the hypervisor and cloud management system recognizes the additional physical server(s) and begins launching VMs on it. (Figure 3-5 shows the physical servers that would run hypervisors and host guest or customer VMs.)

Figure 3-5 shows a notional example of a private cloud installed into a single physical equipment rack. The configuration includes:

- Two network switches for fiber Ethernet and fiber SAN connection to the datacenter infrastructure

- Three cloud management servers that will run the cloud management software platform

- A SAN storage system with seven disk trays connected through SAN switches to server chassis backplane

- Two high-density server chassis, each with 16-blade servers installed, running your choice of hypervisor and available as customer VMs (also called capacity VMs)

Additional expansion cabinets would be installed next to this notional cloud configuration with extra capacity servers and storage. Cloud management servers do not need to be repeated for every rack, but there is a limit, depending on the cloud management software vendor you choose and the number of guest/capacity VMs. When this limit is reached, additional cloud management servers will be needed but can be federated—meaning that they will be added under the command and control of the central cloud management platform and function as one large cloud that spans all of the expansion racks.

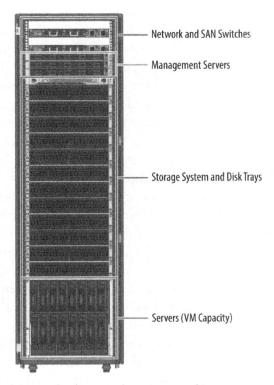

Figure 3-5. A notional private cloud in a single equipment cabinet

STORAGE SYSTEMS

Storage for large datacenters and cloud providers has come a long way from the days of simple hard drives installed within each server. This is fine for desktop workstations, but the performance of any one hard drive is too slow to handle hundreds or thousands of users. Modern disk drives are faster and certainly hold more data per physical hard drive than ever before, but do not confuse these newer hard drives with a true datacenter storage system. Even solid-state drives (SSD) are not always as fast as the multiple, striped disk drives that a SAN provides. Of course, combining striping and SSD provides the best disk performance—but at significant cost.

Anatomy of a SAN

The SAN consists of one or more head units (centralized "brains") that manage numerous trays of disk drives (refer back to Figure 3-5). A single SAN can hold thousands of physical disk drives, with the head units managing all of the striping, parity, cache, and performance management. As you need more storage capacity, you simply add more trays to the system, each one holding 8 to 20 drives. Most large SANs can scale from less than one, to six or eight racks full of disk trays. When one SAN head unit (or pair of head units for redundancy) reaches its recommended maximum number of disk drives or performance threshold, you can add additional head units and drive trays, forming another SAN in its own right. The management of multiple SANs from the same manufacturer is relatively easy because they use the same software management tools and can even make multiple SANs appear as one large SAN.

Within a SAN, there are often multiple types of disk drives. The cheapest ones used are SATA (serial AT attachment) drives. Although these types are the slowest, the trade-off is that they usually have the highest raw capacity. The next level up in performance and price is SAS (serial attached SCSI) drives; however, SAS drives do not have as much capacity as SATA drives. The next higher level of performance is from Fiber Channel disk drives but these are quickly being phased out due to cost and size limitations—SAS being a better mid-tier disk option in many cases. The premium level disk drives for performance and cost are SSDs. Depending on your performance and capacity needs, you can configure a SAN with one or all of these drive types. The SAN head units can automatically spread data across the various disk technologies to maintain optimum performance, or you can manually carve up the disks, striping, and RAID levels to meet your needs.

The latest SAN systems have an additional type of temporary storage called a cache. Cache is actually computer memory (which is even faster than SSDs) that temporarily holds data until it can be written to the physical disks. This technology can significantly improve the SAN performance, especially when pushed to its maximum performance limits. Some SAN manufacturers are now beginning to offer pure memory-based storage devices for which there are no actual disk drives. These are extremely fast but also extremely expensive; you need to consider if your servers or applications can actually benefit from that much performance.

Here are some factors you should consider when selecting and deploying storage infrastructure:

SAN sizing and performance

> When selecting a SAN model and sizing, consider the servers and applications that your customers will use. Often the configuration of the disks, disk groups, striping, RAID, size of disk drives, and cache are determined

based on the anticipated workload the SAN will be servicing. Each individual SAN model will have a maximum capacity, so multiple sets of head units and drive trays might be needed to provide sufficient capacity and performance.

I highly recommend utilizing the SAN manufacturer's expertise to help you pick the proper configuration. Inform the SAN provider of the amount of usable storage you need and the servers and applications that will be using it; the SAN experts will then create a configuration that meets your needs. All too often, organizations purchase a SAN and attempt to configure it themselves, ending in poor performance, poorly configured RAID and disk groups, and wasted capacity.

Key Take-Away

Most cloud providers and internal IT organizations tend to overestimate the amount of initial storage required and the rate at which new customers will be added. The result is over-purchase of storage capacity and increased initial capital expenditure. Careful planning is needed to create a realistic business model for initial investment and customer adoption, growth, and migration to your cloud.

Fibre Channel network

There are various types of cabling, networks, and interfaces between the SANs and servers. The most popular is a Fibre Channel network, consisting of Fibre Channel cables connecting servers to a Fibre Channel switch. Additional Fibre Channel cables are run from the switch to the SAN. Normally, you have multiple fiber connections between each server with a switch for increased performance and redundancy. There are also between two and eight Fibre Channel cables running from the switch to each SAN, again providing performance, load balancing, and redundancy. You can also connect Fibre Channel network switches to additional fiber switches to create a distributed SAN environment, connect to Fibre Channel backup systems, and even implement replication to another SAN.

There are additional cabling and network technologies to connect servers to a SAN. iSCSI and FCoE are two such technologies, utilizing traditional network cabling and switches to transmit data between servers and SANs. To keep disk traffic separate from production users and network applications, additional NICs are often installed in each server and dedicated to the disk traffic.

RAID and striping

There are numerous RAID techniques and configurations available within a SAN. The optimum configuration is best determined by the SAN manufacturer's experts, because every model and type of SAN is unique. Only the manufacturers really know their optimal combination of disk striping, RAID, disk groups, and drive types to provide the required capacity and performance—the best configuration from one SAN manufacturer will not be the same for another SAN product or manufacturer. Here are some key recommendations:

Striping

Striping data across multiple disk drives greatly speeds up the performance of the disk system. To provide an example, when a chunk of data is saved to disk, the SAN can split the data onto 10 striped drives as opposed to a single drive held within a physical server. The SAN head unit will simultaneously write one tenth of the data to each of the 10 drives. Because this occurs at the same time, the chunk of data is written in one-tenth the amount of time it would take to write the data to a single nonstriped drive.

RAID

I won't cover all the definitions and benefits of each RAID technique; however, I should note that SAN manufacturers have optimized their systems for certain RAID levels. Some have even modified a traditional RAID level, and essentially made a hybrid RAID of their own to improve redundancy and performance. One common mistake untrained engineers often make is to declare that they need RAID 10 —a combination of data striping and mirroring—for the SAN in order to meet performance requirements. The combination of striping and mirroring defined in a RAID 10 configuration does give some performance advantages, but it requires twice the number of physical disks. Given the complexity of today's modern SANs, making the blind assumption to use RAID 10 can be a costly mistake. Allowing the SAN to do its job, with all its advanced striping and cache technology, will provide the best performance without the wasted drive space that RAID 10 requires. Essentially, RAID 10 was necessary years ago, when you used less expensive, lower-performing disks and had to maximum performance and redundancy; SAN technologies are now far better options to provide even more performance and redundancy along with scalability, manageability, and countless other features.

Key Take-Away

When using a modern SAN, making the blind assumption to use RAID 10 can prove to be a costly mistake. Allowing the SAN to do its job, with all its advanced striping and cache technology, will provide the best performance without the wasted drive space. Each SAN device will have its own recommended RAID, striping, and caching guidelines for maximum performance, so traditional RAID concepts might not provide the best results.

Thin provisioning

Thin provisioning is now a standard feature on most modern SANs. This technology essentially tricks each server into seeing X amount of disk capacity without actually allocating the entire amount of storage. For example, a server might be configured to have a 100 GB volume allocated from the SAN, but only 25 GB of data actually stored on the volume. The SAN will continue to inform the server that it has a total of 100 GB of available capacity, but in actuality, only 25 GB of data is being used; the SAN system can actually allow another server to utilize the free 75 GB. When done across an entire server farm, you save a huge amount of storage space by providing the servers with only the storage they are actually using. One important factor is that cloud providers must monitor all disk utilization carefully so that they don't run out of disk capacity because they have effectively "oversubscribed" their storage allocations. When actual utilized storage begins to fill up the available disk space, they must add disk capacity.

De-duplication

When you consider the numerous servers, applications, and data that utilize a SAN, there is a significant amount of data that is duplicated. One obvious example is the OS files for each server or VM; these files exist on each and every boot volume for every server and VM. De-duplication technology within the SAN keeps only one copy of each data block, yet essentially tricks each server into thinking it still has its own dedicated storage volume. De-duplication can easily reduce your storage requirements by a factor of 5 to 30 times, and that is before using any compression technology. Critics of de-duplication claim it slows overall SAN performance. Man-ufactures of SANs offering de-duplication are, of course, aware of this criticism, and each have put in technologies that mitigate the performance penalty. Some SAN manufacturers claim their de-duplication technology, combined with caching and high-performance head/logic units are sophis-ticated enough that there are zero or unnoticeably small performance pen-alties from enabling the technology, thus making the cost savings appear even more attractive.

Key Take-Away

Consider using thin provisioning and data de-duplication when possible to reduce the amount of storage required. By embedding thin provisioning and de-duplication functionality within the chipsets of the SAN head units, most SANs now suffer little or no performance penalty when using it. Any penalty you might see is more than acceptable, given the amount of disk space you can potentially save.

Reclamation

When a VM boots up its OS, it allocates a certain amount of temporary swap or working disk storage capacity (e.g., 20 GB) to operate. When the VM is no longer running, it no longer needs this temporary working space from the SAN. The problem is that the data for the inactive VM still exists on the SAN. To reclaim that space, a process known as *reclamation* is used. Most SANs can perform this function, some automatically, and some requiring a software application to be manually executed or using a sched-uled batch job. This technology is crucial, or you will run out of available disk space because of leftover "garbage" data clogging up available SAN storage even after VMs have been turned off.

Snapshots and backup

SANs have the unique ability to take a snapshot of any part of the storage. These snapshots are taken while the disks are online and actively in use, and are exact copies of the data—taking only seconds to perform with no impact on performance or service availability. The reason snapshots are so fast is because the SAN is technically not copying all of the data; instead, it's using pointers to mark a point in time. The benefits of this technology are many; the cloud provider can take a snapshot and then roll back to it anytime needed. If snapshots are taken throughout the day, the data vol-ume can be instantly restored back to any pointer desired in the case of data corruption or other problems. Taking a snapshot and then performing a backup against it is also an improvement in speed and consistency compared to trying to back up live data volumes.

Replication

Replication of SAN data to another SAN or backup storage system is very common within a datacenter. SANs have technology embedded within them to initially seed the data to the target storage system, and then send only the incremental (commonly referred to as *delta*) changes across the fiber or network channels. This technique allows for replication of SAN data across wide area network (WAN) connections, essentially creating a copy of all data offsite and fully synchronized at all times. This gives you the ability to quickly recover data and provides protection should the primary datacenter's SAN fail or become unavailable. Replication of SAN data from one datacenter to another is often combined with redundant server farms at secondary datacenters. This way, these servers can be brought online with all of the same data should the primary servers, SAN, or datacenter fail. This SAN replication is often the backbone of geo-redundant servers and cloud storage operations, facilitating the failover from the primary to a secondary datacenter when necessary.

BACKUP AND RECOVERY SYSTEMS

As a cloud provider, you are responsible for not only keeping your servers and applications online and available to customers, but you must also protect the data. It is not a matter of if, but when, a computer or storage system will fail. As I discuss throughout this chapter, you should be purchasing and deploying your servers, storage, and network systems with redundancy from the start. It is only when redundancy and failover to standby systems fail that you might need to resort to restoring data from backup systems. If you have sufficient ongoing replication of your data (much preferred over depending on a restore from backup), the only occasion in which you need to restore from backups is when data becomes corrupt or accidentally deleted. Having points in time—usually daily at a minimum—to which you have backed up your data gives you the ability to quickly restore it.

Backup systems vary greatly, but traditionally consist of software and a tape backup system (see Figure 3-6). The backup software both schedules and executes the backup of data from each server and disk system and sends that data across the network to a tape backup system. This tape system is normally a large multitape drive library that holds dozens or hundreds of tapes. All data and tapes are indexed into a database so that the system knows exactly which tape to load when a particular restore request is initiated.

Backup software is still a necessary part of the backup and restore process. It is normally a two-tier system in which there is at least one master or controlling backup software computer (many of these in large datacenters) and backup software agents installed onto each server. When the backup server initiates a timed backup (e.g., every evening during nonpeak times), the backup agent on each server activates and begins sending data to the target backup system. Backups can take minutes or hours depending on how much data needs to be transmitted. Often, they are scheduled so that a full backup is done once per week (usually on nonpeak weekends), and each day an incremental backup of only the changed data is performed. The problem with this is that you might have to restore from multiple backup jobs to get to the data you are trying to restore. Full backups are sometimes so time consuming that they cannot be performed daily. One solution is to use SAN replication and snapshot technology rather than traditional incremental/full backup software techniques.

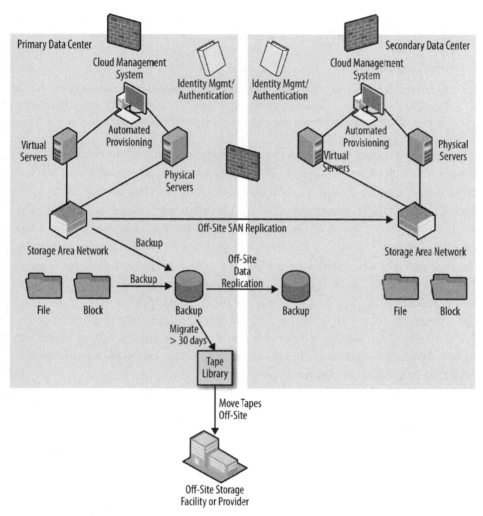

Figure 3-6. A traditional tape-based backup/recovery architecture

Modern backup systems are moving away from tape-based backup in favor of disk-based systems. Disk drives—particularly SATA-type drives—have become so inexpensive and hold so much data that in most cases they have a lower overall cost than tape systems. Disk drives provide faster backup and restoration than a tape system, and a disk-based system does not have the problem of degradation of the tape media itself over time; tapes often last only five to seven years before beginning to deteriorate, even in ideal environmental conditions. The next time you have a customer demanding 10 or more years of data retention, advise them that older tapes will be pretty much worthless.

Key Take-Away

Modern backup systems are moving away from using tape-based backups in favor of de-duplicating, thin-provisioned, compressed disk-based backup systems. Many modern SANs now include direct integration with these disk-based backup systems.

Figure 3-7 shows SAN and/or server-based data initially stored in a backup system at the primary datacenter. This backup system can be tape, but as just explained, it's better to use a disk-based backup media. The backup system, or even a dedicated SAN system used for backup, then replicates data in scheduled batch jobs or continuously to the secondary datacenter(s). This provides immediate offsite backup safety and facilitates disaster recovery with standby servers in the secondary datacenter(s) when a failover at the primary datacenter occurs. There is often little value in having long-term retention at both datacenters, so a best practice is to hold only 14 to 30 days of backup data at the primary datacenter (for immediate restores), with the bulk of long-term data retained at secondary datacenter(s). This long-term retention could use tape media, but as explained earlier, this is not necessarily cheaper than disk storage, especially when you consider that tape degrades over time.

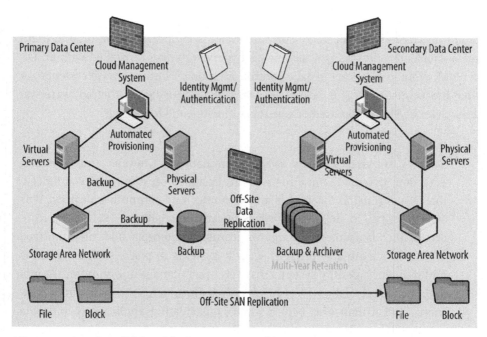

Figure 3-7. A modern disk-based backup/recovery architecture

Backing up VMs

A technique that is unique to virtualized server and SAN environments is the ability to back up VMs *en masse*. Rather than installing a backup agent onto every VM, the agent is only installed once on the physical server's hypervisor system. The backup agent takes an instant snapshot of each VM, and then the backup of the VM occurs based on this copy. This makes backups and restorations much faster.

Key Take-Away

New backup techniques and software that knows how to back up VMs in bulk (rather than per-VM software backup agents) is critical to success in backing up the cloud environment.

Replication of data, often using SAN technologies, is preferred and is now the new "gold standard" for modern datacenters compared to traditional backup and recovery. Given SAN capabilities such as replication, de-duplication, thin provisioning, and snapshots, using traditional backup tapes or backup software agents is no longer economical or desirable.

SOFTWARE SYSTEMS

Cloud providers need dozens of software systems to operate, monitor, and manage a datacenter. Servers typically have a hypervisor system installed with an OS per VM, with applications installed within each one. These software systems are what most consumers of the cloud are aware of and use daily. Other software systems that need to be deployed or considered include the following:

Security

Security software systems range from network firewalls and intrusion detection systems to antivirus software installed on every server and desktop OS within the datacenter and customer end-computing devices. It is also essential to deploy security software that gathers event logs from across the datacenter looking for intrusion attempts and unauthorized access. There are also physical security systems in place, such as cameras and biometric identity systems that you must manage and monitor. Aggregation and correlation of security events from across the system is now more critical than ever before when consolidating applications and data into a cloud environment.

Network

Network management software is used to both manage routers, switches, and SAN or converged fabric devices, as well as to monitor traffic across the networks. This software provides performance trending and alerts to any device failures. Some network software is sophisticated enough to automatically scan the network, find all network devices, and produce a computerized map of the network. This is very useful not only for finding every device on the network, but also when troubleshooting a single device that has failed and might be affecting an entire section of the infrastructure. As in security, the correlation of multiple events is critical for successfully monitoring and managing the networks.

Backup and recovery

Backup software is essential in any large datacenter to provide a safe copy of all servers, applications, and data. Hierarchical storage systems, SAN technologies, and long-term media retention are all critical factors. Integrating this into the overall datacenter management software tools provides better system event tracking, capacity management, and faster data recovery. As described earlier, consider backup software that integrates with

SAN and VM technologies—legacy backup software is often not suitable for the cloud environment.

Datacenter systems

A large modern datacenter has numerous power systems, fire suppression systems, heating and cooling systems, generators, and lighting controls. To manage and monitor everything, you can deploy software systems that collect statistics and statuses for all of the infrastructure's machinery. The most advanced of these systems also manage power consumption to allow for long-term capacity planning as well as to identify power draws. Although rare at this time, future datacenters will not only monitor power and environmental systems, but also utilize automated floor or ceiling vents to change airflow when a rack of servers is detected as running hotter than a set threshold. This type of dynamic adjustment is vastly more cost effective than just cranking up the cooling system. Some of the newer "green" datacenters utilize a combination of renewable and power-grid energy sources, dynamically switching between them when necessary for efficiency and cost savings.

CLOUD MANAGEMENT SYSTEM

The key purposes of a cloud management system are to provide the customer a portal (usually web-based) to order cloud services, track billing, and automatically provision services that they order. Sophisticated cloud management systems will not only provision services based on customer orders, but also can automatically update network and datacenter monitoring and management systems whenever a new VM or software application is created.

Key Take-Away

A cloud provider cannot operate efficiently without a cloud management system. Without the level of automation that a management system provides, the cloud provider would be forced to have so much support staff that it could not offer its services at a competitive price.

Cloud management systems are so important a topic, with significant issues and flexible options, that Chapter 7 has been dedicated to this subject.

REDUNDANCY, AVAILABILITY, CONTINUITY, AND DISASTER RECOVERY

Modern datacenters—and particularly cloud services—require careful consideration and flexible options for redundancy, high availability, continuity of operations, and disaster recovery. A mature cloud provider will have all of these systems in place to ensure its systems stay online and can sustain simultaneous failures and disasters, without customers even noticing. Cloud service quality is measured through service-level agreements (SLAs) with your customer, so system outages, even if small, harm both your reputation as well as your financials. People often confuse the terms "redundancy," "high availability," "continuity," and "disaster recovery," so I have defined and compared them in the following list:

Redundancy

Redundancy is achieved through a combination of hardware and/or software with the goal of ensuring continuous operation even after a failure. Should the primary component fail for any reason, the secondary systems are already online and take over seamlessly. Examples of redundancy are multiple power and cooling modules within a server, a RAID-enabled disk system, or a secondary network switch running in standby mode to take over if the primary network switch fails.

For cloud service providers, redundancy is the first line of protection from system outages. As your cloud service grows in customer count and revenue, the value of network, server, and storage redundancy will be obvious when you experience a component failure.

High availability

High availability (HA) is the concept of maximizing system uptime to achieve as close to 100% availability as possible. HA is often measured by how much time the system is online versus unscheduled outages—usually shown as a percentage of uptime over a period of time. Goals for cloud providers and customers consuming cloud services are often in the range of 99.95% uptime per year. The SLA will determine what the cloud provider is guaranteeing and what outages, such as routine maintenance, fall outside of the uptime calculation.

For purposes of this section, HA is also something you design and build into your cloud solution. If you offer your customer 99.99% uptime, you are now looking at four minutes of maximum outage per month. Many VMs, OSs, and applications will take longer than this just to boot up so HA configurations are necessary to achieve higher uptime requirements.

Key Take-Away

To keep your systems at the 99.99% level or better, you must design your system with redundancy and HA in mind. If you are targeting a lesser SLA, disaster recovery or standby systems might be adequate.

You can achieve the highest possible availability through various networking, application, and redundant server techniques, such as the following:

- Secondary systems (e.g., physical or VMs) running in parallel to the primary systems—these redundant servers are fully booted and running all applications—ready to assume the role of the primary server if it were to fail. The failover from primary to secondary is instantaneous, and causes no outages nor does it have an impact on the customer.

- Using network load balancers in front of servers or applications. The load balancer will send users or traffic to multiple servers to maximize performance by splitting the workload across all available servers. The servers that are fed by the load balancer might be a series of frontend web or application servers. Of equal importance is that the load balancer skip, or not send traffic to a downstream server, if it detects that the server is offline for any reason; customers are automatically directed to one of the other available servers. More advanced load-balancing systems can even sense slow performance of their downstream servers and rebalance traffic to other servers to maintain a performance SLA (not just an availability SLA).

- Deploy clustered servers that both share storage and applications, but can take over for one another if one fails. These servers are aware of each other's status, often sending a heartbeat or "are you OK?" traffic to each other to ensure everything is online.

- Applications specifically designed for the cloud normally have resiliency built in. This means that the applications are deployed using multiple replicas or instances across multiple servers or VMs; therefore, the application continues to service end users even if one or more servers fail. Chapter 4 covers cloud-native applications in more detail.

Figure 3-8 illustrates an example of an HA scenario. In this example, a VM has failed and secondary VMs are running and ready to immediately take over operations. This configuration has two redundant servers—one in the same datacenter on a separate server blade and another in the secondary datacenter. Failing-over to a server within the same datacenter is ideal and the least likely to impact customers. The redundant servers in the secondary datacenter can take over primary operations should multiple servers or the entire primary datacenter experience an outage.

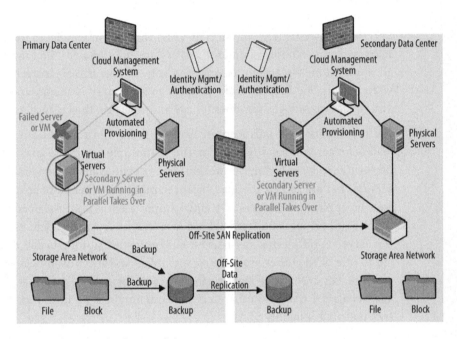

Figure 3-8. Example of HA: a failover

Continuity of operations

Continuity of operations (CoO) is the concept of offering services even after a significant failure or disaster. The dictionary definition is more generic, stating CoO is the ability to continue performing essential functions under a broad range of circumstances. For the purposes of being a cloud provider, CoO is a series of failover techniques to keep network, servers, storage, and applications running and available to your customers. In the real world, CoO refers to a broader range of keeping your entire service online after a significant failure or disaster. Many cloud providers will specifically identify events that are of a more significant nature, such as natural disasters; some spell out different SLAs or exceptions to SLAs when major, unavoidable events occur, versus normal system failures that are common within a datacenter.

A continuity plan for a cloud provider would typically involve failing-over to a secondary datacenter should the primary datacenter become unavailable or involved in a disaster. The network infrastructure, server farms, storage, and applications at the secondary datacenter are roughly the same as those in the primary, and most important, the data from the primary datacenter is always being replicated to the secondary. This combination of having prestaged infrastructure and synchronized data is what make it possible for you, as the cloud provider, to move all services to the secondary datacenter and resume servicing your customers. The failover time in such a scenario is sometimes measured in hours, with the best, most advanced environments failing-over within minutes. This CoO failover might not be as immediate as in a true HA configuration. If you can failover to a secondary datacenter and still function within your guaranteed SLA, that is, by definition, a successful CoO plan and execution.

Another part of a continuity plan deals with your staff and support personnel. If you must failover to a secondary datacenter, how will you adequately manage your cloud environment at that time? Will your staff be able to work from home if the primary office or datacenter location is compromised? The logistics and business plans are a huge part of a complete continuity of operations plan—it isn't only about the technology.

Disaster recovery

Similar to continuity of operations, disaster recovery (DR) is both a technology issue and a logistics challenge. As a cloud provider, you must be prepared for a disaster that could involve a portion or all of your datacenter and systems. When building your cloud system, you typically have two or more datacenters so that you can failover between your primary and secondary in the event of a disaster. If your cloud system design is more advanced, you might have three or more datacenters, all peers of one another, with none of them acting as the "prime" center. If an outage occurs at one, the others immediately take over the customer load without a hiccup (essentially, load balancing between datacenters).

A DR plan is similar to a CoO plan, but with one important addition. As a result of your CoO plan and technologies, you can continue to service your customers. A DR plan also includes how to rebuild the datacenter, server farms, storage, network, or any portion that was damaged by the disaster event. In the case of a total datacenter loss, the DR plan might contain strategies to build a new datacenter in another location, or lease space from an existing datacenter and purchase all new equipment. The recovery, in this worst-case scenario, might take several months to resume normal operations.

This leads to another aspect of your DR plan: while you are now running in your secondary datacenter, are the systems the same size and performance as your original, now-failed, primary datacenter? Maybe you have slower systems or storage with less capacity in your secondary datacenter; this is actually fairly common, because most providers assume that they will never remain operational within a secondary datacenter for very long before switching back to the primary.

Key Take-Away

The DR plan needs to document steps to bring the secondary datacenter up to its "primary" counterpart's standards in the event that there is no hope of returning operations back to the primary.

Figure 3-9 presents a scenario in which the primary datacenter has failed, lost connectivity, or is otherwise entirely unavailable to handle production customers. Due to the replication of data (through the SAN in this example) and redundant servers, all applications and operations are now shifted to the secondary datacenter. A proper CoO plan not only allows for the failover from the primary to secondary datacenter(s), but also documents a plan to either switch back all operations to the first datacenter after the problem has been resolved. Finally, as previously stated, the CoO plan should include procedures to make the secondary datacenter the new permanent primary datacenter should the first (failed) datacenter be unrecoverable.

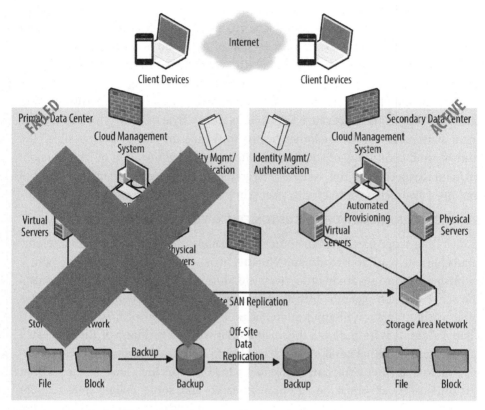

Figure 3-9. Example of disaster recovery—a continuity scenario

Managing Scope, Releases, and Customer Expectations

Lessons learned in the area of project scope management, schedules, and release management are not necessarily technical issues and not unique to cloud computing. This being said, experience teaches us that many transitions to a cloud environment failed or were significantly delayed due to mismanagement of customer expectations and scope creep.

SCOPE CREEP

Cloud technologies, portals, online ordering, and automated provisioning are new capabilities that customers begin to really appreciate and better understand when they begin to pilot and use the system. Past experience informs us that cloud customers very quickly begin expressing their desire for additional features and more customization—especially because on-demand, elastic, automatically deployed cloud services is such a new capability. Just as in any IT project deployment, it is absolutely critical to manage customer expectations and stick with a solid proven plan for releasing a 1.0 version of the cloud service and then decide what customer requests can or should be accommodated through future releases of the cloud management platform portal or XaaS offering. Although any IT project has the potential for this scope creep, private cloud deployments seem to take this to an extreme because the cloud is a new style of IT service delivery for most customers. As the customer begins to realize the "art of the possible" the number and complexity of additional features and customization quickly gets out of hand—especially if the systems integrator or cloud provider has already bid and been awarded a contract with a set scope and price already established.

RELEASE MANAGEMENT AND CUSTOMER EXPECTATION MANAGEMENT

Controlling scope creep and customer expectations can be done through a release management plan and roadmap. Whether it is a public cloud provider with a published feature roadmap or a private cloud implantation, it is critical to control the scope and complete the initial 1.0 release of the environment. As the cloud is built or the transition of applications begins, it is a matter of how many (not if) changes and feature requests the customer(s) will make. Many of the requested changes are legitimate and should be added to a future release of the cloud service or management software—possibly added cost to the cloud service. Other customer requests must be carefully assessed and some politely rejected; for example, when the customer asks to implement a legacy technique that is not suitable for the automated cloud environment, or too specific a requirement that satisfies only one customer (particularly for public clouds).

One lesson among the many that experience has taught us repeatedly is that scope creep can be the death of a successful customized private cloud deployment. You can control customer expectations and scope by pushing new features to future releases, but before you officially commit to the future roadmap, evaluate the impact of these new capabilities on price and ROI. Other lessons learned are that cloud customers seem to forget that customization and new features costs money. The published or contract-stipulated pricing from the cloud provider or systems integrator is only accurate when the scope is managed and new feature requests are under control.

Deployment Best Practices

Based on lessons learned and experience from across the cloud industry, you should consider the following best practices for your organization planning.

CONSUME VERSUS BUILD

The basic acquisition question for any organization is whether to consume an existing service, usually from a public cloud provider, or to build and operate your own private cloud. Here are some considerations:

- You can usually consume services from an existing public cloud with little or no capital expenditures or term commitment. Private clouds must be configured and deployed and therefore often require capital expenditures or minimum commitments.

- Public clouds offer standardized services to a large quantity of customers and are therefore limited in customization. Private clouds can be significantly customized but often require an initial investment. Some cloud providers offer managed private cloud services in which the cloud is actually hosted and operated at the provider's facilities instead of the customer's datacenter.

- If you want to use both a private cloud and some public cloud services, you should strongly consider focusing on a private cloud management platform that has embedded hybrid or bursting capabilities to provision to public cloud providers—creating a hybrid cloud. With this configuration, you have a single cloud management platform in your private network that controls automated provisioning, aggregates billing, and manages operations for both your private cloud and any and all connected public clouds.

- Be mindful that if you purchase cloud services from multiple public providers, you can end up having different ordering and management portals for every provider. A hybrid cloud management platform is often better suited to handle both the internal private cloud all connected public cloud services with a unified customer portal.

CLOUD MODELS

Although most customers desire the pay-as-you-go elastic scalability and ease of management you get with public clouds, organizations with unique customization and security requirements must often consider deploying a private cloud (hosted within customer or third-party facilities). Here are some considerations:

- Lessons learned have shown that larger organizations and government customers benefit most from a private cloud. Soon after deployment, organizations then seek to use additional cloud services from other private, virtual-private, community, or third-party public cloud providers; thus, a hybrid cloud is quickly becoming the most prevalent model in the industry.

- Virtual private clouds (VPCs) have not seen the uptake that was originally expected in the industry. Customers either do not understand VPC or just don't want their private cloud and data hosted by a public cloud provider—essentially the definition of VPC. Thus, the use cases in which customers do want to have VPC seem to be limited. Public and private/hybrid clouds are still, by far, the primary forms of cloud being deployed. Where VPC really could shine is in the future community clouds in which shared capacity is available to multiple customers with the same level of security and requirements.

- Community clouds have not had a lot of adoption in the initial four to five years of the cloud industry. Peer organizations have had significant political and governance issues (e.g., policies, finances, procurement, operational control, individual fiefdoms) that have delayed or killed the community cloud initiative. The biggest concern between community cloud owners is that peer organizations have little or no control over one another—what happens if an organization loses funding or changes its mission in ways that jeopardize critical applications it once provided to the rest of the communities? Cloud brokering might turn out to be a better alternative for organizations wanting multiple cloud providers and aggregated cloud service portals.

DATACENTER INFRASTRUCTURE

Modernizing a legacy datacenter with virtualization or automation does not equal a cloud, but it is an excellent start. There are numerous best practices for modernizing a datacenter that also prepare the environment for cloud services. Here are some considerations:

- Many organizations have now realized that the expense of infrastructure, facility, and staff is too much to justify building or continuing to operate a datacenter. This is due in part to the fact that many datacenters have excess capacity and the perfect return-on-investment (ROI) model only works when a datacenter is completely occupied. Then, when you achieve full occupancy, you have little or no room to grow. Often, the best advice is to get out of the datacenter owner/operator business unless that is your core business offering to customers. If you are not an IT provider company, why take on such a large expense and responsibility?

- Organizations that do need a datacenter should consider leasing out a pod or section of capacity from an existing datacenter provider. You can lease bulk-rate power, cooling, and space at a fraction of the cost of a full datacenter and without the hassle of purchasing and operating the physical facility, equipment, and staff.

- Some organizations now find that pods or shipping containers that contain preinstalled servers and storage (a datacenter in a box) are a good value and can facilitate quick expansion.

- You should try to avoid using the legacy existing network infrastructure (routers, switches, fabrics, physical servers, tape backup media) for the new cloud for two primary reasons:

  — Legacy infrastructure systems are often not as capable of automation, software-defined configuration, multifabric/protocol, and higher densities and performance as modern cloud-enabled systems.

  — As you build and grow your new cloud, you want to avoid the need to seek approval from change control boards, legacy customers, and other operational IT departments—the legacy systems and processes often slow down the new cloud-based processes and configuration needs. After the cloud services are built in the datacenter, you should consider the migration process of bringing legacy infrastructure and applications over to the cloud, not the reverse.

CLOUD INFRASTRUCTURE AND HARDWARE

When building your own cloud infrastructure, many components and technologies are similar to any modern datacenter. Although using the highest density servers and network infrastructure is clearly advantageous, there are technologies that do make some servers, storage, and networking hardware better able to support a cloud-enabled environment. Here are some considerations:

Server infrastructure

> Focus on blade- or cartridge-based servers that install into a common chassis or cabinet—usually 10 to 20 servers fitting in each cabinet, with 3 to 4 cabinets per equipment rack. Look for providers that maintain multiple levels of redundancy in power, cooling, and modular components, such as network and SAN host adapters built into the shared cabinet. Software-based mapping of network, SAN fabric, and other shared cabinet features afford the capability to swap out server blades, which automatically inherit the virtual configuration of that slot; thus no reconfiguration of the network or storage mappings is required. Lights-out and out-of-band management and monitoring tools should also be embedded in the modular servers and shared cabinets. Unique features specific to the cloud also include the ability to perform bare-metal configuration and hot swapping of resources (storage, network adapters) that support a fully automated cloud environment.

SANs

> Avoid local hard drives embedded on each server blade/cartridge—the benefits of booting from a shared storage device such as a SAN far outweigh local storage in terms of flexibility, performance, and reliability. Though some manufacturers might claim that having multiple cheap modular servers each with inexpensive local storage is a good thing, in reality each physical server or blade server now hosts multiple VMs and thus any failures have an impact on multiple applications and multiple customers. Ignore the manufacturer: local, cheap, and slow hard drives are not desired in an on-demand, elastic, automated cloud environment.

Sizing of infrastructure

> Purchasing an overly large initial cloud infrastructure can result in such high capital expenses that the ROI model cannot show a profit for several years. So, start reasonably small with the infrastructure, but use modular

and highly scalable server, storage, and networking equipment for which you can expand capacity by adding modules—automation will take care of configuration and installation of software in most cases. Negotiate quick terms and contracts with hardware vendors to have new equipment pre-staged at no cost until utilized or at least shipped to you and ready to install within 24 to 48 hours from the point at which you make the call. Continuously monitor capacity on your infrastructure so that you can predict when new hardware is needed without over-purchasing excessive new capacity. Even if you can get vendors to supply prestaged, free-until-you-use-it servers and storage, don't forget that sometimes it costs money to power and cool these systems. However, with some of the newer hardware, you can take advantage of *autopower-on* capability with which you can keep the devices idle until they are needed—for truly on-demand capacity.

SANS

Not all SANs are the same. There are unique features that some SANs have—embedded virtual storage controllers and embedded hypervisor VM support—that specifically support a cloud environment. Here are some considerations:

- SANs provide the maximum amount of performance, reliability, scalability, and flexibility to connect disk volumes to your high-density server farms and applications. As stated earlier, avoid local disk drives embedded on each server: you need server blades to be interchangeable, so a software-defined mapping to the SAN storage is desired for both boot and data volumes.

- Utilize thin-provisioning features of your SAN, with which you can over-allocate storage—a primary reason why shared virtualized storage costs less in a cloud environment. Note that VM hypervisors can also perform thin provisioning, and you can only have one or the other (the SAN) perform thin provisioning at the same time.

- Dismiss arguments that thin provisioning, de-duplication, snapshots, and other SAN-based features reduce overall performance; SAN controller units are far faster than disk I/O; therefore, these SAN features have almost no impact on performance (or such a small impact that it's nearly impossible to measure), especially with flash-based caching turned on.

- Utilize a combination of flash cache, solid-state disks, and traditional disk drives within the SAN. SAN controllers are able to automatically move data, and when properly configured, provide you with the maximum performance possible. Follow the advice of the SAN manufacturer to get the best configuration of disk striping, RAID, flash cache, and LUN allocation—every SAN manufacturer's embedded software is unique, so be wary of SAN performance advice from legacy storage operations staff, especially when they are not experienced with the latest SAN hardware and configurations.

- Never assume that RAID 5—or any level of RAID configuration—is appropriate or will provide the best performance without checking with the SAN manufacturer. Countless lessons learned prove that every SAN manufacturer implements their own disk striping, caching, and internal algorithms to achieve maximum performance and redundancy. Assuming RAID 5, for example, would be similar to turning off four-wheel drive in an SUV because you think you can do a better job driving in snow than the intelligent all-wheel-drive system.

- Avoid splitting disks into too many volumes. There is a limit within every SAN on the number of volumes that you can configure. When using a VM hypervisor, one large volume can easily service dozens of VMs. A one-volume-to-one-VM design is an antiquated model and likely will limit performance.

- Do utilize SAN-based, point-in-time snapshots or backups for daily, or even hourly, checkpoints to which data can be restored (recovery points). Use snapshots and VM technology to perform backups of all VMs rather than individual backup software agents on each VM. Remember that snapshots do require some additional storage capacity but have little or no impact on performance when each snapshot is taken.

- Use SAN-based data replication—potentially in real time or based on snapshot intervals—to send a copy of data to another local or remotely located storage device for immediate offsite backup capabilities. This technology is also very useful when configuring multi-datacenter redundancy and continuity of operations, replicating data to a secondary datacenter(s) in near real time if desired.

CLOUD MANAGEMENT PLATFORM

All cloud providers, or operators of a private cloud, utilize a cloud management software system that provides a customer ordering portal, subscription management, automation provisioning, billing/resource utilization tracking, and management of the cloud. Here are some considerations:

- Always deploy the cloud management platform and as much of the automation as possible when initially building any cloud. Avoid the temptation to deploy the cloud management platform and automation at a later time—after the cloud infrastructure, hypervisor, storage, and VMs are installed. Experience teaches us that it is exponentially more difficult to deploy the cloud management platform and automation afterward. And although provisioning and all management is temporarily performed manually, all of the cloud ROI models for pay-as-you-go, capacity management, patching and updates, and support personnel labor are negated.

- You can perform integration with every backend network, server, security, service ticketing, or application management system in a secondary phase after initial cloud capabilities are brought online. This is often the reality, given many datacenters already have these operational management tools and staff that can slowly transition to the cloud. Lessons learned have shown that trying to integrate with every legacy datacenter management tool upon initial launch can significantly delay the go-live date for your new cloud.

- There should be an ongoing effort to improve the cloud portal, reports, and statistical dashboards. Begin with at least a basic cloud portal and consumer-facing dashboard but try to avoid scope creep when customers ask for so many new features that you end up missing your initial launch timing goals.

SCOPE AND RELEASE MANAGEMENT

Because the cloud is new to both your organization and the consumers of the cloud services, avoid blindly accepting every request for improvements and enhancements. Get the first version of your cloud launched and push new feature requests to future releases as part of a published roadmap. Here are some considerations:

- Avoid scope creep. As in an IT project, scope creep can and will get out of control if not managed. Every new feature request can have a significant impact on costs and the cloud infrastructure, so avoid making quick decisions and approval of new features to the roadmap until you have made a full and careful analysis.

- Customers will ask for feature after new feature in the cloud portal—a particular area of scope creep—so be careful and ensure that customers understand the cost of such enhancements, especially if you, as the cloud provider, have already bid on or published service pricing.

- Many of the new features and capabilities of your private cloud will be available from the manufacturer of the deployed cloud management platform. Thus, follow its roadmap and request new features from the cloud management platform manufacturer when possible rather than overly customizing the cloud platform, which could result in difficult future upgrades.

- Customers often have multiple "gold" or standardized operating system templates of images that they'd like to use with their cloud VMs. Always evaluate and test their images for suitability and remember, as a cloud provider, you now own all future updating, patching, and support of these new OSs and configuration. You might want to provide a certain number of image templates within your pricing plan, with additional cost to import, test, and support the lifecycle for every new OS or VM image your customer requests. Often, it is best to have a minimal number of OS templates and use the software distribution and automated installation tools to install variations, updates, and applications rather than trying to manage so many unique combinations of OS and application through templates.

USING EXISTING STAFF

In Chapter 2, in the Operational Lessons Learned section, I discuss the use and possible reorganization of existing operational personnel to support your new private cloud. In this section, I provide best practices for using existing operational staff for the deployment of your cloud. Here are some considerations:

- Existing operational personnel are often hired and expected to perform only routine tasks following runbooks based on the current legacy infrastructure and applications. These individuals are not usually the best personnel to employ for new cloud technologies, processes, and techniques (if they had all the required knowledge for cloud and automation, they likely wouldn't be in a lower-paid operations role).

- Existing operational personnel already have what should be a full-time job, so asking them to deploy and properly configure new systems using new techniques often results in poor build quality, poor configuration consistency, and old bad habits being brought into the new cloud environment.

- Engage new, highly skilled personnel—as employees or contractors—to perform the deployment and configuration of the new cloud hardware. Existing personnel can participate in the hardware staging of systems, as they might need to assume responsibility for operating these systems, but ensure that the primary configuration is performed by the new team with a handoff to the legacy operations staff further down the road.

- Use only new, highly skilled personnel on the cloud automation software platform configuration and ongoing continuous automation improvements. Legacy staffers usually do not have the skills or experience to configure these systems. Over time, you can train these people and have them work alongside the newer staff to automate all legacy manual processes.

SECURITY

Assessing, certifying, and managing a private cloud environment is not very unique compared to a modern datacenter. The new cloud portal might require further vetting and testing, especially if it accepts payments or can be accessed from the public Internet. The actual VMs, storage, and applications all operate from behind one or more firewalls. As a result, there are often few aspects that are unique to the cloud for security personnel to certify at the infrastructure level. Here are some considerations:

- Security should focus on the configuration and how the automated cloud management system configures VMs and OSs, applies patches and updates, and manages the virtual networks to which each VM is configured to communicate. When the templates and network zones are preapproved, the automation software should maintain consistent and reliable configurations when ordered by customers.

- Security should evaluate and preapprove each "gold" or VM image along with its OSs and baseline patch levels. When approved, the automated cloud management platform will consistently deploy VMs based on these images.

- Continuous monitoring should already be a primary goal of the security operations team within the datacenter. The cloud brings in a new level of automation and consequently new VMs and applications brought online 24-7; therefore, all new systems should immediately be added to the change control logs and inventory systems, and trigger immediate scans and ongoing monitoring by security after the VMs are online.

- For additional best practices, read Chapter 6.

Application Transformation

Key topics in this chapter:

- Application evolution to the cloud
- Application categories and characteristics
- The new approach to application development and delivery
- Continuous application delivery automation
- Application transformation methodology
- Application operational considerations
- Application assessment
- Application transformation best practices

Although many clouds initially focused on Infrastructure as a Service (IaaS), enterprise organizations often have applications listed as their top business priority. The reality is that a private or public cloud requires a base infrastructure of server, storage, and networking in order to begin hosting anything—an IaaS, Platform as a Service (PaaS), or Software as a Service (SaaS). In earlier chapters, I covered architectures for baseline IaaS clouds, but the largest task in the journey from enterprise IT to the cloud is in application transformation.

Key Take-Away

IaaS virtual machine services are now considered the very minimum capability for a public or enterprise private cloud. Application transformation is the longer-term goal and will take the most amount of time.

Application transformation is a fancy term for assessing the current applications and then planning and conducting migrations. When planning for your cloud transition or deployment, assessing your existing applications will lead you to decisions on what to migrate to the cloud, what apps to redesign, which to maintain in the existing enterprise, and the priorities for an eventual transition to the cloud. Before planning any application transition, it is essential to understand the basic characteristics and features of traditional and cloud-native applications.

Evolving Your Applications for the Cloud

Chapter 1 discusses the evolution of computers, including a graphic depiction in Figure 1-1. Figure 4-1 repeats that illustration, but this time let's focus on the evolution of applications that are shown below the trend line.

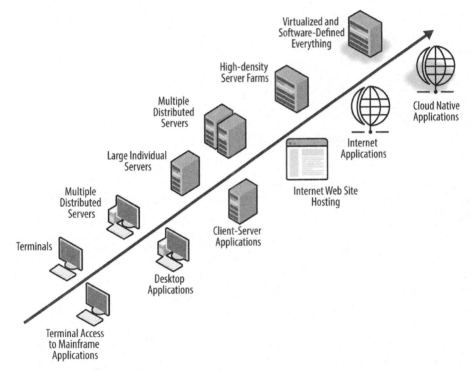

Figure 4-1. The evolution of cloud applications

Though computer hardware has evolved at a continuous and rapid pace, software traditionally has been slower to progress—until now. Although cloud computing is a new style of IT delivery, a new style of application architecture, development, and delivery is upon us. The pace of application development and delivery of new features to consumers is now expected at a pace never seen before in the history of the IT industry. In fact, I will go as far as saying that software is now outpacing hardware in terms of innovation and impact to business and everyday life.

Coming back to Figure 4-1, there are some very important software architecture concepts of particular note:

- Desktop applications are still common but remain inefficient to support and upgrade. Remote desktops or Virtual Desktop Interface (VDI) is often still too expensive as well and still a compromise in ease of use for many organizations. Application publishing essentially pushes desktop applications into the cloud-enabled app category for at least a temporary bridge until a true cloud-enabled application is available.

- Client-server applications have been considered legacy since as early as 2010 (in case you didn't get your official notice in the mail). They are considered too chatty or noisy for efficient network communications and scalability, and they are expensive to deploy in high availability/resilient configurations. These applications are good candidates for *refactoring* (this term is defined later in this chapter) to the cloud.

- Internet applications are really a combination of multitiered client-server applications and web applications hosted on the Internet—this is the Internet service provider (ISP) and application service provider (ASP) era in the years up to 2009 before the cloud. These were rarely very efficient, but they were profitable for the providers and software developers and considered bleeding edge at the time. Most of the software languages, application programming interfaces (APIs), and tools used to create these applications are effectively dead. These applications, providers, and software companies either already upgraded to cloud applications and SaaS or went out of business because they didn't upgrade fast enough in the early days of the cloud.

- Cloud-enabled applications, also referred to as *cloud-native applications*, are designed to take advantage of a cloud infrastructure and all of its capabilities. Cloud-native is fully defined later in this chapter.

Application Categories

Applications can be categorized in many ways, but for this discussion, I will group them into four categories for clarity and relevancy in a cloud service environment:

COTS

> COTS applications are readily available from numerous software vendors, but their suitability for implementation in the cloud is not always straightforward. Many software vendors are rewriting their applications to both fit into a multitenant cloud environment and adapt their licensing models for pay-as-you-go cloud usage models; however, there are still software vendors that do not have properly designed cloud-native applications that work in a multitenant environment.

Open source

> These applications are often not shrink-wrapped or ready for purchase "on the shelf" such as with COTS products. As the name indicates, open source also means that the source programmed code is freely published so any party can customize it for its own needs, scan it for security vulnerability, and integrate other software components. Open source applications are often considered a community project with numerous (meaning hundreds or thousands) of developers, contributors, and integrators across the world. These open source applications are free for anyone to download and use, but they sometimes have licensing limitations such as not being able to use them for profit without permission or royalties paid. Some software companies take an open source application, enhance it with their own software, and sell their own distribution of the system. One key advantage is that open source applications often utilize industry standards and APIs or end up becoming a standard after sufficient adoption and industry acceptance. Besides the cost, one primary benefit to open source is that you avoid vendor lock-in. This is when you purchase and use a proprietary product and find that you are stuck with that product or it would be too costly to migrate away from it in the future.

Custom applications

> Also known as homegrown applications, these are what many large organizations have the most difficulty with when planning the transition to the cloud. These applications can range from legacy mainframe programs, all

the way to heavily modified COTS systems. Because there are often no integration standards and often little integration among these custom applications, there is also no single method of integrating or porting them to the cloud. Careful assessment and planning for each major application is required. A significant portion of this chapter is dedicated to this assessment topic.

Cloud native

Cloud native applications are designed to be hosted in a cloud environment and take advantage of a cloud infrastructure. This means the applications can, for example, remain online during planned or unplanned infrastructure outages and scale up or scale down to meet workload demands. Cloud applications are designed to work with other components and services within a cloud, such as databases, frontend web services, transaction queuing, payment engines, and so on, all working together in what appears to be a single cloud application or service. Cloud native apps consist of *composable* services (more on this term in the sidebar that follows) designed to be dynamic with respect to the infrastructure and other services with which they integrate—essentially discovering and dynamically registering services with other applications and components within the cloud rather than hardcoded mappings or static configuration. Cloud-native applications are developed to be elastic so that they can scale out automatically based on defined workload parameters. Finally, cloud applications are designed to be resilient so that the system can recover or self-heal when a problem is detected in the infrastructure, such as temporary hardware, software, or communications failures.

Composable Services and Applications

Composable

As the cloud continues to evolve, along with it has developed a small dictionary of new words and terms that, although they might not pop up in day-to-day conversation at the supermarket or while you're watching your kid's soccer game, they are common within the industry and often indispensable at getting an idea across concisely. *Composable* is one such term. Essentially, a composable service or application is one that is not hardcoded. Instead, it is flexible and adaptable, and can sense and detect its surroundings and nearby applications and services so that it could function in any cloud or environment in which it's functioning.

Think of a composable as somewhat like creating a form using sculpting clay (whose shape is inherently flexible and responsive), as opposed to using wood or some other inflexible materials; when a wood sculpture is completed, it's nearly impossible to shape it into anything else, but a composable, like clay, can adapt to its environment and whatever new form that entails.

Application Characteristics

There are numerous characteristics that an application should have when transitioning to a cloud infrastructure. A public cloud provider will design these attributes into their application and cloud offerings, whereas a private cloud operator will have to assess and migrate legacy applications. Key characteristics of cloud-enabled (cloud-native) applications include the following:

Secure multitenancy

This means that the application is configurable so that multiple customers can share the same instance of it, while maintaining separation of all data and user accounts. Customers and users within the shared application instance cannot see one another nor any data other than their own by using security access controls lists (ACLs), role-based permissions, and sometimes separation of databases (the application is still shared but can access and utilize separate databases when appropriate).

Elasticity

Applications should be elastic as traffic, demand, and usage increases. Elastic means that an application can scale out (adding more compute resources or additional virtual machines) to handle an increase in workload or utilization. A properly designed cloud-native application should be able to automatically detect high utilization and trigger the necessary steps to start up new VMs or application services to handle peak workloads. Then, when peak utilization diminishes, it should reduce VMs or compute instances. Legacy applications that were not specifically designed to run in the cloud can often use a VM hypervisor to monitor processor and memory utilization, triggering more VM instances when a manually defined peak-utilization threshold is attained. These elasticity techniques make it possible for the applications to take advantage of the power of the cloud infrastructure to dynamically scale—even if the application wasn't originally designed as cloud-native; although, a cloud native application is more efficient.

Resiliency

Resiliency refers to the application's ability to survive and remain online during an infrastructure outage or failure. A properly designed cloud-native application would have multiple techniques to retry failed transactions and there would be multiple instances of the application services running on other servers or VMs. Legacy applications that were not designed for a cloud can use tools within a hypervisor or cloud infrastructure such as traffic load balancing, clustering, and server/VM failover, but these are not as effective and transparent to the end user as a cloud-native application's resiliency. There are many other aspects of resiliency and cloud-native application design benefits that will be covered later in this chapter.

Authentication systems

Applications that might have run within existing enterprise datacenters often utilized the internal corporate Microsoft Active Directory or some other identity management system to authenticate user logons. Ideally, applications hosted in a cloud should not assume Active Directory or the internal identity system is available; instead, they should favor an industry standard for authentication and directories such as Lightweight Directory Access Protocol (LDAP) or Security Assertion Markup Language (SAML). Both provide authentication capabilities—SAML is a bit more robust and appropriate as part of a single sign-on (SSO) system.

Universal access

The applications must be accessible from anywhere on the Internet or other wide area network (WAN) circuit. The application should be compatible with any and all access methods, from web-based access, virtual private network (VPN) access, and every variety of desktop, notebook, tablet, and mobile device. This also means that the user data must also be immediately available when moving from one computing device to another. As a general rule, you should follow the same philosophy as software-defined networking: never hardcode any network addresses or assume anything; always assume applications, users, and data could exist or operate from anywhere in the world through any network connection and any form of user interface or device (see also the section "Mobility" that follows momentarily).

Multitiered applications and platforms

Many cloud applications employ a multitiered design wherein there are multiple layers, or tiers, of services. These tiers separate the backend database, middleware and applications, and frontend processing. This tiered design facilitates higher levels of security, application upgrade modularity, and independent scalability of individual tiers as needed, based on utilization. Tiered applications also benefit from shared platform or PaaS applications in the cloud, such as a database service, that multiple applications can share for lower cost of maintenance, licensing, and operations.

Mobility

With the increasing number of applications hosted in a cloud environment, users or consumers often use mobile computing devices such as tablets or smartphones. The legacy assumption that end users only have desktop PCs or a particular PC operating system (OS) is no longer true. The concept of *mobile first* was adopted over the past few years but is more recently replaced with *ubiquitous access*—the intention of both being that applications need to be designed with the ability for users to access the system through any form of computer device, from any location, and have the same experience. Mobility might also require additional security and asset configuration management features and tools to ensure identity, data encryption, data privacy, and synchronization to mobile devices for offline viewing.

Key Take-Away

Ubiquitous access, elasticity, resiliency, and persistent data are the keys to successful cloud-native applications. Applications and data must always be accessible, from any form of computing device and any location, and with a consistent user experience.

As described later in this chapter, you should consider these characteristics when developing any new applications that you plan to host in the cloud. Also, evaluate your current applications to determine if any of the features are already embedded or how legacy applications could be modified to incorporate them.

The New Approach to Application Development and Delivery

Today's newest and most modern approach to application development is focused on rapid and continuous delivery. Private organizations and software developers are now considered "legacy" and uncompetitive, following previously traditional practices such as releasing applications once or twice a year. It is not just a trend but an expectation of business users to get more frequent updates and new software releases—as often as quarterly or monthly. Many commercial software manufacturers are already using software release cycles measured in weeks if not days, launching not just bug fixes but true new features regularly rather than saving up these enhancements for a big "annual product launch."

Now, enter the public cloud providers and their software applications. Cloud providers have used their infrastructure and automation to further increase the pace of software delivery, sometimes daily if not multiple times per day, particularly because there are so many cloud offerings and subcomponents within each offering. The point here is that the automation and cloud management systems used by the public cloud providers can also be used in a private or enterprise cloud to facilitate rapid application development, testing, and continuous pushing to production as quickly as you and your organization can muster. Figure 4-2 compares notional application delivery cycles for a traditional application to a cloud-based continuous delivery application (future state).

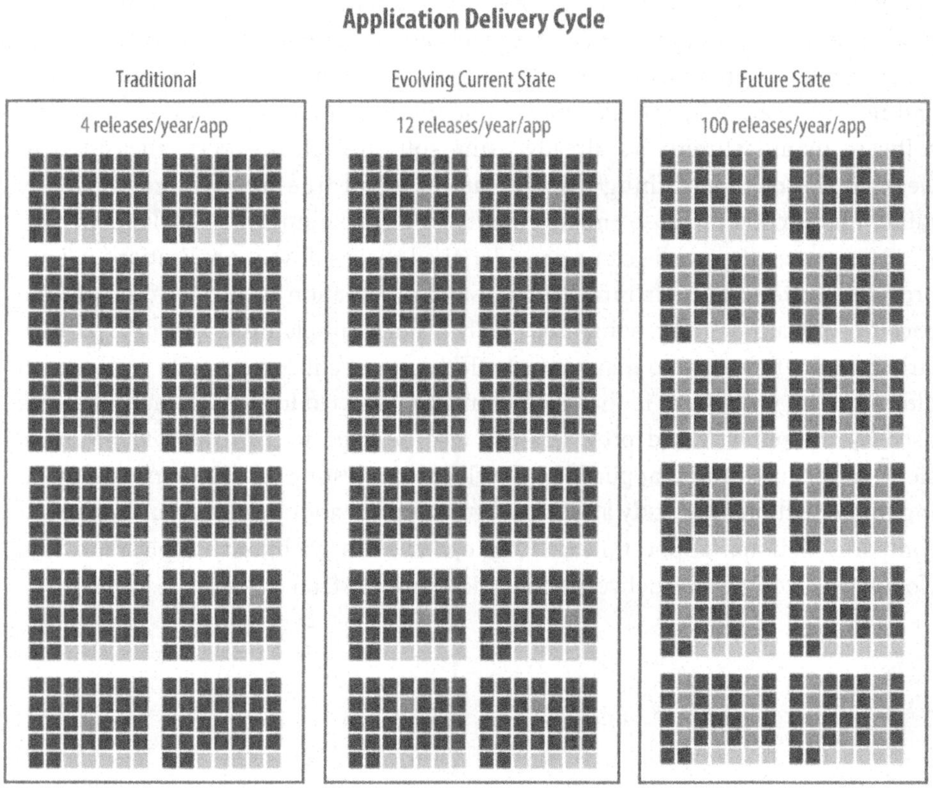

Application Delivery Cycle

| Traditional | Evolving Current State | Future State |
| 4 releases/year/app | 12 releases/year/app | 100 releases/year/app |

Figure 4-2. Notional application delivery cycle—traditional and with continuous delivery

Welcome to the new style of IT—developer style!

Figure 4-3 presents a comparison of traditional application development compared to cloud-based development. Technically, this new pace and style of application development is not specific to the cloud; however, the cloud does provide unique capabilities such as elasticity, software-defined networking, on-demand Development/Testing as a Service (Dev/Test), shared application lifecycle platforms and tools, and an enormous worldwide hybrid infrastructure. Many of the other cloud-based development characteristics shown in the figure were described earlier in this chapter.

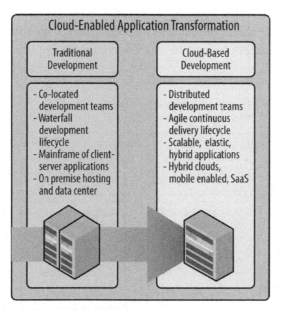

Figure 4-3. Cloud-based application development

CONTINUOUS APPLICATION DEVELOPMENT AND DELIVERY

Although not unique to the cloud, the term *continuous delivery, sometimes called continuous application development,* is now considered the modern methodology for application development and delivery. Continuous delivery employs an Agile-type approach to deliver continuous small software releases into production. To facilitate this application development lifecycle, continuous delivery in a cloud environment takes advantage of automation and software-defined networking to speed application development and promotion to production.

Through the use of VMs and cloud automation, new development environments—consisting of one or more VMs—you order, can provision services on-demand within minutes. You can create multiple sets of VMs so that multiple development teams can work in parallel or on different versions of the same application. Using VM snapshots and automation, these development VMs can be copied to a separate network segment/subnet for testing purposes while the original VMs remain intact for the developers to continue their work. Again, using snapshot technology, you can run multiple testing scenarios and then reset the application back to the previous snapshot for more testing. Finally, you can promote the test VMs or copy them to a production network or subnet through the application development automation—thereby launching the new application for production users. This lifecycle is repeated over and over again while also allowing continuous development and testing activities on the next application release. Figure 4-4 offers an overview of the continous application development and delivery process.

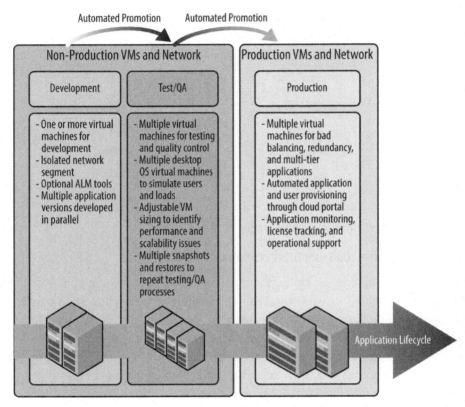

Figure 4-4. Continuous application development and delivery process

Now, consider adding preconfigured VMs with your favorite application life-cycle management (ALM) tools that automatically launch when you order a new Dev/Test subscription. Combine this with automated OS and VM templates, and you can truly appreciate how drastically cloud automation can improve a development team's efficiency. Maybe the best part is that you can easily pause, archive, or terminate your Dev/Test environments when they are not needed and thus stop paying for the service—no servers to disassemble or clear, and your VMs are ready to become active whenever you need them again.

Although the continuous delivery process is nothing new to software teams, the integration of cloud automation and multiple software-defined network segments greatly speeds up and governs an Agile software development lifecycle. This new style of application development has essentially replaced the legacy processes of delivering major software releases in one- or two-year increments. Although the cloud is not necessarily responsible for this shift, it certainly provides further automation and elasticity to facilitate the continuous delivery model.

Application Transformation Methodology

Every modernized datacenter or cloud will provide, at a minimum, the basic VM infrastructure, storage, and network services. When you transform mission-critical applications for use in the cloud, your applications can avail themselves of the unique benefits that the cloud offers. Purchasing or deploying a basic IaaS-focused cloud service is just an initial step in an overall enterprise IT transition to cloud. *It is the application porting or redevelopment that will become the long-term path to complete the transition to cloud.*

Key Take-Away

You must assess each application to determine whether a simple porting is possible or if the application will require a complete redesign to migrate to the cloud.

APPLICATION MODERNIZATION STRATEGIES

There are four types of application modernization strategies to migrate legacy applications in the cloud (see Figure 4-5). You first need to carry out a careful analysis of each legacy application to determine the best method to maximize long-term benefits, taking into account time, costs, and user impact. Some legacy applications are mission critical and unique to your business such that the long-term effort to redesign and recode them is worth the time and cost. Then, there will be relatively simple applications that you can quickly port (i.e., rehost or refactor) to a cloud platform, or even eliminate and replace with a SaaS offering from a cloud provider.

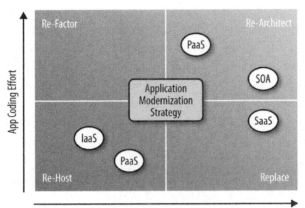

Figure 4-5. Application modernization strategies

Rehosting

Rehosting (or porting) of applications is essentially a "copy and reinstall" technique to take relatively simple legacy applications and host them in the cloud. These applications typically include one or more VMs and, possibly, a database that includes traditional applications which were not originally designed for the cloud. In a perfect scenario, a physical-to-virtual (P2V) migration is possible. Testing and minor configuration changes are often required, but the overall effort to port a single application is usually measured in only days or weeks. Although you might be able to rehost on the cloud quickly and without modifying the application architecture, many of the cloud characteristics (e.g., scalability, resiliency, and elasticity) might not be fully realized.

Refactoring

Refactoring an application is similar to rehosting, but some components of the application are enhanced or changed. You might break up the application into components such as frontend web servers and backend databases so that you can cluster each tier and load balance to provide higher availability, elasticity, and handle more traffic and workload. In this scenario, the core application itself needs little or no reprogramming, because the cloud infrastructure and hypervisors provide some of the scalability without the application having any of the "awareness" that a cloud-native app would.

Redesign

If there are legacy applications that you cannot rehost or refactor (because doing so would not produce the desired performance, quality, or ROI), you should consider redesigning. These applications are often the oldest and most complex legacy applications, possibly mainframe-based, that might require multilayered platforms, databases, middleware, and frontend application servers to be deployed in the cloud. More complex legacy software might require significant assessment and planning just to come up with a project plan and budget to determine the feasibility, risk, and business decision to proceed with the reprogramming. The long-term benefits of a new, properly designed cloud-native application include dynamic elasticity, resiliency, distributed processing, high availability, faster performance, and lower long-term code maintenance.

Replace

Purchasing services from an existing SaaS cloud provider and retiring the legacy application is often a fast and effective cloud-transition strategy. If the ROI to transition a legacy application to the cloud is poor, the organization should consider if the application is truly mission critical or necessary, and whether you could use a COTS or SaaS cloud provider, instead. Technically, you can consider an application hosted in a private cloud as SaaS, but most SaaS applications in the industry are hosted with public cloud providers. Excellent examples of this are public cloud email providers such as Microsoft Office 365 and GoogleApps, or customer relationship management software such as Salesforce.com. Sometimes these SaaS applications provide more features than your legacy software, but they also might not be as configurable as you are accustomed to because they are normally hosted on a shared public cloud infrastructure.

OPERATIONAL CONSIDERATIONS FOR APPLICATIONS

Regardless of which application modernization strategy you use, organizations must also consider operational factors. For example, applications that have been ported to a public cloud might still need database maintenance, code updates, or other routine administrative support. Applications that are hosted as a PaaS or SaaS offering might need less support because the cloud provider will have responsibilities for updating and patching OSs and software components. Of course, in a private-enterprise cloud, your staff (or hired contractor) continue to provide this support but hopefully in a more automated manner than a traditional datacenter. Consider your current staffing levels, outsourced support, and overall IT organizational structure. Most organizations that have already deployed a private cloud or use some public cloud have not reduced their IT staffing levels; however, they have changed the skillsets and team structures to better accommodate a more service-oriented model that is best suited to support a cloud ecosystem. For more details on recommended operational and support staff changes and best practices, refer to Chapter 2.

Application monitoring

When it comes to mission-critical applications that are core to your organization's customers and livelihood, you might keep these applications hosted within a private enterprise cloud or a secure public provider. In either situation, you should still be concerned with monitoring the performance and user experience (UX). The private or public cloud management tools will provide some level of VM, and maybe some limited application-level, utilization monitoring but this is usually not adequate for truly mission-critical applications (they're likely OK for normal business productivity systems). So, regardless of where your mission-critical apps are hosted—public or private cloud—you should still use your own application monitoring tools and techniques that include synthetic transactions, event logging, utilization threshold alerts, and more advanced UX simulated logon tools. For lessons learned and best practices for IT operations, monitoring, and process changes related to cloud-based application hosting, refer to Chapter 2.

Service levels

Consider the service-level agreements (SLAs) for applications hosted in the cloud. I cover contracts, terms, and SLAs in Chapter 5; however, specific to this chapter's subject, you might need a higher SLA or specific terms for some of your mission-critical applications. Many public cloud providers provide a default level of service guarantee and support that is insufficient for mission-critical applications. In some cases, the public cloud provider does not even guarantee that it will back up, provide credit, or be liable for data loss. Be careful how cloud providers word their SLAs because they might only guarantee network availability in their uptime calculations instead of PaaS or SaaS platform service levels. Other vendors claim extensive routine maintenance windows (in other words, potential outages) that are also excluded from their SLA. Refer to Chapters 2 and 5 for more information on service levels and contractual terms as well as how and what changes to demand from the provider before signing an agreement.

Federated authentication

Consider user authentication and access controls for cloud-hosted applications. You might want to federate an enterprise user directory and authentication system (e.g., Microsoft Active Directory or LDAP) to the cloud for an always up-to-date and consistent user logon experience. As stated earlier, a preferred method is to use a vendor-agnostic industry standard for authentication, such as SAML, especially when federation and SSO is required. For more information about federation and authentication systems, refer to Chapter 6.

Scalability

When migrating applications to IaaS or PaaS-based cloud services, you might gain scalability features that were not easy, cheap, or available in the legacy enterprise environment.

Scale out

Depending on the type of application modernization undertaken for a given application, the cloud-based system might now be able to take advantage of dynamic or automated scale out of additional VMs—technically, scale out is called elasticity. It is preferable that the application be cloud native or cloud enabled so that it is capable of detecting peak utilization and triggering scale out automatically. For legacy applications moved to the cloud, you can use the hypervisor and cloud infrastructure to measure utilization with defined thresholds that will trigger scale out, even though the application is unaware of these events. Scaling down after peak utilization subsides is just as important as scaling out. Again, cloud-native applications that handle this automatically are more efficient and faster to react than legacy applications that rely on the hypervisor to scale.

Scale up

Scaling up an application refers to increasing the size of a server, or more common in cloud computing, a VM with more memory and processors to handle increasing workload. Whereas the aforementioned scale out involves launching new VMs to handle peak utilization, scale up involves enlarging the configuration of the same physical server or VM(s) running your applications (up to the maximum number of processors and memory capacity for that particular physical server or VM).

Scale up is considered a legacy technique for scaling. Scale up does not provide cloud-level resiliency or redundancy and is not as efficient compared to scale out. Scale up is considered a legacy technique whose underlying philosophy is "just buy a bigger server" rather than smaller more purpose-built servers and services in a scale-out cloud configuration. Another downside of scale up is that you often need to reboot the VMs to recognize the new processor and memory configuration. However, the need for this additional step will likely recede because some hypervisor platforms are beginning to support dynamic *flexing* of additional processors and memory.

Finally, consider scalability of your applications in terms of geographic access and performance. Although I discuss geographic data sovereignty and redundancy in Chapters 3 and 6, respectively, here I'm referring to load balancing and/or hosting applications in multiple geographic locations to maximize performance and reduce network latency (inherent delays in the communications path over the network). You might want to deploy your application in multiple cloud datacenters on opposite sides of the country in which you reside or in different regions of the world so that end users of your applications are automatically routed to the closest and fastest datacenter. Be aware, however, that many cloud providers charge additional fees for data replication, geo-redundancy, bandwidth, scale up/scale out, and load-balancing capabilities. For an enterprise private cloud, these geo-redundant communication circuits are often cost prohibitive.

Application performance and benchmarking

When you migrate applications to the cloud, you should keep in mind that most public cloud providers do not guarantee the performance of your custom applications nor for any customer-managed PaaS databases or platforms. The cloud provider is simply trying to avoid the argument of who is at fault if an application—particularly one that they didn't create or manage—is not performing the way the customer believes it should. Hosting your own cloud keeps you in complete control of your applications and their performance.

Poor application performance in the cloud is often an indicator of a legacy application ported to the cloud that has not been optimized. For example, just because an application might be copied to a technically faster cloud—"as is" with little or no modifications—does not mean the legacy application will perform well. Performance testing—using live test users and possibly load-testing tools—is recommended for all applications before and after porting them to the cloud.

Having the original application performance baseline measured before any transition to the cloud will give you valuable data to determine expected performance levels. You might be able to use the scale-up or scale-out techniques described earlier to improve performance and meet acceptable levels without redesigning the entire application.

Network bandwidth

Most public cloud providers do not charge for uploading or importing data but do charge transaction, metered bandwidth, or storage input/output fees for network bandwidth. Given that your applications are moving to the cloud for the first time, it is often very difficult to estimate the bandwidth over the Internet or other network circuit. This can result in a bit of a surprise at the end of the first month that the application goes into production use. This bandwidth issue is a much lesser issue for private clouds, because they are usually hosted within your organization's datacenters or via private network circuits. Some public cloud providers offer an optional direct connection option whereby you pay for a private circuit into the provider's network, bypassing most of the normal variable bandwidth fees in lieu of the fixed, direct connect fee. This is well worth it for high utilization/bandwidth needs.

Application Assessment

Assessing or evaluating your existing applications is often the most time-consuming part of the cloud transition. Implementing a private cloud, or procuring some public cloud services, is often completed within one year; however, assessing and then migrating a dozen and up to 100 applications could take a couple of years. The time it takes to perform assessments depends on (at least) three factors:

- Internal technical capabilities versus hiring external application transformation consultants

- Quantity of legacy applications and how many are complex or custom built

- Available budget as it relates to how many parallel assessment teams and work streams

Although hiring application transformation specialists will greatly improve and speed up the assessment and migration planning process, there are steps that many organizations can take to at least begin their application assessments using internal resources. Using the guidelines and checklists that follow, you might be able to self-assess many of your basic applications—saving you precious time and money—and defer hiring external application transformation-to-cloud experts for only the most complex requirements. If your organization is very large or has hundreds or thousands of applications, seriously consider using these application transformation experts who specialize in *app modernization factories* that have numerous experienced teams and proven processes for analyzing and migrating large quantities of applications in parallel work streams. There really is a special art to doing this type of application transformation in mass, across multiple work streams with the same standards, same governance, and same customer/cloud infrastructure requirements.

Figure 4-6 shows a recommended high-level, five-step application assessment plan.

1	**List and Prioritize Applications** List all legacy applications, business purpose/use case, and priority. Note applications that might be retired and those that are newer or already deployed in the cloud.
2	**Data Classification** Determine sensitivity of data, risk and damage of corruption, deletion, competitive theft, intellectual property, risk to customers, corporations, shareholders, etc.
3	**Requirements and Compliance** List top business and technical goals for cloud-based app. Examples: improve performance, high-availability, reduce licensing costs. Note any compliance requirements.
4	**Assess Application** Assess each application based on priority list. Determine, as best as possible, legacy application's existing architecture, server/hosts, programming language, database of middleware, network configuration, authentication/user controls, end-user interface, etc.
5	**Preliminary Decision** Discuss/determine initial list of applications that are good candidates for cloud migration. Consider complexity, risks, costs/effort to migrate, ROI priority and criticality to the business.

Figure 4-6. Application assessment steps

Table 4-1 contains a checklist of tasks and items to consider during the application assessment process. Even if your organization decides to hire experts for more formal application assessments or actual application migrations, the information gathered by completing this self-assessment can be a significant head start.

Table 4-1. Initial application assessment checklist

Category	ASSESSMENT ITEMS/DATA GATHERING
List and prioritize applications	• Create a list of all COTS and custom-built applications along with the primary use case or business function performed by each • Specifically note the name of each application, the manufacturer/software vendor, and version of the application, if known • Note any significant customizations to COTS applications that have been made and any updates that might have been intentionally skipped or avoided due to potential conflicts with these customizations • Prioritize these applications lists based on criticality to the business, how broadly the application is utilized across the business (i.e., how many users), and if this is a customer-facing or internally focused application • Flag applications that are seldom used, are candidates for retirement, have been considered for replacement already, and any workloads for which the cloud has been considered already
Data classification	*Lower Impact Level* The unauthorized disclosure of information might have a limited adverse effect on the organization. *Moderate Impact Level* The unauthorized disclosure of information might have a serious adverse effect on the organization. *High Impact Level* The unauthorized disclosure of information might have a severe or catastrophic adverse effect on the organization. • Consider each application and particularly its data; rank the impact to the organization if the data is corrupted, or completely lost (requiring a data restore); repeat this data security assessment for all applications and data using the same ranking and criteria

Category	ASSESSMENT ITEMS/DATA GATHERING
	• Assess the impact to the internal organization but also to your customers; in addition, weigh the potential harm to your company reputation • Consider the cost and impact of data (e.g., trade secrets) lost to competitors • Consider loss or corruption of customer data, the impact on your customers, and the impact to your organization that this can cause (damage to your reputation, legal issues, monetary damages, and other liabilities) • Classify applications to determine which model they should follow (i.e., the highest-risk applications/data are likely candidates for a private cloud, whereas less-risky applications/data are candidates for public or community cloud models) • Rank each application using one of the following impact categories:
Requirements and compliance	• Briefly list the top business and technical goals (if known) for the application—and possible next generation of the application • Goals or requirements might be to improve application performance problems, reduce licensing purchasing costs, improve user experience/usability, and improve reliability/high-availability • Also note any compliance or similar requirements such as industry or government regulations that might impact the application design, security controls, where data is stored or who has access to and administration of the application and data
Application architecture	• Is the application currently hosted on a single server, spanned across multiple services? Is there a backend database? Can frontend services (web, client-facing application interfaces) be separated into their own network segment from the rest of application, database, middleware? • Does the current application use a multitiered architecture such as separate database, middleware, and frontend processing services? Can the application and middleware be separated into its own network segment, forming two or three tiers of networks?

Category	ASSESSMENT ITEMS/DATA GATHERING
	• Can or should the application share a common database, middleware, or other application or PaaS-type services? Shared services could increase security but reduce licensing costs and easier to manage in an automated environment. • What application platform or programming language was used as the basis for the application (if known)?
Application modernization and migration	• For every application, consider the cost, effort, and risks to redesigning/recoding and if the application is worth the effort, cost, and risk; consider moving commodity applications, such as email, to hosted or even public cloud services • Hire outside consultants and experts in application transformation, if needed, to provide more detailed analysis (even down to code level) if necessary • Which applications could be ported "as is" to the cloud using scaled-up (more computer power) cloud servers? Which applications could be ported to the cloud and use hypervisor-level scale out (such as additional frontend servers) without the application having to be recoded? • Evaluate which applications would benefit from application redesign to take advantage of automation, elasticity, on-demand pay-as-you-go cloud services
Application management	• Always consider how consumers will order applications, how automation will provision them, and how other automated processes will upgrade and monitor them • What application settings, customizations, and self-service controls should be available to administrators and users? Is there a commercial control panel already available on the market or will this need to be programmed as part of the application transformation and deployment in the cloud? Avoid relying on individual app management consoles for each application. • Will there be billing or financial chargeback of application, data, transactions or data fees to the consumers or other departments? Consider how the cloud management platform will handle this. • What application statistics and reports will need to be presented in the cloud management portal to the customer/consumers?

Category	ASSESSMENT ITEMS/DATA GATHERING
	• What user roles and groups need to be created/managed? • How will user authentication and identity for logon to each application be managed and federated through cloud management or other systems? • Consider how you should treat user accounts and data, in each application, when the user no longer exists in the organization, the account is removed, and so on.
Operations and governance	• Evaluate who is currently, and who should in the future, be performing all application upgrades, data maintenance, and monitoring. Are there existing challenges that could be addressed as part of application transformation (change in personnel responsibilities, governance, etc.)? • Consider grouping similar application profiles from an operations standpoint into the same cloud model (i.e., private cloud with operations/management by internal employees) versus applications that are commodities (meaning, they could be operated by anyone internal or outsourced) versus mission critical (meaning, they should only be run/operated by specific persons or department). • Consider advantages and disadvantages of outsourcing application management and upgrade to an external cloud provider (public cloud model) or peer agency (community model); consider which applications are commodities and where an existing SaaS or PaaS cloud provider has a similar or better offering
Mission criticality	• Assess how critical the application—and particularly the data—is to your customers and/or the mission of the organization. This can be a combination of data availability, slow performance, or potential loss of productivity:

Availability	• Low impact to the business if application is unavailable for more than eight hours	• Moderate impact to the business if application is unavailable for	• High impact to the business if application is unavailable for more than five minutes

Category	ASSESSMENT ITEMS/DATA GATHERING		
		• No significant financial or measurable productivity impact to employees or customers • Alternative methods exist during extended system outage	more than one hour • Potential financial and productivity losses internally • Potential customer impact including minimal loss of revenue and customer satisfaction • Alternative methods are not adequate during extended outage	• Significant financial and productivity losses internally • Significant customer impact including substantial loss of revenue and damage to reputation • No alternative methods exist during extended outage
	Performance	• Application response time (latency) to user requests is not a concern • Real-time processing of records/data is not required • Application does not require high availability • Application disaster	• Application response time (latency) to user requests is a concern and must be measured and monitored • Processing of data must be completed as soon as possible but not necessarily in real time	• Application response time (latency) is critical with strict monitoring, threshold alerting, and remediation • Real-time processing of data is required • Application must be configured for

Category	ASSESSMENT ITEMS/DATA GATHERING		
	recovery (DR) to secondary site not required • Recovery point objective (RPO): 24 hours; recovery time objective (RTO):8 hours	• Application must be configured for high availability within single datacenter • Data replication and/or snapshot every 8 hours • Application DR to secondary site required • RPO: 8 hours; RTO: 4 hours	high availability across multiple datacenters with immediate failover • Data replication in real time is required across datacenters
Preliminary decisions	• Form an initial decision as to which applications are good candidates for a cloud migration, which apps should remain hosted within internal datacenters, and which workloads should not be migrated or dealt with immediately • Consider which applications and workloads are best fits for hosting within an internal private cloud and which might be appropriate for a public cloud • This preliminary decision should be based on the assessment steps described earlier compared to the effort (cost, time, ROI) that the migration will require and ultimately the priority to the corporation • Consider hiring external application transformation-to-cloud consulting services to handle the most complex or mission-critical workloads. Have them perform detailed assessments and systems redesigns, select cloud providers/models, develop a cloud migration plan, and conduct a pilot.		

Category	ASSESSMENT ITEMS/DATA GATHERING
	• Most organizations have numerous applications and business priorities, so aligning these is crucial to forming a realistic cloud migration plan that meets available budgets and timelines. A common approach is to "continuously reprioritize" the application migration efforts over time to keep up with evolving business priorities.

Application Transformation Best Practices

Based on lessons learned and experience from across the cloud industry, you should consider the following best practices for your organization's planning.

LEGACY APPLICATION ASSESSMENT

Assessing each legacy application is an essential part of your cloud planning and transition strategy. Use the following guidance when evaluating each of your existing applications:

- Analyze each application to determine which architectures, multitiered applications, or legacy applications you could move quickly to a cloud (public or private) and which will require more significant transformation.

- Consider data security and risks on an application basis. Are there applications and data that would be at risk if hosted by a cloud provider or possibly in another state, territory, or country?

- Consider breaking up legacy applications into multitiered platforms as part of the transition to cloud. For example, separating application data and databases from middleware and frontend application servers will allow more elasticity, reliability, scalability, and possibly an ability to use the data platform by other applications that are also transited to the cloud. In this analysis, consider which applications you can transform and have share a common platform rather than moving every legacy workload to the cloud as individual applications.

- Remember, you can always leave an application back in the legacy/enterprise datacenter and deal with it another day. Some organizations and businesses need to show a more immediate benefit and adherence to cloud-first standards so don't necessarily take on the difficult applications first.

- Application assessment checklist:

  List and prioritize applications
      List all legacy applications, their business purpose and use cases, and priority to the business. List applications that might be retired or are seldom used.

Data classification

> Determine the sensitivity of the data for each application. Assess the risk of data corruption and competitive theft of intellectual property compared to the harm this might cause the corporation, your customers, or shareholders.

Requirements and compliance

> List your top business priorities and technical goals for each application. Do legacy applications have performance problems or require change regardless of the cloud migration? Note any regulatory or security compliance requirements.

Assess applications

> Assess each application based on the priority list. Determine as best you can the legacy application's software architecture, servers/hosts, programming language, database or middleware, network configuration, authentication/user controls, end-user interfaces, and so on.

Preliminary decision

> Discuss and determine your initial list of applications that are good candidates for cloud migration. Consider application complexity, risks, costs/effort to migration, ROI and priority and criticality to the business.

APPLICATION MODERNIZATION TECHNIQUES

Evaluate each legacy application to determine if, when, and in what priority to migrate the system to the cloud. Based on the assessment, select from the four application modernization strategies:

Replace

> Depending on your business priorities, it might not be cost effective to recreate some legacy applications for the cloud, so consider porting these "as is" to a cloud provider or replacing the legacy application entirely with a new public-provider hosted SaaS offering.

Rehost

It might be possible to copy and reinstall less complex applications in a cloud environment with little or no changes. Testing and network address changes are often required.

Refactor

You can redeploy multilevel applications into the cloud using multiple VMs to gain more performance, reliability, or scalability.

Redesign

When legacy applications are critical to the business and you cannot use the other migration techniques, a redesign and reprogramming of the software might be required. Although the advantages of the new modern application in a cloud are numerous, you need to make a financial decision to determine if the effort and cost are worth such investment.

CONSIDER CLOUD ARCHITECTURES FOR NEW APPLICATIONS

You should consider a cloud-based design and operations approach for all new applications and IT systems to achieve scalability, elasticity, and resiliency. Do not forget that the business outcomes and consumers of the applications is also critical. Here are some considerations:

- You should build applications with embedded multithreading, multitenant, highly scalable architectures to span across multiple servers, VMs, datacenters, and cloud providers.

- Though new applications can start on a small infrastructure, having these inherent capabilities will greatly improve the ability to make applications redundant, resilient, and scalable—all part of reduced operational, management, and support costs in the long term.

- Implement new application development practices around continuous development and delivery.

- Consider cloud-native application characteristics in every new application—and as a goal for all applications that are being redesigned as part of your cloud migration.

OPERATIONAL CONSIDERATIONS

Consider the following recommendations when evaluating your legacy applications and transitioning them to a new cloud operating environment. Remember that simply moving or porting applications to the cloud without modification is certainly possible, but may not provide the best performance, scalability, or long-term supportability.

- Consider establishing unique service levels for mission-critical applications rather than accepting the default cloud-wide service level proposed by the cloud provider.

- Implement federation tools to connect your enterprise user directory and authentication system to any public or managed private clouds to provide SSO capabilities to your users. This also greatly helps maintain security and permissions by having an always up-to-date user directory.

- Use scale-out and scale-up techniques to increase or decrease system capacity and application performance as applications workloads change. You might be able to use these scaling techniques to improve migrated legacy application to achieve better performance even if the app was not rewritten specifically for cloud hosting.

- Measure application performance of your existing enterprise applications before and after you migrate or port them to the cloud. This will make it possible for you to properly set scaling options and avoid the "blame game" with the cloud provider if application performance problems are found.

- As part of testing and during the initial days, weeks, and month of a new application hosted in the cloud, pay careful attention to network bandwidth utilization so that you are not surprised when the end-of-month invoice is calculated. Remember that most public cloud providers charge for network bandwidth (sometimes after a base allowance is exceeded).

REPLACE COMPONENTS AND LEGACY LICENSING AGREEMENTS

While evaluating your legacy applications and determining whether or when to move them to the cloud; consider renegotiating any software licenses, replace components of the system with COTS software, or use cloud-based platform/PaaS offerings. Here are some considerations:

- As part of the migration to cloud, consider replacing certain components of the system with COTS software of a PaaS offering from the cloud provider.

- Consider changing or renegotiating a legacy software license with a different vendor or in a more pay-as-you-go model—chances are that the legacy software platform and license agreements haven't kept up with modern licensing practices or pricing models.

- Consider what commercially available SaaS offerings are available in the industry and whether your organization could save money on internal software development, maintenance, and hosting. Many SaaS offerings might even provide more features than your current applications and might be able to assist in data importing/transition.

Billing and Procurement

Key topics in this chapter:

- Capital versus operational expenses
- Concerns with the "build it and they will come" model
- Ordering cloud services, procurement challenges in an automated service catalog
- Fixed price XaaS versus variable scaling and pricing
- Metering versus allocated pricing models
- Cloud billing versus accounting and invoicing systems
- Usage forecasting
- Legal and contract agreements
- Top cloud providers
- Billing and procurement best practices

Cloud services represent not only a new style of delivering IT services, but also a change in the way they are procured, resource usage is measured, billing is carried out, and the way organizations maintain budgets. In this chapter, I focus on lessons learned and best practices relating to the resource tracking, billing, contract terms, and public cloud vendor guidance. This chapter covers topics relating to both a private enterprise cloud and also procuring public cloud services as many organizations consider or end up with a combination of both cloud models.

Because some large organizations serve as a central IT for other departments or peer agencies, this would put central IT into a cloud service brokering role—making these other departments or agencies essentially "customers," which is a term that will sometimes be used in this chapter. You can read a full description of cloud brokering in Chapter 8.

Capital Versus Operational Expenses

We begin this chapter with a brief discussion on the potential benefits and trade-offs of using operating funds rather than capital to procure or build your cloud. Some organizations do not have a clear delineation between these two "colors" of money but it is pretty common in government and public sector organizations.

Many organizations procure information technology using capital funds on a three- to five-year depreciation schedule for information technology hardware, software, and sometimes installation and maintenance. At the end of each lifecycle, which varies depending on the asset type, more capital funds are allocated and the cycle repeats. In this example scenario, there are operational funds for ongoing IT-related services labor, datacenter facility (e.g., electricity and HVAC maintenance), but often these operations funds are far more scarce. Whatever the length of this capital model and lifecycle, the one constant is how all IT assets are depreciated, retired, and replaced with newer technologies in a never-ending circle of expense. Many industry analysts and business leaders—right or wrong—now call this the *old traditional style* of IT and point to the cloud and an operational cost model as the *new style* of IT.

One of the core benefits or promises of the cloud service model is that there is little or no up-front expenditure of capital funds to procure, deploy, and operate the cloud. Certainly in a public cloud model, the cloud service provider invests all of the necessary money and time to deploy its cloud and then market it to consuming organizations. As a consumer organization, you would pay for public cloud services similar to a monthly utility bill and use operating funds instead of capital—again, if color of money is a concern for you. Major benefits of this cloud consumption operational expense (OpEx) model are little or no expenditures of precious capital funding, little or no term commitment, and easy scalability up and down as cloud services are needed and utilized.

When a private cloud is required, the pure capital expense (CapEx) or OpEx decisions are more complicated. You could contract with a systems integrator or cloud provider to deploy a private cloud within your datacenter; however, this continues the CapEx cost mode. The exception is if you can negotiate a deal with a systems integrator or similar IT vendor to essentially lease you a utility-based or pay-as-you-go private or managed private cloud for which your costs are spread out and paid through operational funds.

Regardless of the organization, the key advantage with public cloud services is that you can increase or decrease the selected services (and thus costs) at any time, normally without penalties from the cloud provider. This pay-as-you-go approach makes public cloud more flexible and more of a monthly utility bill rather than large long-term capital IT asset or expense. The bottom line is this: there are trade-offs between OpEx and CapEx, and the use of public cloud versus managing your own private cloud.

Concerns with "Build It and They Will Come"

Public cloud providers invest funds and considerable effort to build a cloud infrastructure and then market their service to potential customers. They are making a calculated investment that customers will want their services and at some point they will surpass the break-even point and rocket to profitability. For enterprise customers, this is important to understand. Procuring and deploying too much hardware and software initially will increase the initial cost of your private cloud infrastructure. This will delay your break-even point on whatever return-on-investment (ROI) model you or your company's financial manager has created. The reality is that it is often difficult to guess future demand for a service you and your company's business users haven't utilized before. As soon as your users (your customers) are aware of all the new Infrastructure as a Service (IaaS), Platform as a Service (PaaS), and Software as a Service (SaaS) capabilities, will there be a lot of new demand. If your organization's goals are to migrate solely the existing IT systems you already have with no additional capacity, estimating the initial size for your enterprise private cloud will, of course, be much easier. But, you will still need some amount of additional capacity to accommodate elasticity.

The key problem with any cloud, properly sized or not, is the potential that applications are not migrated or users and consumers do not sign up in the early stages as expected. Any delays in expected revenues or chargeback within your organization will quickly destroy an ROI model. So, the lesson learned from countless customers—and I caution all of the customers with whom I work personally—is that the "build it and they will come" model has failed repeatedly, more often than not.

Key Take-Away

Countless organizations and agencies have overestimated the migration, or new service adoption rate of their new cloud. A best practice is to size the initial private
cloud conservatively and rely upon disciplined capacity management to keep up
with demand.

So, the best practice is to size the initial private cloud conservatively unless
you have a particular reason to expect explosive growth (with which you will not
be able to cope). Remember, as is detailed in the first three chapters of this book,
a cloud infrastructure is all about elasticity to the consumers and (reasonable)
capacity management from your IT operations team. Following the operational
best practices in Chapter 2, there should be sufficient spare capacity, monitoring
and alerts, and vendors and contracts in place for rapid addition of new hardware
and software licenses to keep up with demand.

Some large organizations such as public sector government agencies have IT
departments that service as a centralized IT "everything" for multiple subagencies or peer organizations. The relationship between these organizations and
these peer or subagencies might be officially mandated or more of a cooperative
agreement. Regardless of which it is, the central IT essentially supports the needs
of each "customers."

Use-Case Scenario: A Large, Public Sector Organization

A large, public sector organization plans to use the cloud transition
project as the core of an overall consolidation of legacy datacenters,
applications, and sometimes IT responsibilities that might have been distributed at the subagencies or departments. In this scenario, the intention of central IT is to create a central—often hybrid cloud broker—that
all department and peer agencies will share. This also means that funding goes to the central IT and little or no moneys are distributed to the
subagencies so that they do not continue maintaining their own IT systems and staff. The legitimate business justification is that the centralized IT and cloud automation, service brokering, cloud infrastructure,
and shared operations staff will save significant money and reduce dupli-
cation across the greater community or agencies.

So, let's assume that central IT does an absolutely phenomenal job
of planning and implementing a cloud brokering system consisting of an
on-premises private cloud with the hybrid ability to connect to external

public cloud providers if and when needed for certain applications or workloads. They create a very intuitive and robust range of cloud services into a web-based cloud service catalog portal for all subagencies to place their orders. They also begin a consultative effort to assess all legacy applications across each subagency to begin migrating legacy workloads.

The problem is that each subagency really isn't happy that they are not in control of their own IT. They feel they are not in control of the cloud offerings (which they aren't) and they had little or no input into how the cloud was designed. Finally, their IT budget was cut and redirected to the central IT department who clearly wasted money (in their opinion) building this large cloud that nobody is using—in reality, nobody is using it because it is brand new. The result is that the subagencies might try everything in their power to avoid cooperating with the cloud transition and central IT. They might play the passive-aggressive role, simply ignoring central IT, or outright object to senior management. Either way, they are holding up progress on behalf of their entire subagency. Sometimes, the IT leader making these objections has more influence or friends in senior management than central IT does. Consequently, this situation could further delay the overall cloud transition, call central ITs project into question, and cause this discontent to spread to other subagencies.

By the way, I'm not making this up: this is less a case "example" than it is an actual case, and I've seen it happen multiple times within large organizations.

To amplify the issues, the IT security managers at one or more of the subagencies now chime in—a month or two too late in the project plan—with objections about new servers or virtual machines (VMs) launching through automation at all hours of the day and night. They claim that this is against standard policy and they will not approve moving forward. One or two business-application owners, within a subagency, also speak up and indicate that their application cannot be moved to the cloud and must be kept at the subagency's existing legacy datacenter. The application software vendor does not have a cloud-enabled version of their software so they, too, cannot move to the cloud.

The result of all of this is a significant delay in utilization of the new private/broker cloud. The hardware and software is under utilized for many months, the ROI model is continually "pushing right" on the timeline, and project migration cost overruns begin to mount up. You need to keep in mind that in this scenario there was no technology problem. The security objections within one or more of the subagencies were largely because central IT either didn't include them early enough in the cloud planning or the subagency security personnel chose to ignore those meetings—either way, their objections are easily resolved through best practices (as I detail in Chapter 6). As for the business-application owner's objections, no application assessment has even been attempted yet, so maybe there is an alternative SaaS application that can be used or some other application modernization technique applied, as is detailed in Chapter 4.

The lessons learned from this case example are the following:

- Even when a parent organization has an official mandate to provide cloud services to peer or subagencies, don't underestimate the ability of a reluctant "customer" to stall, delay, or otherwise avoid adoption of your new enterprise cloud.

- Forcing your authority has proven to make matters worse in the long run.

- Using a "carrot" instead of a "stick" method to entice subagencies to join the central IT cloud and support organization is statistically shown to have little difference in results.

- Involve your subagencies and peer organizations early in the cloud-planning process. Ensure that they are involved and even if you do not follow some of their ideas, they need to feel that they were heard and their ideas addressed. Yes, this new style of IT sometimes includes "hugging it out."

- Consider consolidating subagency IT hardware and software assets based on their next three- to five-year refresh cycle so that central IT is not "taking" anything but rather deploying services on the newest, best, fastest system— that happens to be the cloud during this refresh cycle.

- Build your initial cloud small and with a reasonable amount of features and complexity. Overbuilding the size and spending a lot of time and money configuring dozens of Anything as a Service (XaaS) offerings is often wasted when you have few if any initial "customers." Follow best practices for capacity management to keep up with demand rather than oversizing the initial cloud.

- You will have plenty of time to configure new cloud services in the future. Any cloud services that you configure before bringing on a new subagency's users and applications is likely not going to be exactly correct anyway (i.e., before you meet and fully discuss goals and requirements with each new subagency or "customer," you are really guessing as to which cloud services and applications to create in your cloud).

Key Take-Away

Countless organizations and government agencies have overestimated the adoption or consumption rate of their new cloud service offerings. Even with the promised benefits of cloud, never underestimate the ability for consuming peer or suborganizations to delay or avoid consolidating their legacy IT or reducing their fiefdoms.

- Form a consultative team to work with each subagency as early as possible in the planning process (and on an ongoing basis thereafter) to assess their existing applications based on the guidelines for application transformation described in Chapter 4. Application assessments and migration take the most time and effort and are often the highest concern for your customers. You can begin applications assessments even before an initial cloud is staged.

Online Ordering and Approval Workflow

As stated earlier, every cloud will have some form of a cloud management system that provides a customer-facing portal for ordering, billing, and service management along with significant backend workflow, automated provisioning, and systems management capabilities that control all aspects of the cloud environment. The capabilities and level of maturity of these cloud management platforms is highly proprietary and often is what differentiates one cloud provider from another—or in the case of a private cloud, what differentiates a cloud management platform from another. For full details, lessons learned, and best practices, refer to Chapter 7.

Key Take-Away

There are two basic rules when procuring and building an enterprise private cloud: (1) the hardware and software for the infrastructure are not nearly as important as the cloud management software; and (2) because you have a favored hypervisor does not mean you should use that vendor's cloud management platform. Rarely is the best hypervisor product also the best heterogeneous multiprovider hybrid cloud management vendor.

Common functionality within these cloud management platforms is a customer-facing (normally web-based) portal on which customers are presented with a service catalog of available cloud services along with pricing and specifications from which to choose.

SERVICE CATALOG

The cloud portal's capabilities often begin with an online ordering system. Here, an authorized user or manager can browse through a catalog of service offerings. This catalog is essentially the storefront to begin cloud service orders and then manage subscriptions. It is critical that the service catalog be easy to use and have complete specifications for each offering, including an optional price field if your organization wishes to use a billing or chargeback function. For IaaS compute services, as an example, the primary service normally begins with a VM, with options underneath offering a choice of operating system (OS), processors, memory, VM size, and the amount of storage. The total price for the service with options is normally displayed on a shopping cart for customers to confirm their purchase.

Industry Trend

Public cloud providers rarely provide pricing within a service catalog, opting instead to keep pricing published on separate static web pages. This makes it difficult to understand pricing for cloud services and transaction fees when ordering new services via the cloud management portal. In an enterprise private cloud, pricing or chargeback features are optional and can be shown within the service catalog of most cloud portals.

Behind the scenes of each service catalog item is a service design, although each cloud management system might have a different name for this. These service designs define the specific applications, compute resources, automation workflows, and pricing for each item shown in the service catalog. Service designs can be a simple VM automated workflow or a complex multitiered application that launches multiple VMs and virtual networks. Finally, each service design can have optional features defined to give customers the ability to customize their order, such as selecting their preferred OS for a VM, the amount of memory, processors, disk, and so on, with each option potentially having an additional cost associated with them in the service catalog shopping cart.

APPROVAL WORKFLOW

Some cloud portals offer an optional and configurable approval process. This is common to private enterprise cloud portals, because they can be more customized than public deployment models. For example, the cloud management system automatically sends an email to one or more predefined approvers within the organization indicating that an order has been placed and needs approval. A link in the email launches the cloud management system web portal, where the approver can log on and see a list of pending orders. Upon her approval, services are automatically provisioned by the cloud management system. When the provisioning is completed—usually within minutes—the customer billing cycle is started with a notification sent to the person who ordered the service.

Lessons learned have demonstrated that some organizations benefit from multiple levels of approval, such as basing it on order-price thresholds, the user's role within the organization, and depending on the specific cloud service being ordered. Some cloud portals offer passive and active approvals so that some cloud services are preapproved for ordering and do not need human vetting or layers of approval.

SUBSCRIPTION MANAGEMENT

Although the actual term "subscription" can vary from one cloud management portal to another, the basic concept is important to understand. When ordering your first IaaS VM, for example, you are placing an order for a VM at the agreed-upon pricing. This price is usually measured and invoiced on a monthly (or daily, weekly, or yearly) recurring charge that automatically renews for each billing period until canceled (or a specific end date if chosen). When your order is processed, it becomes a new subscription to which most cloud portals allow you to assign a unique name.

Using the cloud management portal, you can always view the status of your subscriptions, view configurations information (e.g., IP address and system status), or add and remove features within a subscription (such as adding an additional VM to an existing subscription).

Financial Tracking and Billing

Depending on the chosen cloud management platform vendor, you can bill cloud services to customers or internal departments or agencies in many ways (you can also disable billing if it's not needed). With some cloud providers, users can place orders and pay using a credit card; whereas others produce invoices or charge-back reports. Billing periods are typically on a monthly basis, although the actual metered and charged cloud services accumulate based on hourly, daily, weekly, or monthly pricing plans.

Regardless of the cycle and payment methods, the actual charges accumulated are based on one or both of the following:

Fixed fee

A fixed fee is charged and shown in the service catalog for each cloud service, or optional service (e.g., additional storage or memory). The cloud management system will charge this same fixed price for each billing period.

Variable fees

Variable charges are billed based on the resources that were used during the billing cycle. These itemized resources would normally be a base price for each VM, charge per processor, per gigabyte of memory, per gigabyte of storage, and network options. The customer is only billed for what it uses, but there might be a minimum charge per billing cycle. These variable fees per usage could result in unexpected high fees—some cloud management systems allow high limit thresholds to prevent unexpectedly large bills.

Cloud portals can get extremely granular in the way subscriptions are metered. Some public providers offer VMs by the minute or hour. Regardless of the granularity, the billing cycle usually does not change (monthly is most common), with the overall charges totaled up and reported to the customer at the end of the billing cycle. Most cloud services automatically renew or move to the next billing cycle until the customer cancels the service. Again, all of this is highly configurable in an enterprise private cloud management platform that you own or operate, and is only somewhat configurable as a customer for a public cloud.

METERED VERSUS ALLOCATED RESOURCES

When cloud compute resources (processors, memory, and storage) are bundled into a service catalog, it is common for IaaS applications to be offered as VMs in small, medium, large, and additional sizes. The specifications for each of these VM sizes will specify or allow you to choose the number of processors, memory, storage, networking, and OS for each VM bundle or catalog item—each at the pricing shown within the service catalog. As a consumer or user of the cloud, it is important to know whether these resources are metered or allocated; as a private cloud manager, it is important to understand the difference between these and choose which method, or both, to use when configuring resource metering.

Continuing with the VM use case, in a resource allocation model, each VM purchased has a set amount of compute resources that is charged regardless if all of the resources are utilized or not. Even if you do not use all of the allocated storage space, you are paying for it. This is pretty much standard policy and practice for all public cloud providers and the default model for private cloud management platforms unless you configure it otherwise.

Metered resource management means that the cloud provider or management system measures the actual utilization of storage, for example, and only bills for the amount used. This metered resource model is more in line with the overall pay-as-you-go and elasticity characteristics of cloud computing. Metering of resources also means using variable fees (as described earlier) whereby the cloud management system will calculate billing based on actual utilization at the end of each billing period.

Key Take-Away

Pay-as-you-go is a basic economic benefit for cloud services. To truly pay only for what is utilized, resource metering is necessary so that the consumer is billed only for actual utilization instead of traditional flat/fixed fees for service each billing period. This results in variable pricing, which is sometimes difficult for maintaining budgets and preventing unexpected overage charges.

Allocated resources—storage in particular—is a common practice in most legacy datacenters. Metered resources—again in storage—are most common in a public cloud model. Within a private-enterprise cloud, many organizations do not want to deal with the extra configuration hassle necessary for metered storage, and instead use the allocation model.

BILLING REPORTS

One key feature within the cloud management system is the ability for the organization or customer to see their billing history and current balance through the cloud portal. Most organizations do not want to rely solely on the billing cycle to see a report of their detailed charges; they prefer the ability to view resource utilization at any time, even in the middle of a billing cycle. You should look for public cloud providers that offer a detailed dashboard view of service utilization and financial forecasting or a private cloud management system with similar capabilities.

Of course, even enterprise organizations that do not bill their users or departments for IT services utilized can benefit from detailed billing and chargeback reports. Using these reports, you can see which services are being heavily utilized, which are not being utilized, and which are left running but not in use (i.e., being wasted). Many early-adopter cloud customers have used these billing reports to justify new purchases and expansion of cloud services, staffing, software, and so on, or just to plan an annual operating budget.

DRAW-DOWN ACCOUNTS

One unique billing feature that some cloud providers and private cloud management platforms offer is the ability for a customer to submit a contract or purchase order document with a maximum funding level. This is very popular with large organizations and government customers. In this billing method, the ceiling of the contract amount is entered into the cloud management system, and the customer then places orders against this spending limit. After each billing cycle, an invoice is generated and the available contract funding is reduced by that amount. When the account nears zero, warning notices can be sent to customers reminding them that their contract ceiling is about to be reached. Customers can also submit multiple purchase orders that can be utilized by department(s) or project team(s), with the costs of each subscription invoiced against a specific purchase order.

Some public sector customers are required to track and limit their purchases so that they cannot exceed their budgeted purchase order limits. Although rare for public cloud management systems, a private cloud portal is more customizable and might be able to support this type of budgeting process. An example of this would be the cloud portal prompting for a purchase order when services are ordered, and automatically warning the customer of potential budget shortfalls if the pending order is actually processed and approved.

IMPLEMENTING GRACE PERIODS AND SERVICE SHUTDOWNS

With successful public cloud providers hosting thousands of customers, one key feature of good cloud management software is the ability to automatically detect when a funding pool or purchase order goes to zero. A feature to consider in an enterprise private cloud management system is the ability to allow services to function while being in a grace period. The customer is told that they are overdue on their account and warned of an imminent service cut-off if payment is not received. After a configurable grace period has expired, the cloud management system can automatically pause or shut down services. One word of advice is to not destroy the account immediately after the grace period; instead, pause the services temporarily and keep the data. Payment might be on the way, the customer might want the service reinstated, or the customer intends to export their data to another provider. Whatever the situation, you don't want to have to resort to re-creating the service and restoring it from backup if you can avoid it. You can perform a destructive deletion of old data after 30 or 60 days, for example. When you do finally clean up the data, the cloud management platform will automatically allow those resources to be assigned to the next new customer or subscription. When you consider how many cloud services are being ordered, changed, or renewed—multiplied by hundreds or thousands of customers or users—you can begin to understand how the cloud management system must include financial and resource utilization billing as a core function, even if you do not actually charge your enterprise consumers.

CLOUD BILLING VERSUS ACCOUNTING AND INVOICING SYSTEMS

The cloud portal and billing system are a system of record (i.e., billing and utilization data) and not an invoicing or accounting system. A cloud management portal calculates cloud subscriptions, renewals, and resource utilization to generate the billing data and a printable or exportable report. Some cloud systems will call this an invoice but there is rarely a backend accounts payable or receivable system, such as a real accounting system would have. You could integrate this billing data into your organization's accounting system, if desired, to generate official invoices or chargebacks.

Legal and Contract Agreements

When consuming services from a public cloud, the provider will have standardized service terms, service-level agreements (SLAs), and limitation agreements that you must accept before service can begin. One of the basic tenets of a public cloud service is that each customer is paying for a service to be delivered, based on a SLA. One common assumption in the industry is that cloud customers are not supposed to be concerned with all the details and technology used by the public cloud provider, only the results of the cloud service, as measured in availability of the service. Most public cloud SLAs include a financially backed, guaranteed percentage of time, per month, that the services will be available—typically this is 99.9% or 99.95%. The cloud provider will provide credits should it fail to meet the defined SLA. For your enterprise private cloud, consider what terms and conditions you want to establish and if you need to have an agreement at all if all of your "customers" are internal employees. Many organizations use some of the contractual language of the top public cloud providers to create an internal SLA.

Other terms that you should consider when evaluating or creating a cloud service agreement include the following:

Performance guarantees

Will the VMs, storage, and networking performance be guaranteed? Some cloud providers "oversubscribe" their customers, and during peak periods of usage, this could have a negative impact on your service performance. Look for guarantees from the public cloud provider that your services will not be affected by oversubscription or the peak workloads of other customers. Within a private cloud, you might not want to do this, because you might intentionally want to oversubscribe as a way to lower costs and increase overall server utilization.

Minimum service term or commitments

Ensure that you are aware of any minimum level of services or term duration required by the cloud provider. Some providers might publish attractive pricing, but there is a minimum cost or amount of services to which you are committing. Public cloud providers often do have special low-priced cloud services if you agree to a certain minimum commitment.

Migration terms and costs

Some cloud providers will charge additional fees for importing or exporting your data, applications, and VM templates out of their system. Most cloud providers do not charge for data import labor or data transfer but do charge for exporting the data if you attempt to terminate services. Make sure that you understand the process, costs, and amount of time the cloud provider will take to facilitate your service termination and subsequent export of your data so that you can move it to another provider or internal cloud.

Transaction and data input/output fees

Some public cloud providers have a significant number of transaction or data input/output transfer fees that are either hidden or not well understood. These fees can quickly add up during normal usage each month, often surprising new customers when they see their first full month's invoice. This should not be an issue for enterprise private clouds.

Liability

Most cloud providers will have service agreement terms that attempt to limit their responsibility for data loss and consequential damages. Attempt to negotiate better terms for both the data loss and consequential damages clauses. The service agreement should include some liability on the provider's part for maintaining, protecting, and ensuring the availability of your data, and should outline penalties in case the provider fails to meet the terms specified in the SLA. This should not be an issue for enterprise private clouds.

Maintenance windows

All clouds require maintenance of the infrastructure, including network, hardware, and software upgrades. Some providers might try to declare that they may have several hours of potential outages each month without incurring a penalty against the SLA. You should have no problem negotiating that term out of any agreement. The top cloud providers, and hopefully your enterprise private cloud, are designed with resilient applications and services so that there are no scheduled maintenance outages, because the services should automatically failover without interruption.

When building your own enterprise private cloud, you should also create a standardized service agreement to your customers, peers, or subordinate organizations that intend to use the service. In addition to the aforementioned legal and contract considerations, here are additional terms that you should consider specifically for a private cloud:

- Consider specifying different SLA availability guarantees for optional fully managed services versus user-managed services. A common example of this is with VMs wherein a provider might not support the OS or applications in its default pricing unless the user purchases a fully managed up-lift support program.

- Clearly define if and when services will be terminated, and data deleted, when a service subscription expires or the customer forgets to renew. As mentioned earlier, you might want to simply stop services, but not delete any data for a specified grace period. This makes restoration of services very simple if the customer determines that it wants to continue.

- Ensure that you define what level of support is provided to your users. Customers using a Dev/Test service, for example, might unreasonably expect support on their application programming efforts that is out of scope. You should be clear that support is only for the availability of VMs and the OS or patches, depending on whether you are offering fully managed or customer-managed VMs.

- You should specify if any departments or subagencies you support are able to bring or transfer their own software licenses to your enterprise private cloud, possibly reducing the overall cost of the services.

Licensing

In a cloud environment, application licensing has some unique challenges compared to traditional enterprise IT procurement and lifecycles. A traditional software vendor usually requires a customer to prepurchase a quantity of licenses upfront, even though those users are not yet accessing the system. In a cloud environment that is supposedly an "on-demand" style of IT delivery, this would be considered an "over purchase," likely resulting in commitment of money up front, with potentially unpredictable revenue streams coming in the future. As a cloud service provider, even a private cloud owner or provider, you might need to negotiate (or more accurately, convince) each of your preferred software vendors to change their licensing models to support the pay-per-use and elasticity characteristics so important to cloud computing. There are many software vendors who still refuse to adapt to this new on-demand or pay-as-you-go model; however, the size of your organization and amount of potential revenue you represent can help influence the software vendor's terms.

It is important to note that, depending on the cloud deployment model and software vendor, you might or might not be able to use legacy noncloud enterprise licensing agreements. For example, in a private cloud, it is much more likely that the software vendor will allow an existing enterprise software license to be used, assuming that you have a cost advantage in doing so. In a public or community cloud scenario, it is much more likely that the software vendor would not allow the transfer or use of the legacy enterprise licensing agreement. Although this license reuse issue often favors organizations deploying a private cloud, public cloud providers usually have the leverage of massive quantity and scale on their side to extract a good software licensing price, which ostensibly results in a competitive, if not lower, price to public cloud consumers.

The Current Cloud Industry: A Summary of the Leading Providers and Integrators

Although you might begin your cloud transition with an enterprise private cloud, it is important to understand the cloud industry, what cloud providers are offering, and in which areas each provider specializes. There are numerous successful cloud providers, so I will attempt to summarize the capabilities and target market for the most well-known and established providers in the industry. As stated earlier, for enterprise private clouds, the cloud management platform is the primary system to evaluate and deploy. Chapter 7 includes a list and description of the leading cloud management products and vendors.

Because these vendors constantly upgrade their features and capabilities, it is almost impossible to keep the information that follows completely up to date in a published book. Before you make any decisions, I recommend visiting the vendors' websites to view the most current information.

AMAZON WEB SERVICES

Amazon remains the leading public cloud provider measured by the number of customers and capacity of its infrastructure. Amazon was originally focused on IaaS applications and has the largest web content delivery network, cloud storage, and VM server capacity in the industry. Amazon now has significant PaaS applications, including multiple databases, mobile, analytics, media, transaction processing, and application development platform services. Amazon also offers a virtual private cloud (VPC) offering, whereby it still owns and manages the cloud but provides a dedicated instance of its cloud system to each customer. This VPC offering does not include all of Amazon's cloud service options.

It is fair to say that Amazon is the current 800-pound gorilla in the cloud industry with by far the most customers. It is the largest and was the first to deploy a massive cloud service environment to the public, and it continues to add new cloud-based service offerings. Amazon was one of the first cloud providers to form a large reseller network and publish its own (proprietary) API. Amazon has a growing list of third-party SaaS and PaaS applications available through its public cloud service portal. The marketplace of third-party solutions makes it possible for customers to mix and match both Amazon and third-party vendor software offerings through the same public cloud portal and billing.

Amazon continues to lead the public cloud industry with numerous new service offerings announced each year. Amazon also leads public cloud providers in achieving security accreditations up to a year before many of its competitors. Amazon's commercial public cloud service has achieved FedRAMP accreditation as well as its more secure and specialized GovCloud service.

GOOGLE

Google Compute is a more recent entry in the large-scale public cloud market. Its services were originally focused on IaaS but have quickly added application development tools, databases, and cloud storage options. Google's depth of features is not yet at the level of those of Amazon or Microsoft; however, the services in place are very fast, easy to configure, and low cost. For example, Google VMs have fewer OS (e.g., minimal Windows Server OS options), platforms, and sizing options compared to Amazon and Microsoft. Given Google's history and stated intentions, Google is expected to continuously roll out improvements and new features to catch up to the leading competitors and is likely to become a significant player in the public cloud IaaS and PaaS market, all while expanding its SaaS offering through natural growth and acquisition.

MICROSOFT

Microsoft originally focused on "behind the firewall" internal enterprise installations of its Windows desktop, Windows Server, and numerous other platforms and applications. Around the time cloud computing was coined, Microsoft began selling a SaaS offering based on its Exchange and SharePoint platforms. It then embarked on a tectonic shift to the cloud, transforming its large portfolio of enterprise software into cloud-based services.

Microsoft continues to expand its IaaS and PaaS offerings through its Azure public cloud service. Azure offers a complete line of public cloud services, including infrastructure VMs, storage, Dev/Test, web hosting, and database platform hosting. Given Microsoft's success in developing its own hypervisor, virtualization, database, OSs, and numerous enterprise applications, adapting these for the cloud and hosting in a public cloud service offering is a logical step. With regard to the number and completeness of the cloud offerings, Microsoft's key competitors are Amazon and Google. Microsoft has such a significant portfolio of development, productivity, and enterprise platforms and applications that it is using—as expected—to differentiate itself from other IaaS-focused providers with a large suite of integrated platforms and enterprise applications hosted in the cloud.

The Azure offerings are primarily public cloud in nature, but Microsoft also offers private cloud integration to its Azure platform. This private cloud integration shows great potential given the huge customer base Microsoft already has running its products within on-premises datacenters. This hybrid integration from the public Azure service back into on-premises enterprise servers and applications is sold and configured as optional offerings, including backup, server replication and failover, federated identity, virtual desktops, and application publishing. Although Microsoft has publicly stated that it will remain competitive to Amazon prices now and in the future, it appears that Microsoft will focus more on enterprise customers—keeping a focus on transitioning enterprise IT to the cloud and hybrid integration of the Azure public cloud back to these existing enterprise applications.

RACKSPACE

Rackspace offers a range of public cloud IaaS and PaaS applications as well as a separate line of private and hybrid cloud solutions. Rackspace was one of the first providers to offer public and private cloud services. Its claim to fame is superior customer service, but online pricing indicates this is offered at a significant premium over its base cloud service. Rackspace is one of the few public cloud providers that also offers private and hybrid clouds. Rackspace also utilizes OpenStack as its primary management platform for public cloud. Rackspace also offers multiple SaaS offerings, such as Microsoft Exchange and SharePoint hosted services. This combination of IaaS, PaaS, SaaS, and private cloud shows the maturity of Rackspace as a public and private cloud provider.

IBM

IBM provides public cloud services as well as private/hybrid consulting and deployment as part of its long history as a systems integrator. IBM announced it would retire its SmartCloud public cloud offering in 2014, with a plan to migrate all current customers to its newly acquired SoftLayer platform. IBM's SoftLayer, which is based on the CloudStack open source cloud platform, offers all of the expected IaaS VM and storage services, but it is not yet considered an industry leader for public cloud. IBM has more recently announced the launch of two new datacenters in the United States that will host a new SoftLayer-based public cloud designed to meet FISMA and FedRAMP security standards, but no go-live target date was provided. Expect IBM to remain a significant industry player, particularly in private cloud, and expand its market presence in both public and private/hybrid enterprise cloud in the future. IBM most closely competes with CSC (Computer Sciences Corporation) and Hewlett-Packard as an enterprise cloud systems integrator. It is not known if IBM will attempt to directly compete with Amazon or Google or just continue building upon its enterprise customer base, transforming customers to private and hybrid clouds.

HEWLETT-PACKARD

Hewlett-Packard has a long history of hosting datacenters, building large networks, manufacturing servers, storage, and creating software for leading Internet and cloud providers. It has traditionally functioned as a systems integrator but more recently began its public, private, virtual private, and hybrid cloud solutions. The cloud offerings are now marketed under the HP Helion brand name. HP Helion offers infrastructure VMs, storage, Dev/Test, database, and platform services in public, private, and hybrid cloud models with OpenStack as the underlying technology platform. Hewlett-Packard is both cloud provider and a software developer with private and hybrid cloud management platforms. Its primary competitors are IBM and CSC, both of whom also provide transitioning service to enterprise customers moving to private and hybrid clouds.

SYSTEMS INTEGRATORS

Systems integrators (SIs) such as Hewlett-Packard, IBM, CSC, Accenture, Computer Associates, and many others now offer a portfolio of customized private and hybrid cloud services to enterprise customers. Most integrators do not compete with the likes of Amazon, Microsoft, or Google in public cloud. The differentiators between competing SIs are their migration and consultative deployment expertise, experience and reputation, and willingness to build highly customized private or hybrid clouds that most public cloud providers do not offer. More recently, there is a trend whereby these SIs are partnering or acquiring open source or commercially available cloud management platforms that they use as a baseline architecture that heavily influences each SIs approach to cloud, XaaS offerings, and competitive differentiators.

SERVICE AGGREGATORS

Companies that aggregate and host several third-party software applications include Apptix, 1and1, and Intermedia. These cloud providers, previously known as application service providers, focus on web-based storefronts, online ordering, and the hosting and administration of COTS and third-party software applications over the Internet. Now called SaaS providers, these companies usually do not create applications themselves; rather, they host, manage, and provide support to customers by integrating numerous applications into readily consumable low-cost cloud service subscriptions. Some of these traditionally SaaS providers are now expanding into PaaS and IaaS offerings but are unlikely to ever compete with large-scale public cloud providers such as Amazon, Microsoft, and Google. Overall, as an industry, these SaaS aggregators have been most successful in the small and medium-sized business market.

Billing and Procurement Best Practices

Based on lessons learned and experience from across the cloud industry, you should consider the following best practices for your organization's planning.

CAPITAL VERSUS OPERATING EXPENSES

One of the benefits of consuming an existing public cloud service is the ability to use operating funds for a recurring hosted service with no capital expenditures and minimum commitments. When building and deploying your own private cloud, the capital investment and ongoing operations can be extensive. Here are some considerations:

- When procuring a private cloud infrastructure, organizations often attempt to utilize existing server farms, storage systems, and networks; however, lessons learned have demonstrated that mixing the new cloud services with legacy systems can create significant change control, security, customization flexibility, and performance problems. It is more desirable to build a new infrastructure and then, when operational, consider migrating the legacy systems into the cloud as the legacy systems lifecycles expire or need refreshing.

- When procuring hardware and software for your private cloud, avoid purchasing too much and thus deploying more capacity than you need. The result is an overly expensive initial cloud service—you are starting with a steep expense curve and a long path to achieving your ROI. Leasing of the initial hardware and software are certainly options, but also try to negotiate pay-as-you-grow agreements with hardware vendors, in which you only pay for a portion of your equipment immediately, yet extra capacity is prestaged in your datacenter. Your agreement will only begin charging you for the prestaged equipment as you begin to use the extra capacity. Often, you can seek a similar agreement with software license vendors so that you don't prepurchase a large pool of licenses while waiting for new customers to actually consume them.

- In some situations, you might be able to negotiate an agreement with a systems integrator to deploy and host a private cloud that is dedicated to your organization. This systems integrator would be taking on some or all of the risk of funding and building the cloud but will likely require minimum term commitments from the customer. Lessons learned have shown that this model of a systems integrator building a private dedicated cloud for free can result in profit losses almost immediately and the systems integrators ROI model rarely recovering in future years. Although this might appear as an advantage to the end customer of this cloud, the systems integrator will eventually have to cut corners, provide reduced quality, and ultimately the customer suffers from lack of new features, new XaaS offerings, application migration assistance, and so on.

BUILD IT AND THEY WILL COME

Many organizations and public cloud providers have relied on the "build it and they will come" approach to attracting customers and growth of the cloud. Real-world experience is in clear conflict with this approach. Rather, this can lead to significant financial loss as lack of customer adoption can make the planned ROI model worthless. Here are some notes:

- Organizations that plan to host a private cloud and sell or chargeback service costs to peer or suborganizations often predict only the best-case adoption and growth scenario and cost model that results in financial losses and an under utilized cloud environment.

- Organizations tend to overestimate their ability to entice, coerce, or force subagencies and departments to utilize and migrate to the new cloud environment. Lessons learned are to never underestimate a department or subagency's ability to resist, delay, or find other methods to not migrate to the new environment that they don't feel they control or that would reduce their political power or trusted staff.

- Create a plan for internal marketing of the cloud service and attempt to get confirmed/signed agreements for migration and funding from subagencies or departments. This would be the equivalent to a public cloud provider obtaining some preorders so that there is a backlog going into production, thus helping the planned ROI model.

- Do not create a financial model with the traditional "hockey stick" pro forma financial model in years three or four when suddenly everyone is perfect with customer adoption and ROI: don't use the best-case scenario to plan your cloud pricing, staffing levels, and customer growth rates.

- The bottom line is that when there is no customer backlog of orders, no minimum commitments contracted, and no capital or "skin in the game," the "build it and they will come" model has not been successful even if the product (the cloud, in this case) is a technical success.

ONLINE ORDERING

The cloud management platform of a public or private cloud, will normally be the engine behind a customer-facing portal, service catalog of available XaaS, pricing, and a checkout or order confirmation process. Here are some key points to keep in mind:

- For public cloud consumers, you have little or no choice but to customize the ordering or portal experience. Private cloud owners can often pick from available cloud management platforms and therefore evaluate capabilities, features, usability, and customization options.

- Evaluate and walk through sample procurement use cases, such as using purchase orders and draw-down accounts (pools of funding) with the cloud management platform to determine if it meets your needs or if you customize it.

- You will need to determine and provide to the cloud management platform the usernames or a defined group in LDAP or Active Directory who are allowed to place orders in the cloud portal. These usernames, and sometimes several group names, are used to define each role in the cloud portal. These roles-based permissions determine what exactly users of the portal can and cannot do.

PROCUREMENT PROCESS FOR ORDERING CLOUD SERVICES

When an order is placed within a private cloud service catalog, the approval and/or the financial obligation of funds are processed through a customizable workflow engine. Many organizations find that their traditional procurement processes do not allow for distributing authorizations for these purchases; thus, requiring the procurement or finance department approval of every order is inefficient. A successful cloud environment depends on automated ordering, pay-as-you-go, and rapidly provisioned services, which also means that the procurement of individual cloud services needs to be preapproved or automated, as well. The procurement or finance team within an organization likely cannot or does not want to be involved in every order or micro-transaction that might occur through the online service catalog and cloud portal. Here are some consiserations:

- It is recommended that you creat funding pools, multiple purchase orders, or other forms of preapproved allocations of money with assigned personnel allowed to order services against these funds.

- In addition to the initial procurement of cloud services, the ongoing cost allocation or chargeback to one or more consuming organizations is also critical. Some cloud management platforms and portals provide sufficient reports with the granularity of data necessary to assign costs to each consuming organization or user.

- Even for organizations that do not directly charge costs to the consumers and thus provide reports and usage statistics along with the invoice, it is still important to track costs and track system usage, plan for system growth, and to remove or shut down services that are no longer actively in use.

APPROVAL WORKFLOW

Most cloud portals, particularly private clouds, have some form of customizable approval workflow. This makes it possible for specified individuals to log onto the cloud portal and place orders that then trigger a notification to one or more persons in your organization who must approve the order. Each tenant or organization can usually have its own set of approvers by department or subagency. Here are some considerations:

- Avoid having too many approval steps or individuals involved. Remember that the intent is to quicken the pace for obtaining cloud services.

- You might want to use a combination of passive and active approval services listed in the portal service catalog. Passive items do not need a person to actively approve the order, so it automatically provisions and starts billing of that service when ordered. Active approval requires someone to approve each order before provisioning and billing begins.

- It is recommended that the contracting departments not be involved in the numerous micro-transactions of every order; instead, they should issue and track pools of approved funding such as purchase orders where every cloud order draws-down against the contract funding ceiling.

- An existing service ticketing or service management system might already be deployed in some organizations and datacenter operations. Most cloud management portals can easily integrate with existing service ticketing systems for approvals and other event notifications.

FIXED AND VARIABLE PRICING

Both in consuming a public cloud service or building a private cloud, you need to determine which of the cloud services will need to be billed at a fixed price for each billing period and which will be at a variable price. Here are some considerations:

- Variable pricing also means that the resources utilized for the particular cloud service will be measured or metered with usage charges accumulated and then billed at the end of each billing cycle. Thresholds or limits can be set within the cloud management system and portal, but otherwise the end customer might be surprised with a higher-than-expected invoice when using variable pricing during a high-utilization period.

- Fixed pricing provides a more predictable and stable price for each cloud service for each billing period. The only way the cloud service expands to use more resources (processors, memory, storage, etc.) is for the customer to manually order expanded services from within the cloud portal. Although fixed pricing means predictable and controlled bills, the cloud management platform will not automatically expand resources to accommodate the increase workload. This can result in poor performance or even system failure when an XaaS application reaches its defined resource limits.

- A combination of fixed and variable pricing is possible, even in the same service catalog. Sometimes it is best to configure the variable-pricing options in the service catalog for active approval to ensure management is aware of potential costs of the newly ordered cloud service.

AUTOMATIC ELASTICITY OR SCALING

The ability for a cloud service to expand in resource utilization or capacity is a core benefit of cloud. Enabling automatic expansion means that the cloud management system will attempt to add more VMs, memory, processors, or disk space to a given XaaS subscription in order to keep up with peak workloads. Here are some things to keep in mind:

- Enabling automatic elasticity can result in a surprisingly high variable cost at the end of the billing period. The alternative is for the cloud platform to be configured to enforce the maximum resources (processors, memory, storage, network, or application licenses) that were ordered and never automatically expand the service or charge more for that elasticity.

- Many legacy applications can benefit from more processing power and memory when the amount of workload increases. The individual VMs running these applications can be scaled up, but expanding to additional VMs might or might not be as effective. It takes a newer cloud-enabled application to be easily or automatically scaled out across multiple VMs to increase capacity. The very best and most advanced cloud applications can both expand and contract themselves across multiple VMs and multiple networks, providers, and multiple instances of the application. We will begin to see these new styles of dynamic applications in the coming years, but they are rare right now.

CLOUD BILLING VERSUS ACCOUNTING SYSTEMS

The cloud management portals and integrated billing should be used as a source of data that can automatically or manually feed into a true accounting system.

Government public sector customers often require the accounting systems be certified for invoicing the government. Cloud management platforms usually do not qualify as an accounting system; therefore, the invoice or bill generated by a public or private cloud management platform might not always be suitable to actually invoice or chargeback to the end-consuming organization of the cloud. Use the data from the cloud management system to input (manually or through some customized automated import process) into the real accounting and invoicing system.

DETAILED CLOUD SERVICE COST MODELS

In a traditional IT department or managed service model, all of the costs of the physical datacenter facility, network infrastructure, server farms, applications, software licenses, support vendors and internal IT staff are often consolidated into the budget. In this legacy managed service model, the costs of providing an individual service to a consuming end user were rarely known to any level of accuracy; the overall budgets were usually not broken down to the service level but were maintained at a much higher level. Here are some considerations:

- In a cloud model, it will be important to recalculate the costs of providing each application or cloud service on a per-unit basis. These units are typically a consuming end user of an application or per-VM/server hosted in the cloud. As more users and services or more VMs are activated, in this example, the costs for providing these services must be known in order to properly scale the environment, potentially charge the consuming user/organizations, and to provide support services using the IT staff.

- Create a financial model during the planning phases of a private cloud deployment. Calculate the costs of equipment, software, deployment, licensing, and support and operations labor for the initial months and out to two to three years at a minimum.

- Your formulas should allow insertion of customers and user adoption rates (purchases of services) against your cost model so that you know your break-even period, your average revenue per user (ARPU), and cost of every infrastructure component as you scale up the environment to meet demand.

- Keep adjusting this model as actual customer orders come in, reset your customer demand curves, and adjust your infrastructure and support cost models every 6 to 12 months.

LEGAL AND SERVICE AGREEMENTS

Whether consuming a public cloud service or deploying your own enterprise private cloud, service terms and legal agreements are essential to defining the scope of the service, defining service-level guarantees, and limiting liability. Specific legal and service terms to consider, both as a consumer of cloud and as a private cloud operator include the following:

Defined SLA and availability guarantee

Ensure that there is an active SLA, not just a service-level objective. Do not be surprised if the SLAs are different from one service to another within the same cloud provider.

Minimum service term or commitments

Some providers offer the lower pricing only if customers commit to significant minimum terms, volume discounts, and so on.

Migration terms and costs

Always review termination procedures and fees that might be associated with migrating away from the provider.

Import, export, and non obvious transaction fees

Many public cloud providers have significant transaction fees that are not obvious on their price lists and are often not included in their cost-of-service estimation tools. Most providers do not charge for data importing/uploading but do charge fees for downloading and migration away from the provider's cloud.

Liability limitations

Cloud providers often include terms in their service agreement that attempt to limit the provider's liability for data loss or consequential damages. Some cloud service agreements even state that they have zero responsibility or guarantee to even maintain or back up your data. Ensure that these service terms are changed and negotiate a better agreement with appropriate protections and liability limits.

Declared maintenance windows

Consider the provider's definition of maintenance outages (planned and unplanned) and how service credits are to be requested. When it comes to maintenance windows, verify that the cloud provider will deploy updates through rolling updates and not total system outages every week or two, as a legacy datacenter operation might have done.

Support limitations and exclusions

Consider what basic level of support is included with the cloud service and what support options are available at additional cost. For more advanced services such as Dev/Test, does the cloud provider offer support to developers and application development tools or is this entirely the responsibility of the end user and developers?

Cloud Security

Key topics in this chapter:

- Cloud security planning and design
- Governance and operations
- Multitenant security
- Security in an automation cloud environment
- Identity management and federation
- Data sovereignty and on-shore operations
- Cloud security standards and certifications
- Cloud security best practices

In this chapter, I will focus on cloud security planning, system design, governance, and operational considerations. Rather that cover IT security from a general perspective, we will concentrate on areas unique to cloud environments. Information technology security and cloud security are such sweeping and important topics that they could easily require multiple books to cover everything. It is important to understand that all general IT security best practices still apply but few books and industry standards organizations have provided real-world guidance and lessons learned on cloud-specific security. That being said, I recommend reading the National Institute for Standards and Technology (NIST) *Special Publication 500-299* as a good baseline cloud-security reference model and detailed specifications. In this chapter, I will focus more on real-world lessons learned and best practices rather than a government-style reference model (I will leave that to NIST and other government organizations).

This chapter is divided into several sections: we'll take a look at security planning and design, infrastructure security, security standards, and best practices. Let's dig in.

Cloud Security Planning and Design

As an organization begins to plan for a cloud transition or deployment, certain security-specific considerations should be discussed. These security considerations should be part of the overall cloud planning process and not just a security audit or an assessment after everything is deployed. You should include these topics that are covered in this chapter as part of the appropriate governance, policies, and systems design planning for your cloud.

PLANNING

The first step to consider is what IT systems, applications, and data should or must remain within a legacy enterprise datacenter. Not all workloads are ideal candidates for transition to the cloud due to data sensitivity concerns, mission criticality, or industry regulations on security and data controls. Security experts need to work with application and business owners to determine which applications and data you can easily move to a cloud and which you should evaluate further or even delay moving to a cloud. You need to repeat this assessment on all key applications and data repositories to develop a priority list with specific notations on the desired sensitivity, regulatory, or other security classifications (Chapter 4 presents a detailed application assessment process). Having this information is critical for the IT and financial business units of any organization to help determine the type of cloud to be used or deployed, calculate initial infrastructure capacity, financial and return-on-investment (ROI) models, and to establish overall operational governance decisions.

Key Take-Away

You should perform assessments of each application and data repository to determine the security posture, suitability, and priority for transition to the cloud. Match security profiles to the cloud architecture, controls, and targeted security compliance standard.

A logical next step in planning is to consider the cloud model(s) to be procured or deployed. Although public cloud services provide solid infrastructure security, they often do not have the level of security or customization your organization might need. A private cloud can be heavily customized to meet security or feature requirements, but you still need to control costs, scope creep, and over-building the initial cloud.

In a hybrid or multivendor cloud, security becomes even more complicated when evaluating, selecting, and using cloud services that are not all at the same level of security or accreditation. If you know from the beginning that your organization is likely to form a hybrid cloud with multiple cloud providers, consider establishing a minimum-acceptable security posture that all providers must meet. Then, evaluate and select certain cloud providers that offer stronger security compliance for mission-critical applications or workloads, allowing the hybrid cloud management system to provision services to the appropriate cloud provider(s). Note that the hybrid cloud management system or a cloud broker might have access to the data stored on each of the multiple cloud providers; thus, the cloud broker or hybrid provider needs to be accredited at a level equal to your highest provider security requirement. For more information on cloud management, hybrid cloud, and brokering, refer to Chapters 7 and 8.

GOVERNANCE

The first and most obvious consideration is to define who establishes the security posture, policies, and potential accreditation of the system. Based on the assessment of each application and data repository, determine the overall cloud security model including any industry standard you will follow. Remember that you can select a security model or standard with which to be compliant, but you do not necessarily need to go through the actual certification process unless you're required to by industry or government regulations. Table 6-1, later in this chapter, provides a listing of the most common security standards and organizations.

Organizations should determine who the consumers of the cloud services will be. If multiple departments or peer agencies will be using the cloud service, determine which security team or organization controls the standards for the overall cloud or each application. You might want to form a committee of security experts from each consuming agency, but ultimately some of the overall security strategy—and a tie-breaker for difficult decisions—will need to come from the organization that is leading or sponsoring the cloud effort. I recommend that a baseline security posture be adopted and that other agencies or departments be more involved in settings the security standards for their unique applications and mission-critical workloads.

You should also consider daily security operations, response to events, and ongoing security reviews. Regardless of where the cloud services are hosted (a provider or on-premises enterprise datacenter), you need to determine whether a third party or your internal staff will be responsible for continuous monitoring, incident response, and reporting. Often in a multitenant cloud environment, it is difficult to involve every consuming organization's security personnel in daily operational activities (described in more detail later), so publishing the security operations process, ownership, and visibility, or statistics, events, and reports should be documented and well understood to ensure acceptance of the cloud by consuming agencies and users.

MULTITENANT SECURITY

One of the fundamental benefits of a cloud is the ability to host multiple consuming organizations on a shared pool of network, servers, storage, and application resources. Even though public clouds heavily rely on multiple tenants to achieve a profitable scale of economy, a private cloud might or might not be deployed for use by multiple consumer organizations; however, there can still be multiple departments or project/application development teams that desire isolation of cloud services, data, network traffic, or billing and chargeback.

Key Take-Away

Multitenancy features apply to almost all cloud environments.

Public clouds heavily rely on a multiple tenant sales and data isolation model. Private clouds can be deployed for just one organization but there might be multiple departments, project, or application development teams that require isolation.

From a security standpoint, it is critical to understand how multitenancy is configured so that each consuming organization or department is isolated from all the others. The cloud management system, including customer-facing portal and backend automation systems, is the primary mechanism to manage multiple tenants. The cloud management system can integrate or synchronize with an identity-management system that is either hosted by the cloud provider or connected to an internal enterprise directory services such as Active Directory or a Lightweight Directory Access Protocol (LDAP) service (see "Identity Management and Federation" on page 242 later in this chapter). Using the authenticated user and group hierarchy, you can define multiple organization names in the cloud-management system and create access control list (ACL) groups. Users from the identity-management system fall within one or more of the organizations that are defined or synchronized to the cloud management portal. Each ACL group is then assigned cloud portal permissions for such activities as administration, finance and procurement, approvers, or auditors. When a user or administrator is authenticated into the customer-facing cloud management portal, he only has permissions and a view to cloud services that are assigned to his organization and within the ACL permissions. For detailed information on the cloud portal, ordering, approval, and automation systems, see Chapter 7.

The cloud management system and portal controls which users and ACL groups have access and permissions for ordering and managing services. You can define other unique ACL groups to control access to server remote logon, virtual machines (VMs), applications, and data.

The key aspect to remember here is that all of the aforementioned access controls are software based and do not provide any level of physical separation of servers, VMs, or data in the cloud. In a normal multitenant cloud, there are pools of physical servers and storage that are segregated up using software and permissions to isolate one customer from another. Technically, one physical server will host multiple VMs—each VM being owned by a different customer or department. This VM isolation is managed through ACLs in the cloud management system and the hypervisor platform.

Key Take-Away

Most clouds use software-based access controls and permissions to isolate customers from one another in a multitenant cloud environment. Hardware isolation is an option for some clouds but is also an additional cost.

In a public cloud, the use of software-based access controls, roles-based permissions, storage, and hypervisor separation is commonplace. If more levels of isolation or separation of workloads and data between customers is required, other options such as a virtual private cloud (VPC) or a private cloud are often more suitable. In a VPC, a cloud provider can still host the services, but you can configure your cloud with physically separate networks, physical servers, pools of VMs, and storage. This physical separation, often referred to as an *air gap*, will normally cost more than cloud services in a multitenant shared environment. For a private cloud, you have the most flexibility to customize how networks, servers, and storage are separated, and if or how multiple consuming organizations are isolated from one another. This is where security experts need to match the value of applications and data security against the cost of the cloud infrastructure to find the right match. One of the biggest steps in making these decisions is a thorough knowledge of multitenancy, identity and authentication systems, hypervisor, and storage security controls. With this knowledge, security personnel will begin to realize that clouds are not inherently less secure than legacy enterprise

IT; in fact, they are potentially more secure with more flexibility and more align-
ment of data protection needs to security policy. This leads us to the next topic.

IS YOUR DATA MORE OR LESS SECURE IN THE CLOUD?

The basic concept of cloud computing is the transformation and consolidation of
traditional compute services, data, and, applications to an on-demand, automated, elastic, often third-party hosted cloud. Customers and security industry
experts often ask if their cloud environment is more or less secure than a traditional behind-the-firewall enterprise network. Not surprisingly, there are two
polar-opposite opinions among industry experts on this:

Less secure

> Some industry experts claim that consolidating all customer data and
> servers into a cloud means that a successful hacker could have access to
> massive amounts of proprietary information. This would make the risk of
> data loss or tampering higher in cloud environments, compared to server
> farms and applications in traditional enterprise datacenters because the
> cloud is, in theory, a more attractive and lucrative target.

More secure

> The majority of security industry experts agree that the cloud can be more
> secure than traditional enterprise IT operations. The reason why is because
> a consolidated location for servers, applications, and data is easier to pro-
> tect and focus security resources on than traditional enterprise systems—if
> it is done properly. Public cloud providers and any private cloud owner can
> procure all of the very latest in security appliances and software, centralize
> a focused team of security personnel, and consolidate all systems events,
> logs, and response activities. The quality of security normally increases but
> at a high capital expense to initially procure the newer and better security
> systems and staff upgrades. Industry experts point to consolidated focus,
> and simpler correlation of logs and events as reasons for cloud environ-
> ments being more secure than most legacy server farms. Predictable and
> consistent automated service provisioning of VMs, storage, operating sys-
> tems (OSs), applications, and updates also improves configuration accu-
> racy, rapid updates, and immediate triggering of security monitoring and
> scanning.

Key Take-Away

Cloud automation brings consistency and real-time updating of security and operational systems, improving configuration control, monitoring, and overall security compared to legacy IT environments.

In a cloud environment, the security and mitigation systems are in place protecting the entire network. Cloud providers have sufficient capability and capacity to monitor and react to real or perceived security issues. However, because this is a multitenant environment, any individual customer with higher-than-normal security requirements might be more difficult and expensive to accommodate in a shared cloud model. This is probably the number one reason for private cloud deployments. A private cloud is dedicated to one customer (or group of departments) that have shared goals and, more important, a shared security posture.

Another concern with multitenant cloud security is transparency to the customer. The security and monitoring systems are designed to consolidate and correlate events across the entire environment with a skilled team of security operations personnel managing and responding. Presenting this event data to individual customers in a multitenant environment is difficult because the security software is often not designed to break out the consolidated and correlated data for each tenant.

Security in an Automated Cloud Environment

One of the major differentiators of a cloud environment versus a modern on-premises datacenter with virtualization is the automation of as many processes and service-provisioning tasks as possible. This automation extends into patching of software, distribution of software and OS updates, and creation of network zones. Each of these automated provisioning processes presents a challenge to traditional security monitoring because the software and hardware environment is constantly changing with new users, new customers, new VMs, and new software instances. A cloud requires equal attention to the automation of asset and operational management; as new systems are automatically provisioned, so to must the security and operational systems learn about the new items in a real-time fashion so that scanning and monitoring of these assets can be initiated immediately.

AUTOMATION

The first rule for any cloud is to automate "everything." You should plan and design a cloud system with as few manual processes as possible. Manual processes are inherently less consistent and inhibit the ability for rapid provisioning of new services or expanded capacity on demand, which is fundamental to a cloud. So, a core security concept—and this might be contrary to ingrained principles of the past—is to avoid any security processes or policies that delay or prevent automation.

As described in Chapter 2, the relentless pursuit of automation brings operational efficiency, consistent configurations, rapid provisioning on demand, elastic scale up and scale down, and support cost savings. This pursuit of all things automated also improves security. Lessons learned since 2010 illustrate that the traditional security processes have tended to be manual approvals, after-provisioning audits, and slow methodical labor-intensive assessments—tendencies that must change when building or operating a cloud. Just as we discussed the cloud as a new style of IT, the new style of cloud security is to assess and precertify all cloud services, applications, VM templates, operations system builds, and so on. I will discuss this in depth throughout the remainder of this chapter.

Key Take-Away

You should adopt the theme "relentless pursuit of automation." Eliminate any legacy security processes that inhibit rapid provisioning and automation.

As soon as new systems (VMs, applications, etc.) are brought online and added to the asset and configuration management databases, the security management systems should immediately be triggered to launch any system scans and start routine monitoring.

Key Take-Away

There should be little or no delay between provisioning a new system or application in the cloud and beginning security scans and continuous monitoring.

I'm not going to try and sell you on the merits and necessity of continuous security monitoring other than to say you should not manage a cloud without it. In a dynamically changing and automated cloud, continuous monitoring should be combined with continuous updating of asset and configuration databases. This real-time updating of assets and configuration changes will be fed into the security systems whenever new servers, VMs, and applications are launched and need to be scanned and monitored. Without automated updating of asset, configuration, and monitoring systems in real time as cloud services are being provisioned and de-provisioned, it would be almost impossible to keep up (manually or otherwise) with all of the changes to VMs, virtual LANs (VLANs), IP addresses, applications, and so on.

PRECERTIFICATION OF VM TEMPLATES

Organizations with strict security accreditation processes often struggle with the idea that cloud services should immediately provision new VMs when ordered. I recommend changes in the legacy security process to have the IT security teams precertify all "gold images" or templates that can be launched within new physical devices or VMs. These templates might include a combination of an OS, applications, patches, and agents for network or security monitoring. As soon as the VM is ordered and provisioned by the cloud automation system, the VM or gold image template is copied to a new VM and then booted. Because the security teams have already approved the templates, each new VM that is based on the precertified template should also be considered approved and in compliance. Of course, any future changes to the applications or VM might need to go through additional change control and security scrutiny. One of the best ways to control software application deployment and security management is to create and certify automated application installation packages that can be deployed in combination with VM templates

Certification of gold images is not just an initial step when using or deploying a new cloud. Many organizations and customers will request that existing or future gold images—homegrown or commercial off-the-shelf (COTS) applications and configurations—be loaded and added to the cloud service catalog. I highly recommend that security experts perform scanning and assessments of every new or modified gold image before loading it into the cloud management platform and giving customers the ability to order it. Again, using a combination of VM templates and smaller application installation packages—all precertified by security—will reduce the frequency of having to update the master VM gold image. Also realize that when a new gold image is accepted and added to the cloud, the cloud operational personnel (depending on contract scope) might now be responsible for all future patches, upgrades, and support of the template. Many cloud providers charge a fee to assess and import customer VMs or gold images. Customers might push back on this extra cost, so you should take the time to explain the need for these manually intensive assessments and the ongoing upgrades and support required.

PRECERTIFICATION OF NETWORK ZONES AND SEGMENTATION

Most cloud services, such as a VM or applications running on a VM require, require a default network or virtual network connection as part of the automated configuration. You can configure VMs with multiple virtual network interfaces and connect to one or more production or nonproduction network segments with your datacenter. These network configurations include the VM configuration when your security team performs its precertification.

You might want to offer additional network segmentation as an option through the use of virtual firewalls and VLANs to secure or isolate networks. Applications that need to be Internet-facing should be further segmented and firewalled from the rest of the production cloud VMs and applications. Platform as a Service (PaaS) offerings are very often configured with multiple tiers of VMs and applications that interact and can have several network zones to protect web-facing frontend servers from middleware and backend databases that all form the enterprise application.

Key Take-Away

Pre certify all production and nonproduction network segments so that VMs can be provisioned automatically without manual security approval processes. Also consider preapproving a pool of optional virtual networks that can also be provisioned automatically upon a customer order.

One specific caution here is to not overdo the default segmentation of networks, because this only complicates the offerings and usefulness of the cloud environment, and increases operational management. Stick with some basic level of network segmentation such as a default single network per customer, and then allow customers to request additional network segments. I recommend pre-certifying several network VLANs, firewall port rules, load balancers, and storage options and make these available to cloud consumers via the self-service control panel. By precertifying several options, possibly charging customers extra for these, you can still offer your customers flexibility and rapid provisioning by having all these options already vetted and certified by security personnel. Remember, customers will often seek a future VLAN or opening of firewall ports that go behind the precertified configuration, meaning that these can still be handled by a less-than-automated approval or vetting process.

PRECERTIFICATION APPLICATIONS

As just mentioned, security precertification also extends to all applications and future updates that will be available on the cloud. You should configure applications as automated installation packages where any combination of application packages can be ordered and provisioned and then installed on top of a VM gold image. By separating the VM gold image from application installation packages, you can reduce the number of VM image variations and frequency in updating VM images (compared to fully configured VM images that include applications). Additional packages for upgrades and patching of the OS and apps will also be deployed in an automated fashion to ensure efficiency, consistency, and configuration management. Remember that customers and cloud administrators can also uninstall application packages on demand using the cloud management system orchestration tools.

Key Take-Away

Use a combination of security-approved VM templates and application installation packages. Reduce the quantity of VM image variations and frequency of updates by separating the OS image from the applications.

The point here, just as with VM gold images and network zones, is to precertify everything to facilitate automated deployment—avoid forcing any manual security assessments in the provisioning process. You need to realize that this precertification is not necessarily difficult, but it will be an ongoing effort because new applications and update packages are continuously introduced. Finally, you should understand that more complex multitiered applications (e.g., multitiered PaaS applications) will require significantly more security assessment and also involvement in the initial application design process. If security experts are not involved with the initial multitiered application design, trying to map multiple production-ready application tiers to the automated and precertified network segments or VLANs can be a nightmare.

ASSET AND CONFIGURATION MANAGEMENT

Although I covered asset and configuration management in Chapter 2, from a security standpoint, there are specific processes that should be put into place to support an automated cloud environment.

Many organizations have a mature asset and configuration-management system in place. In a private cloud environment that uses automated provisioning, the key to success is to also automate the updating of asset and configuration databases. This means that you configure the cloud management platform, which controls and initiates automation, to immediately log the new VM, application, or software upgrades into the asset/configuration database(s). Because this is done through automation, there is little chance that updating the asset or configuration databases is skipped and the accuracy of the data will be improved when compared to legacy manual update procedures.

Key Take-Away

The overall goal is to have all inventory, monitoring, and security systems updated in real time so that network, security, and operations teams are continuously monitoring the current state of the environment and all its assets and continuously changing configurations.

Some organizations have very formal configuration control approval procedures and committees in place. Although the need for these is understood, the concept of a manual approval process and committee are contrary to the tenets of cloud automation and rapid provisioning (which includes routine software updates). I recommend that the change control, just as with security, be changed to include preapproving new application patches, upgrades, gold images, and so on to allow the cloud automation system to perform its rapid provisioning responsibilities. As new systems are deployed in an automated manner, so to will the configuration log and database be updated in real time. These automated configuration changes, which are based on preapproved packages or configurations, should be marked as "automatically approved" in the change control log, fulfilling the purpose of a change control log as an auditing tool. In this case, the change log entries are automatically entered, but there will likely be other more significant infrastructure configuration changes throughout the cloud that can and should still follow the manual change control board process.

CUSTOMER VISIBILITY INTO SECURITY AND OPERATIONS

In a public cloud, customers no longer need to allocate precious staff, funds, or time to work on routine systems administration and upkeep of the network. This includes security operations, continuous monitoring, and responding to security events and threats; however, some public cloud customers still want visibility into their hosted cloud.

Public cloud providers were initially reluctant to provide much visibility into what was considered internal operations. As customers have adopted public cloud and managed private cloud services, customers quickly realized that they were effectively blind to the operations that could affect their data and cloud-based systems. Providers periodically provided customers with a summary report, but they almost never provided real-time security event and mitigation information. Customers of any cloud want more visibility into events, alerts, threats, and remediation activities relating to their data and their cloud services.

A private cloud model and management system is far more customizable and therefore capable or integrating with existing or new security software to provide real-time dashboard, statistics, and event alerts and mitigation data.

Key Take-Away

One of the major reasons enterprise customers deploy a private cloud is to have in-depth visibility and engagement with cloud security monitoring, events, and mitigation.

Enterprise customers often want to be aware of security events and remediation, whereas others just want visibility but still remain hands off to the hosted cloud-based activities. The challenge is that most network monitoring and security systems are focused on consolidating triggers, alerts, and critical system events. The data is aggregated and then correlations of multiple related events found, which leads to earlier and more complete detection of the overall event or threat. In a multitenant cloud environment, these same advanced aggregation, analytics, and correlation tools are not perfectly suited to then separate the data for distribution to individual tenants or consuming organizations. This is a primary reason why visibility and real-time access to security monitoring and events is a challenge for many cloud providers and cloud management systems. In a private cloud deployment, multitenancy is not as much of an issue, so there are more tools and options for presenting security monitoring to appropriate personnel within the consuming organization.

Experience has shown that customers do not trust that everything is OK. They don't want to depend solely on a monthly report that shows past events, threats, or vulnerabilities. Real-time monitoring and visibility into systems and security operations is clearly desired by cloud consumers. In the future, I expect to see better tools and improved customer-facing dashboards that provide roles-based configurable levels of continuous monitoring information—we'll even see these with some public cloud providers in the near future.

Identity Management and Federation

User identity management, synchronization of directory services, and federation across multiple networks is very unique in a cloud environment compared to traditional enterprise IT. Chapter 4 covers identity management and authentication for application migrations. Here, I discuss single sign-on and federation, which are unique security considerations in a cloud environment.

SINGLE SIGN-ON

With the single sign-on (SSO) model, applications or other resources in the cloud use the same logon information that an end user provides when she logs on to her computer, precluding the need to prompt the user for any additional logon information. This is done through a variety of techniques depending on the desktop OS, the applications, the network infrastructure, and possibly third-party software that specifically enables this functionality.

Within a traditional local area network (LAN) hosted by an enterprise organization in its own facility, having a single network authentication system, such as Microsoft Active Directory, is not very difficult; in fact, it is a built-in feature of the Microsoft Windows Server OS. LDAP is a more universal industry standard for user directory services and authentication that is not specific to any software manufacturer. Security Assertion Markup Language (SAML) is an even better solution for cloud environments when SSO and federation are used. The challenge is when users access data on multiple server farms, across wide area networks (WANs), and on multiple applications created by different software manufacturers. As you implement cloud services, this becomes even more complex.

A cloud service provider can only do so much to enable SSO from their facilities. There are cloud providers that implement third-party software solutions that broker authentication to downstream applications and networks. This requires each cloud customer and application to integrate with the centralized authentication system that the cloud provider has chosen. There are numerous identity and authentication systems available in the industry that either the cloud provider might have available for customer use, or a customer can deploy its own within its VM. So, there is no one answer to implementing SSO; however, LDAP and SAML are the primary industry standards. All applications and OSs that you want to integrate with the cloud or migrate to the cloud should support one or both of these protocols.

FEDERATION

One area related to SSO and identity management is *federation*, also called *Federated Identity Management* (FIM). Federation is when you connect multiple clouds, applications, or organizations to one or more other parties (see Figure 6-1). The list of users and authentication details are shared securely across all parties of the federation. This makes possible features such as allowing one organization to see another organization in a Global Address List (GAL), or sending an instant message to another person across organizations. The federation software creates and maintains a bridge between the disparate networks and applications, effectively synchronizing and/or sharing user lists between one or more organizations. In a cloud environment with distributed applications, data, and users located potentially all over the world, federation and SSO is what makes this seamless experience possible. Your average daily tasks performed in the cloud might actually involve logging on to a dozen applications, databases, networks, and cloud providers, but all of this is transparent to you due to federation and SSO.

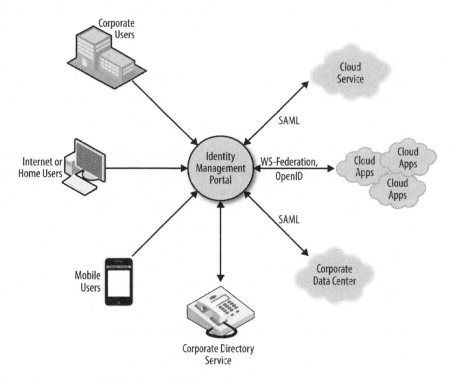

Figure 6-1. An overview of Federated Identity Management

Customer Accreditation of Cloud Services

It is difficult—if not impossible—to get a public cloud provider to give an individual customer access to the provider's network and allow customer IT security staff to perform an accreditation. In fact, to show customers what was happening inside the networks can be considered paramount to showing customers—and potentially competitors—your intellectual property, with too much visibility into the internal security systems and procedures. Although most public cloud providers rarely allow individual customer inspection and accreditation, providers have in some cases allowed a third-party assessment so that the public cloud provider can sell its services to government and other large customers with requirements for an official security accreditation. The U.S. government's FedRAMP accreditation process, which uses third-party assessment vendors, is an excellent example of this approach. For more details on FedRAMP and other international security entities, see "Cloud Security Certifications" on page 246 later in this chapter.

A private cloud deployment is much more accommodating and suitable for customer accessibility and a security accreditation process. The security standards and accreditation process are the same or very similar for a public cloud, with any multitenant cloud getting the highest level of scrutiny for security controls and customer data isolation.

As part of planning your organization's transition to cloud, you need a complete understanding of the cloud models, the security standards that you need to follow, and the personnel who will perform the security accreditation. When procuring a public cloud service, your evaluation criteria should include the designed security accreditation. For a private cloud deployment, ensure that your organization or the systems integrators that does the deployment is capable and experienced in highly secure cloud computing and already has security accreditation experience. Finally, remember that security accreditations normally require annual reassessments and certification renewals (or perhaps on some other time interval). As most public and private clouds mature and add new capabilities over time, these periodic accreditations are not just a quick "rubber stamp" process but involve assessing the entire system again with particular attention to the new services or configuration changes.

Data Sovereignty and On-Shore Support Operations

Data sovereignty refers to where your data is actually stored geographically in the cloud—whether it is stored in one or more datacenters hosted by your own organization or by a public cloud provider. Due to differing laws in each country, sometimes the data held by the cloud provider can be obtained by the government in whose jurisdiction the data is stored, or perhaps by the government of the country where the data provider is based, or even by foreign governments through international cooperation laws. Further government monitoring or snooping (some governments tend to change laws or push the bounds of legality to serve their own purposes) on behalf of crime prevention agencies has also become a concern.

Not everything here is doom and gloom. There are "safe harbor" agreements between key governments such as the United States and the European Union to better enforce data privacy and clarify specific scenarios and data types that can legally be turned over by a cloud provider upon official requests. Organizations using public cloud services should examine the policies and practices of a prospective cloud provider to answer the following questions:

- Where will data, metadata, transaction history, personally identifiable data, and billing data be stored?

- Where will backups or replicated data for disaster recovery be located? What is the retention policy for legacy data and backups? How is retired data media securely disposed?

- Who and where support personnel are located and to what do they have access? How are their personal background checks performed?

- Where is the provider's primary headquarters, location of incorporation, and under which laws and jurisdictions do they fall? How does the provider respond to in-country or foreign government requests for data discovery?

- Is the government authority or third party obligated to notify you that it has taken possession of your data.

Data sovereignty and data residency has become a more significant challenge and decision point than most organizations and cloud service providers originally anticipated. Initially, one of the selling points of the cloud that a cloud service provider would point out was that you, as the customer, didn't need to be concerned with where and how it stored your information—there was an SLA to protect you. Lessons learned are to now ask or contractually force your cloud provider to store your data in the countries or datacenter locations that fit your data sovereignty requirements. Also consider if you require that all operational support personnel at the cloud provider be located within your desired country and be local citizens (preferably with background checks performed regularly)—this in combination with data sovereignty will help to ensure that your data remains private and is not unnecessarily exposed to foreign governments or other parties with whom you did not intend to share it.

Key Take-Away

You should request that data be stored in the country of your choosing to maintain your data privacy rights. Many public cloud providers now offer these options and this is definitely a consideration for building your own private or hybrid cloud environment.

If you are a private cloud operator, you should not only have published policies to address these concerns, but also consider formal written internal policies, such as the following:

- All staff must know the policies with regard to when and if to respond to government and other requests for data release.

- Staff must be fully versed in all data retention policies and procedures for data retirement.

- There must be a clearly articulated policy for cloud data locations, replications, and even temporary data restorations or replications in order to maintain data sovereignty for customers with such requirements and contracts.

- An internal policy review committee must be established as well as a channel into corporate legal department for handling each official data request and overall policy governance.

- A documented plan should be in place for how to handle document requests and other legal events that might occur—be specific with respect to law and government identities and how each will be handled.

Cloud Security Certifications

There are dozens of government institutions in the U.S. and worldwide that have published computer security guidance. U.S. government customers often mandate these security specifications, but these are also excellent guidelines for non government clouds, as well.

There are also a significant number of security policies that come from U.S. government organizations, and certain industries such as healthcare and finance are required to follow them. Commercial and government agencies are required to implement these security standards and often go through a formal security accreditation process before their computer systems can go online.

Table 6-1 lists many of the organizations that have created security standards or accreditation criteria. This is not an exhaustive list, and new security policies are introduced frequently. Use this as a starting point to identify which cloud and security standards your organization wants—or is required—to follow when procuring or building a cloud service.

Table 6-1. Security standards and organizations

STANDARD OR ORGANIZATION	DESCRIPTION
Cloud Security Alliance (CSA)	The CSA Security, Trust & Assurance Registry (STAR) initiative was launched in 2011 to improve transparency and assurance in the cloud. STAR is a publicly accessible registry that documents the security controls provided by various cloud computing offerings, thereby helping companies to assess the security of cloud providers they currently use or with which they are considering contracting. STAR consists of three certification levels that are based on ISO 2001 and CSA's Cloud Controls Matrix (CCM) standards: • Level 1 CSA STAR Self Assessment • Level 2 CSA STAR Certification/Level 2 CSA STAR Attestation • Level 3 CSA STAR Continuous
EuroCloud Star Audit (ECSA)	EuroCloud is an independent nonprofit organization focused on cloud security standards with voluntary participation by most European countries. The EuroCloud Star Audit is a 1-to-5 star-graded certification suitable for any company operating an Infrastructure as a Service (IaaS), Platform as a Service (PaaS), or Software as a Service (SaaS).
E-Government Act	The United States E-Government Act (Public Law 107-347) (*http:// 1.usa.gov/1cCKtkc*) was passed by the 107th Congress in 2002. It is focused on the importance and impact of information security

STANDARD OR ORGANIZATION	DESCRIPTION
	on the economic and national security interests of the United States.
FISMA	Title III of the E-Government Act, titled the Federal Information Security Management Act (FISMA) (*http://1.usa.gov/1ONHcf*), requires each United States federal agency to develop, document, and implement an agency-wide program to provide information security for the systems that support the operations and assets of the agency, including those provided or managed by another agency, contractor, or other source. There are three levels of FISMA controls and compliance: Low, Moderate, and High.
FIPS	The U.S. Federal Information Processing Standards (FIPS) provide guidance and minimum characteristics for areas such as data encryption and IT security (many U.S. federal agencies are required to adhere to these policies): • FIPS 199 Standards for Security Categorization of Federal Information and Information Systems • FIPS 200 Minimum Security Requirements for Federal Information and Information Systems • FIPS 140-2 Security Requirements for Cryptographic Modules
FedRAMP	The U.S. Federal Risk and Authorization Management Program (FedRAMP) is a U.S. government-wide program, created by the General Services Administration (GSA) that provides a standardized approach to security assessment, authorization, and continuous monitoring of cloud products and services. Note that many U.S. government agencies still use FISMA as a standard for their computer security accreditation, but FISMA is an older, more generic law and not as specific to the cloud as FedRAMP. FedRAMP was originally intended to apply to U.S. federal government agencies and public cloud providers offering services to these agencies. Although the basic principles and guidance within FedRAMP is valuable to all cloud environments, it is

STANDARD OR ORGANIZATION	DESCRIPTION
	unclear if or when FedRAMP will be extended to cover other forms of cloud including private clouds.
	The U.S. Department of Defense (DoD) organizations usually follow more robust cloud security guidelines published by the U.S. Defense Information Systems Agency (DISA). DISA has recently added the concept (not an actual standard yet) called FedRAMP+, which calls for additional security controls and requirements—on top of the basic FedRAMP—to meeting DoD cloud security requirements.
National Institute of Standards and Technology (NIST)	NIST is responsibilities for publishing computer standards and guidance under FISMA. There are numerous general information technology and cloud-specific "special publications" published by NIST. Some of the more relevant documents are the following: • Special Publication 500-291 v2. Defines Cloud Computing Standards Roadmap. This updated publication was released in July 2013, and provides a significant number of updated cloud brokering, hybrid cloud, portability, and security standards. • Special Publication 500-292. Defines the Cloud Computing Reference Architecture. • Special Publication 800-146. NIST, which is a part of the U.S. Department of Commerce, has issued a document, titled *Cloud Computing Synopsis and Recommendations*. This document provides definitions of cloud deployment models, cloud characteristics, and recommendations. Although NIST is a government organization, these standard definitions are often utilized throughout the world. • Special Publication 800-12. This document provides a broad overview of computer security and control areas. It also emphasizes the importance of security controls and ways to implement them. Initially this document was aimed at the federal government, although you can apply most practices outlined in it to the private sector as well. Specifically, it was written for those people in the federal government responsible for handling sensitive systems.

STANDARD OR ORGANIZATION	DESCRIPTION
	• Special Publication 800-14. This document describes common security principles, providing a high-level description of what should be incorporated within a computer security policy. It describes what can be done to improve existing security as well as how to develop a new security practice. • Special Publication 800-26. This document provides advice on how to manage IT security, emphasizing the importance of self-analysis and risk assessments. • Special Publication 800-37. This document, titled *Guide for Applying the Risk Management Framework to Federal Information Systems* and updated in 2010, provides a new risk approach. • Special Publication 800-53. This document is titled *Guide for Assessing the Security Controls in Federal Information Systems*. It was updated in August 2009, and it specifically addresses the 194 security controls that are applied to a system to make it "more secure."
STIG	A Security Technical Implementation Guide (STIG) is a methodology for standardized secure installation and maintenance of computer software (*http://bit.ly/1cCLtF0*) and hardware (*http://bit.ly/1PXVxYA*). The term was coined by DISA (*http://bit.ly/1PXVAUa*), which creates configuration documents in support of the U.S. Department of Defense (*http://bit.ly/1ERgkZw*) (DoD). The implementation guidelines include recommended administrative processes and span the device's lifecycle.
ISO	The International Organization for Standardization (ISO) is similar to NIST, but it is a widely accepted international, non government entity, whereas NIST is primarily used by U.S. government organizations.
ISO 27002/ISO 27K1	The ISO 27001 document provides underlying information security management system standards and taxonomy, with ISO 27002 providing best-practice recommendations on information

STANDARD OR ORGANIZATION	DESCRIPTION
	security management for use by those responsible for initiating, implementing, or maintaining Information Security Management Systems (*http://bit.ly/1ERh1Sx*) (ISMS). Information security is defined within the standard in the context of the C-I-A triad (*http://bit.ly/1E9EPSZ*), a preservation of confidentiality (*http://bit.ly/1G3YHaA*) (ensuring that information is accessible only to those authorized to have access), integrity (*http://bit.ly/1IS3mgA*) (safeguarding the accuracy and completeness of information and processing methods), and availability (*http://bit.ly/1HftBeE*) (ensuring that authorized users have access to information and associated assets when required).
IT Grundschutz	A security certification scheme created by the German government's Federal Office for Information Security (BSI), which provides baseline framework and a basic list of security requirements although not specific to cloud.
OBM A-130	The Office of Management and Budget (OMB) through Circular A-130, Appendix III, *Security of Federal Automated Information Resources*, requires executive agencies within the federal government to (a) plan for security; (b) ensure that appropriate officials are assigned security responsibility; (c) periodically review the security controls in their information systems; and (d) authorize system processing prior to operations and, periodically, thereafter.
OMB M-07-16	Defines the "Safeguarding Against and Responding to the Breach of Personally Identifiable Information."
HIPAA	The Health Insurance Portability and Accountability Act of 1996 (HIPAA) defines privacy and security rules protecting individually identifiable health information. Any system that processes or stores personally identifiable health information must adhere to these security regulations.
HSPD-7	Homeland Security Presidential Directive (HSPD-7) defines Critical Infrastructure Identification, Prioritization, and Protection standards.

STANDARD OR ORGANIZATION	DESCRIPTION
PCI DSS	The PCI DSS is a multifaceted security standard that includes requirements for security management, policies, procedures, network architecture, software design and other critical protective measures. This comprehensive standard is intended to help organizations proactively protect customer account data.
FERPA	The U.S. Education Department is releasing a Notice of Proposed Rule Making (NPRM) under the Family Educational Rights and Privacy Act (FERPA). The proposed regulations would give states the flexibility to share data to ensure that taxpayer funds are invested wisely in effective programs.
COPPA	Children's Online Privacy Protection Act of 2000 applies to the online collection of personal information from children under 13. The new rules define what a website operator must include in a privacy policy, when and how to seek verifiable consent from a parent, and what responsibilities an operator has to protect children's privacy and safety online.
CIPA	The Children's Internet Protection Act (CIPA) is a federal law enacted by congress to address concerns about access to offensive content over the Internet on school and library computers. CIPA imposes certain types of requirements on any school or library that receives funding for Internet access or internal connections from the E-rate program—a program that makes certain communications technologies more affordable for eligible schools and libraries.
DIACAP	The U.S. Department of Defense (DoD) Information Assurance Certification and Accreditation Process (DIACAP) is the DoD process to ensure that risk management is applied on information systems. DIACAP defines a DoD-wide formal and standard set of activities, general tasks and a management structure process for the certification and accreditation (C&A) of a DoD IS that will maintain the information assurance (IA) posture throughout the system's life cycle. Note that the directive to DoD agencies is to begin using the newer DoD Cloud Computing Security Requirements Guide

STANDARD OR ORGANIZATION	DESCRIPTION
	(SRG) defined by DISA. This SRG details the latest cloud security standards along with correlation back to the DIACAP, FedRAMP, and other DoD IT and cloud security and risk frameworks.
Defense Information Systems Agency (DISA) SRG	The Defense Information Systems Agency (DISA) is the U.S. Department of Defense (DoD) organization that governs IT standards, guidance, and provides some centralized IT services to DoD organizations. DISA has produced several cloud security guidelines with the latest called DoD Cloud Computing Security Requirements Guide (SRG), initially published in January 2015, which replaces the previous Cloud Security Model (CSM). The SRG defines roles and standards for private cloud and external cloud service providers based on four Impact Levels. This is a relatively new standard and likely to mature over time, this DISA SRG is more specific to the cloud than the DIACAP standard for overall DoD IT. Refer to DoD Cloud Computing SRG at www.disa.gov. This DISA standard is intended for DoD organizations and it contains more security controls and requirements than FedRAMP or FISMA. The four SRG levels are as follows (paraphrased and translated to remove DoD terms and extraneous jargon for this book): • Level 2: All data cleared for public release; includes some private unclassified information not considered controlled or mission critical; some level of minimal access control required. • Level 4: Data that must be controlled or is mission critical; data that is protected under law or policy and requires protection for unauthorized disclosure. Controlled data includes export controlled, personally identifiable information, protected health information, law enforcement, and for official use classifications. • Level 5: Controlled and mission critical data that requires a higher level of protection as determined by the information owner, public law, or other government regulations.

STANDARD OR ORGANIZATION	DESCRIPTION
	• Level 6: Classified data to include compartmented information; data classified due to Executive Orders, or other policies. This impact level might be suitable for the highest-level intellectual property, trade secrets, and similar data that would result in grave harm to an organization if data is lost or compromised.
Common Criteria/ISO 15408	A framework that provides assurance that the process of specification, implementation, and evaluation of a computer security product has been conducted in a rigorous and standard manner. The Common Criteria for Information Technology Security Evaluation (*http://bit.ly/1b4si6b*) (CC), and the companion Common Methodology for Information Technology Security Evaluation (*http://bit.ly/1b4si6b*) (CEM) are the technical basis for an international agreement, the Common Criteria Recognition Arrangement (*http://bit.ly/1aDtIno*) (CCRA), which ensures the following: • Products (*http://bit.ly/1DPYDJd*) can be evaluated by competent and independent licensed laboratories (*http://bit.ly/1NXD3sJ*) so as to determine the fulfillment of particular security properties, to a certain extent or assurance. • Supporting documents (*http://bit.ly/1FS81Zv*) are used within the Common Criteria certification process to define how the criteria and evaluation methods are applied when certifying specific technologies. • The certification of the security properties of an evaluated product can be issued by a number of Certificate Authorizing Schemes (*http://bit.ly/1CWjBkq*), with this certification being based on the result of their evaluation. • These certificates (*http://bit.ly/1DPYDJd*) are recognized by all the signatories of the CCRA (*http://bit.ly/1aDtIno*).
ETSI CSC	The European Telecommunications Standards Institute (ETSI) is an independent, nonprofit standards (*http://bit.ly/1E9HfAY*) organization for the telecommunications (*http://bit.ly/1aDu79E*) industry in Europe. ETSI produces globally applicable standards

STANDARD OR ORGANIZATION	DESCRIPTION
	for Information and Communications Technologies (ICT), including fixed, mobile, radio, converged, broadcast, and Internet technologies. ETSI has commissioned the Cloud Standard Coordination initiative to define and develop cloud standards including nomenclature, terms, operational roles, and use cases for cloud computing.

Cloud Security Best Practices

Based on lessons learned and experience from across the cloud industry, you should consider the following best practices for your organization's planning.

PLANNING

As an organization plans for transitioning to a cloud service or deploying a private or hybrid cloud, the first step from a security standpoint is to consider what IT systems, applications, and data should or must remain within a legacy enterprise datacenter. Here are some considerations:

- Perform assessments of each application and data repository to determine the security posture, suitability, and priority to transition to the cloud. Match security postures to the cloud architecture, controls, and target security compliance standard.

- Work with application and business owners to determine which applications and data you can move easily to a cloud and which you should evaluate further or delay moving to a cloud. Repeat this assessment on all key applications and data repositories to develop and priority list with specific notations on the desired sensitivity, regulatory, or other security classifications.

- Consider the cloud model(s) to be procured or deployed internally:

  — Although public cloud services provide solid infrastructure security, they often do not have the level of security or customization you may need.

  — A private cloud can be heavily customized to meet security or feature requirements, but you need to control costs, scope creep, and over-building your initial cloud.

- Determine who the consumers of the cloud services will be. If multiple departments or peer agencies will be using the cloud service, determine which security team or organization controls the standards for the overall cloud or each application workload:

— Adopt a baseline security posture so that individual consumers or peer agencies will be more involved in settings the security standards for their unique applications and mission critical workloads.

— Publish the security operational processes, ownership, and visibility or statistics, events, and reports to ensure acceptance of the cloud by consuming agencies and users.

MULTITENANCY

Most clouds use software-based access controls and permissions to isolate customers from one another in a multitenant cloud environment. Hardware isolation is an option for private clouds and some virtual private clouds, but at additional cost.

- Understand how multitenancy is configured so that each consuming organization is isolated from all the others. In a public cloud, the use of software-based access controls, roles-based permissions, storage, and hypervisor separation is commonplace. If more levels of isolation or separation of workloads and data between customers is required, other options such as a virtual private cloud or a private cloud are often more suitable.

- Implement or connect an enterprise identity management system such as Active Directory, LDAP, or SAML service. Some cloud providers and management platforms can optionally connect to multiple directory or LDAP services —one for each consuming organization.

AUTOMATION IN A CLOUD

The first rule in an automated cloud is to plan and design a cloud system with as few manual processes as possible. This might be contrary to ingrained principles of the past, but you must avoid any security processes or policies that delay or prevent automation. Here are some considerations:

- Adopt the theme "relentless pursuit of automation."

- Eliminate any legacy security processes that inhibit rapid provisioning and automation.

Experience has shown that traditional security processes have tended to be manual approvals, after-provisioning audits, and slow methodical assessments—tendencies that must change when building or operating a cloud. Precertify everything to allow automated deployment—avoid forcing any manual security assessments in the provisioning process.

- Have IT security teams precertify all "gold images" or templates that can be launched within new VMs. Certification of gold images is not just an initial step when using or deploying a new cloud.

- Have security experts perform scans and assessments of every new or modified gold image before loading it into the cloud management platform and presenting it for customers to order.

- Understand that when a new gold image is accepted and added to the cloud, the cloud operational personnel (provider or support contractor, depending on contractual terms) might now be responsible for all future patches, upgrades, and support of the template.

- Have security precertify all applications and future updates that will be available on the cloud. You should configure applications automated installation packages whereby any combination of application packages can be ordered and provisioned on top of a VM gold image. Additional packages for upgrades and patching of the OS and apps will also be deployed in an automated fashion to ensure efficiency, consistency, and configuration management.

- Realize that this precertification is not so difficult of a task but will be an ongoing effort as new applications and update packages are introduced to the cloud often and continuously. Finally, understand that more complex multitiered applications (e.g., multitiered PaaS applications) will require significantly more security assessment and involvement during the initial application design.

It is common for customers to request additional network configurations or opening of firewall ports. These can be handled through a manual vetting, approval, and configuration process, but you might want to charge extra for this service. Here are some things to keep in mind:

- Segment the network so that each customer (not VM, which is often overkill), at a minimum, has its own virtual network. This is better than physical networks for each customer which is difficult to automate and more expensive.

- You can offer additional network segmentation as an option for each tenant or customer organization by using virtual firewalls to isolate networks. Applications that need to be Internet-facing should be further segmented and firewalled from the rest of the production cloud VMs and applications.

- Avoid overdoing the default segmentation of networks, because this only complicates the offerings and usefulness of the cloud environment, and increases operational management. Stick with some basic level of network segmentation such as the one virtual network per customer by default and then offer upgrades only when necessary to create additional virtual networks.

- Consider precertifying a pool of additional VLANs, firewall port rules, load balancers, and storage options and make these available to cloud consumers via the self-service control panel.

ASSET AND CONFIGURATION MANAGEMENT

The key to success is to also automate the updating of asset and configuration databases. This means that you configure the cloud management platform, which controls and initiates automation, to immediately log the new VM, application, or software upgrade into the asset and configuration databases. Here are some considerations:

- Reconsider all manual approval processes and committees that are contrary to cloud automation and rapid provisioning (which includes routine software updates).

- Update the legacy change control process by preapproving new application patches, upgrades, gold images, and so on so that the cloud automation system can perform rapid provisioning.

- Integrate the cloud management system to automatically update the configuration log/database in real-time as any new systems are provisioned and launched. These automated configuration changes, which are based on pre-approved packages or configurations, should be marked as "automatically approved" in the change control log.

MONITORING AND DETECTION OUTSIDE YOUR NETWORK PERIMETER

Traditional datacenter and IT security had a focus on monitoring for threats and attacks of the private network, datacenter, and everything inside your perimeter. Cloud providers should increase the radius of monitoring and detection to find threats before they even find or hit your network. Here are some things to keep in mind:

- Traditional web hosting services and content delivery networks (CDNs) are a good fit to host, protect, and cache static web content, but many of these providers do not protect dynamic web content (logons, database queries, searches) so all inbound attackers need to do is perform a repetitive search every millisecond and your CDN network can do little about it because it must forward all requests to your backend application or database.

- Consider a third-party network hosting service in which all data traffic to your cloud infrastructure first goes through the provider's network and filters. This provider will first take the attacks from the Internet and forward only legitimate traffic to your network. There is a significant number of configurable filtering and monitoring options available from these providers. In addition, consider using these providers for all outbound traffic from your cloud —thus, truly hiding all of your network addresses and services from the public Internet.

- Consider a third-party provider of secure DNS services that has the necessary security and denial-of-service protections in place. As this provider hosts your DNS services, your internal DNS servers are not the attack vector by having this third-party DNS provider take the brunt of an attack and forward only legitimate traffic.

CONSOLIDATED DATA IN THE CLOUD

As discussed in this chapter, many customers are concerned that data consolidated and hosted in the cloud might be less secure. The truth is that having centralized cloud services hosted by a cloud provider or your own IT organization enables a consolidation of all the top-level security personnel and security tools. Most organizations would rather have this concentration of expertise and security tools than a widely distributed group of legacy or mediocre tools and skillsets. Here are some considerations:

- Technically, a cloud service has no extra vulnerabilities compared to a traditional datacenter, given the same applications and use cases. The cloud might represent a bigger target because data is more consolidated, but you can offset this by deploying the newest security technologies and skilled security personnel.

- Continuous monitoring is the key to good security. Continuous monitoring in the cloud might mean protecting and monitoring multiple cloud service providers, network zones and segments, and applications.

- Focus monitoring and protections not only at your network or cloud perimeter, but begin protections before your perimeter (see "Monitoring and Detection Outside Your Network Perimeter" on page 260). Don't forget monitoring your internal network, because a significant number of vulnerabilities still come from internal sources.

- Focus on zero-day attacks and potential threats rather than relying solely on pattern or signature-based security that only contains past threats. Sophisticated attackers know that the best chance of success is to find a new vector into your network, not an older vulnerability that you've probably already remedied.

CONTINUOUS MONITORING

As soon as new systems are brought online and added to the asset and configuration management databases (as described earlier), the security management systems should immediately be triggered to launch any system scans and start routine monitoring. There should be little or no delay between a new system being provisioned in the cloud and the beginning of security scans and continuous monitoring. Monitoring of the automated provisioning, customer orders, system capacity, system performance, and security are critical in a 24-7, on-demand cloud environment. Here are some considerations:

- All new applications, servers/virtual servers, network segments, and so on should be automatically registered to a universal configuration database and trigger immediate scans and monitoring. Avoid manually adding new applications or servers to the security, capacity, or monitoring tools to ensure that continuous monitoring begins immediately when services are brought online through the automation processes.

- Monitoring of automated provisioning and customer orders is critical in an on-demand cloud environment. Particularly during the initial months of a private cloud launch, there will be numerous tweaks and improvements needed to the automation tools and scripts to continuously remove manual processes, error handling, and resource allocation.

- Clouds often support multiple tenants or consuming organizations. Monitoring and security tools often consolidate or aggregate statistics and system events to a centralized console, database, and support staff. When tracking, resolving, and reporting events and statistics, the data must be segmented and reported back to each tenant such that they only see their private information—often the software tools used by the cloud provider have limitations in maintaining sovereignty of customer reports to multiple tenants.

- There are three key tenets of continuous monitoring:

Aggregate diverse data
> Combine data from multiple sources generated by different products/vendors and organizations in real time.

Maintain real-time awareness
> Utilize real-time dashboards to identify and track statistics and attacks. Use real time alerting for anomalies and system changes.

Create real time data searches
> Develop and automate searches across unrelated datasets to identify the IP addresses from which attacks were originating. Transform data into

actionable intelligence by analyzing data to identify specific IP addresses from which attacks originated and terminated hostile traffic.

DENIAL-OF-SERVICE PLAN

Denial-of-Service (DoS) attacks are so common that it is a matter of when and how often, not if, your cloud is attacked. Here are some recommendations:

- Try to isolate your inbound and outbound network traffic behind a third-party provider that has DoS protections, honey pots, and dark networks that can absorb an attack and effectively hide your network addresses and services from public visibility (see "Monitoring and Detection Outside Your Network Perimeter" on page 260).

- Have a plan for when a DoS attack against your network occurs. Perhaps you will initiate further traffic filters or blocks to try and redirect or block the harmful traffic. Maybe you have another network or virtual private network (VPN) that employees and partners can revert to during the attack and still access your cloud-based services. Remember that the time to find a solution for a DoS attack is before one occurs—after you are experiencing a DoS attack, your network and services are already so disrupted that it is much more difficult to recover.

GLOBAL THREAT MONITORING

Consider implementing security tools, firewalls, and intrusion detection systems that subscribe to a reputable worldwide threat management service or matrix. These services detect new and zero-day attacks that might start somewhere across the globe and then transmit the patch, fix, or mitigation of that new threat to all worldwide subscribers immediately. Thus, everyone subscribed to the service is "immediately" immune from the attack even before the attack or intrusion attempt was ever made to your specific network. These services utilize some of the world's best security experts to identify and mitigate threats. No individual cloud provider or consuming organization can afford the quantity and level of skills as these providers have.

CHANGE CONTROL

Legacy change control processes need to evolve in an automated cloud environment. When each new cloud service is ordered and automated provisioning is completed, an automated process should also be utilized to process change controls that can also feed or monitor be security operations. Here are some recommendations:

- Avoid all manual processes that might slow or inhibit the automated ordering and provisioning capabilities of the cloud platform.

- When new IaaS VMs are brought online, for example, configure the cloud management platform to automatically enter an entry into the organizations change control system as an "automatic approval." This immediately adds the change to the database and can be used to trigger further notifications to appropriate operational staff or trigger automatic security or inventory scanning tools.

- Utilize preapproved VM templates, applications, and network configurations for all automatically provisioned cloud services. Avoid manual change control processes and approvals in the cloud ordering process.

- Remember to record all VMs, OS, and application patching, updates and restores in the change control database. Finally, also remember that the change control and inventory databases should also be immediately updated when a cloud service is stopped or a subscription is canceled.

Cloud Management

Key topics in this chapter:

- Architecture of a cloud management platform
- Orchestration and automated provisioning
- Systems management
- Multitenant self-service control panels
- Software applications and packaging
- System extensibility and APIs
- Build versus buy decision for cloud management platforms
- Open source cloud platforms and industry standards
- Cloud management best practices

The cloud management system is one of the most important components to consider when planning, deploying, and operating (or consuming) a cloud service. In a public cloud environment, the customer might only utilize a fraction of the overall cloud management platform—usually just the ordering and self-service portal hosted by the public cloud. In an enterprise private cloud, the management system makes it possible for organizations to provision, track billing and utilization, and manage the entire cloud infrastructure. Lessons learned from the first generation of cloud providers and private cloud deployment has clearly shown an under-appreciation of the importance of the cloud management platform. The cloud management platform is the true core for automation, orchestration, workflow, resource tracking, billing, and operations.

Key Take-Away

Public and private clouds both use an underlying cloud management platform. Private clouds have significantly more features and customization capabilities but you have to evaluate and chose your cloud management platform and software vendor carefully.

In an enterprise private cloud deployment, cloud management tools are the most underestimated or overlooked component. Using just a hypervisor platform for server virtualization is not the same as a full cloud management system that provides multitenant online ordering, approval workflows, customized automated provisioning, resource utilization and financial tracking, self-service application administration, and reporting.

Throughout this book, I have stressed the importance of cloud characteristics. To achieve on-demand ordering, automated provisioning, and pay-as-you-use billing, a cloud management system is an absolute necessity. Anyone can build a server farm, install some virtualization software, and then declare he has a cloud; however, without a system to manage it there is no multitenant customer interface, no automated provisioning, and no metering of resources for billing. And you can forget about saving money on personnel: you'll have to manually configure networks, servers, virtual machine templates, applications—everything. This would drive your costs too high to be competitive in the industry (public cloud) or control your operational costs in a private cloud.

Understanding the Cloud Management System Architecture

Cloud management systems vary greatly in their features, ease of use, flexibility, and cost. A cloud provider (or private cloud operator) can develop its own cloud management system or purchase an existing system from cloud software management vendors (see the "Cloud Management Platforms: The Build Versus Buy Decision" on page 280 analysis later in this chapter).

Key Take-Away

A well-designed, modular cloud management system provides a cloud portal, orchestration, workflow, automated provisioning, and integrated billing/resource metering capabilities.

Figure 7-1 shows a vendor-agnostic example of the primary functions of a cloud management system. These functions are presented in three functional layers. Each layer integrates with the layer directly above and below it. For the purposes of illustration, the top layer represents the client-facing web portal on which consumers can place orders, manage, and track their cloud service subscriptions. The middle layer represents the automation, orchestration, workflow, and resource management functions. The bottom layer is the network management layer. This is where systems monitoring, security, and capacity management functions monitor the cloud infrastructure and integrate with existing datacenter operational management tools.

It is very important to note one function that is not included in the cloud management system (and Figure 7-1): the hypervisor. There can be several of these including those hosted at other cloud providers.

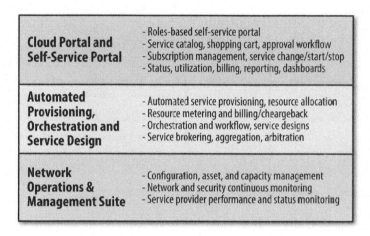

Figure 7-1. High-level functional cloud service management layers

Figure 7-2 depicts a detailed functional architecture of an ideal cloud management system. There are dozens of ways to show a detailed functional architecture and they will vary depending on cloud management software vendor—none are right or wrong, but pay attention to the individual elements shown in this figure that represent functionality any cloud management system should have.

Similar to Figure 7-1, the function architecture presented in Figure 7-2 does not include the hypervisors or actual cloud service provider(s)—this is just the command and control functions for all the cloud ecosystem.

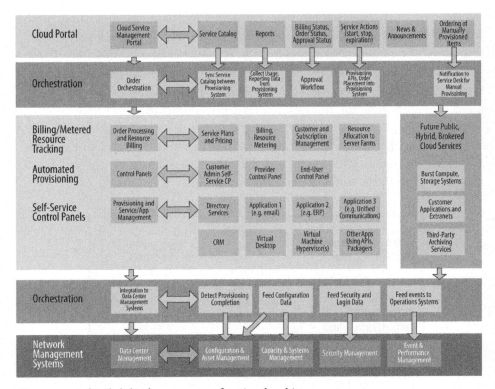

Figure 7-2. A detailed cloud management functional architecture

In this example, the orchestration levels are both above and below the automation system. This is an attempt to show that orchestration activities occur both pre- and post-initial provisioning. This could also be represented as a circle surrounding the boxes in the middle of the architecture diagram. The orchestration system makes the connections, integration, and data interchange between other layers of the architecture, which allows software from various companies to be integrated when necessary. Workflow and business process logic is normally part of the orchestration layer. There can be multiple instances of the provisioning systems shown in those same middle boxes. As new cloud providers or technologies are added, these additional provisioning systems would integrate with the orchestration system, facilitating modular additional functionality to your cloud without changing the other layers that have been integrated and are in production operations for your business.

The network management layer at the bottom represents the operations, security, asset, configuration, and software licensing functions that the cloud provider uses to manage the entire infrastructure, including all legacy IT systems, private cloud, and any hybrid integration to third-party cloud services.

The National Institute for Standards and Technology (NIST) has also published a high-level diagram showing the functional capabilities for cloud service management. Figure 7-3 demonstrates how several of the elements in the NIST model are very similar to those in the more detailed depiction in Figure 7-2.

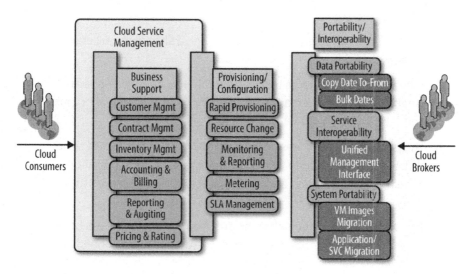

Figure 7-3. NIST model for cloud service management (Source: NIST, Special Publication 5-500-291 version 2, July 2013)

Orchestrating Automated Actions

An orchestrator refers to a software system programmed with workflow rules and business logic that facilitates automated actions and integrated connectors to external software systems. Many IT organizations create scripts to automate manual tasks; however, these are now considered a legacy technique. Scripts are also difficult to maintain and reuse, and their sequential processing limits their flexibility. An orchestration system goes well beyond scripting with parallel tasking, branching workflows, situational-awareness logic, and the ability to back out from or resume workflows that fail or sense an error. You can integrate sScripts and other automated software installation packaging tools into an orchestration workflow; however, the orchestration should always be the primary logic engine at the core of all cloud provisioning and automation workflows.

Use-Case Scenario: Orchestration

To understand the importance of the orchestrator, let's walk through a case scenario.

1. The customer logs on to the cloud service catalog portal and orders one virtual machine (VM) with Linux as the OS, 4 processors, and 16 GB of memory.

2. The customer processes his order through a shopping cart checkout process and submits it.

3. The orchestrator detects this new customer order and sends an email to the designated approver(s) within that customer's organization.

4. The person who approves orders receives the email and clicks the URL within it to log on to the cloud management portal. A list of pending orders awaiting approval appears, and he approves the order.

5. The orchestrator detects that the order is now approved and begins the automated provisioning process. The orchestrator connects to the VMware server farm and instructs VMware to create one VM based on the Linux VM template.

6. VMware creates the VM as instructed. The orchestrator then changes the configuration of the VM so that it has four processors and 16 GB of memory. The orchestrator then instructs the VMware software to boot the VM for the first time.

7. The orchestrator logs on to the VM, knowing to use Linux commands, to confirm that the system is functioning correctly. The orchestrator completes any additional steps the cloud provider has configured, such as installing additional software updates or patches.

8. The orchestrator connects to the cloud provider's change control system and enters a record in the database indicating that a new server—VM in this case—has been brought onto the network. The orchestrator populates the IP address and other configuration infor-

mation into the change control system so that the cloud provider's support staff now knows that this new server ex sts.

9. The orchestrator is aware that the VM has been successfully created, so it sends an email to the customer indicating that the VM service is available. This email notification contains the new VM server name, IP address, and logon information.

10. The orchestrator sends out error notices (or uses an API call to an existing service ticketing system) to the cloud provider's support staff if any step in this process failed to complete or if any of the downstream software systems generated an error. You can configure the orchestration workflow logic to pause if an error or failure is detected (to give cloud support personnel time to resolve the problem rather than generate an error to the customer). Upon fixing the error, the cloud support personnel can continue the workflow, and in some cases the orchestration system can automatically detect the change in status and resume the workflow automatically.

In the preceding example, VMware was the hypervisor technology. There are numerous hypervisor technologies in the industry that would perform similarly; however, a key point to highlight is that the hypervisor software itself is not the same as the cloud management platform. In this example, hypervisors perform only the creation and management of VMs. Note that some hypervisor software platforms can perform some higher-level cloud management functions but are usually not as complete and all-encompassing as a full cloud management platform. It is the cloud management system that performs everything from taking the customer's order from a service catalog to the approval process; to triggering the hypervisor to provision services; updating the network management systems with the new VM configuration and status; starting utilization and invoice tracking, and finally, sending email to the end user and cloud support staff of success.

Key Take-Away

The earliest cloud systems often relied solely on the hypervisor software's portal or configuration tools. These hypervisor configuration portals are good for technical personnel to manage basic VM services for a single tenant organization. Multitenant clouds with more advanced PaaS and Software as a Service SaaS applications utilize full cloud management platforms that automate and orchestrate the entire infrastructure and customer portals—the hypervisor software is now just an underlying component of the cloud management system.

Figure 7-4 shows a diagram published by NIST that maps service orchestration to the NIST Cloud Reference Model (see Figure 8-2). Note that the major functionality shown in this diagram closely resembles that of the more detailed orchestration processes detailed in Figure 7-2 and the functional management layers shown in Figure 7-1.

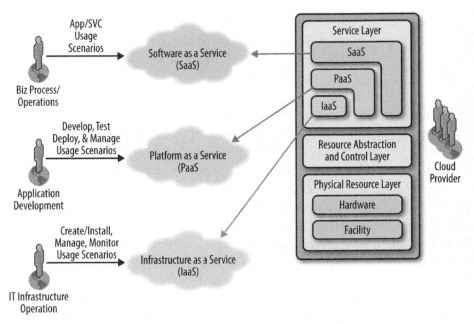

Figure 7-4. NIST model for cloud service orchestration (Source: NIST, Special Publication 5-500-291 version 2, July 2013)

Although I legitimately focus on automation throughout this book, there are actually three common methods for provisioning resources in a cloud infrastructure. Clearly, automatic is the preferred method, but there are scenarios in which you would use the other methods, as well.

Table 7-1. Cloud deployment model definitions

Provisioning Method	Benefits	Risks
Manual, using cloud provider's web portal	• Simple and easy for customer to understand and self-configure • Immediate initiation of provisioning activity and visual confirmation	• Less efficient use of labor • Susceptible to configuration mistakes; human error • Potential for inconsistent configurations, adherence to standards • Cloud provider's management and billing systems might not be aware of manually configured services or changes to subscriptions
Programmatic, using API calls from scripts	• Easily integrates into existing software installation tools and scripts • Often preferred method for software developers, especially for non-production • Low cost to implement	• Concerns and conflicts using hypervisor APIs versus provider's cloud management platform APIs • Sequential scripts are not as dynamic, upgradeable, and flexible as full automation and orchestration • Susceptible to configuration mistakes at a faster scripted pace • All provisioning activities must be synchronized with the cloud provider's management platform and billing.
Automatic, using cloud management	• Fastest provisioning with least amount of labor/support required	• Higher effort to implement and configure full orchestration

Provisioning Method	Benefits	Risks
platform orchestration	• Real-time provisioning status awareness, billing, and operational readiness of new cloud services • Consistent configurations resulting in better quality, improve security and compliance to standards/procedures	• Use caution if automation is configured to allow unlimited elasticity • Potentially steep learning curve for legacy IT staff to implement/use new orchestration/automation tools

RESOURCE ALLOCATION

One key feature of orchestration and provisioning is resource allocation. In this process, the cloud system takes a new order from a customer and determines which servers, storage systems, and subnetworks have available capacity to host this new customer's request for a compute or software instance. As each server and server farm fills up, the system knows to automatically move to the next pool of servers to provision new services (e.g., virtual machines). If there are no available resources, a warning message is generated to the cloud provider's support staff. When additional space is available, the orchestrator will again attempt to provision the new service. All of this is done without human intervention, and potentially hundreds of times each day as new customers order services and existing customers begin to utilize more disk space and VMs.

RESOURCE RECLAMATION

The opposite of automated provisioning is the de-provisioning of services for customers that cancel, or that the support personnel instruct the cloud management system to destroy. The management system knows how to stop VMs, delete user accounts, reclaim disk storage, application licenses, and cease billing for the terminated services. When any customer's subscription is terminated, all of the server, VM, processor, memory, storage, and other resources are cleared, reclaimed, and made available for the next customer. There are some hypervisors and storage systems that do not automatically reclaim the now-unused disk space because of technical limitations in the manufacturer's software. This is similar to moving files to your deleted items or trash can on a desktop computer, but the disk space is still being occupied by the deleted data until you clear the trash can; the disk space is not truly reclaimed or made available for the next customer.

Key Take-Away

The reclamation process, both within a hypervisor and especially storage systems, are not always automatic (various limitations of some software manufacturers). This requires the creation of batch processes scheduled to run daily, weekly, or monthly during nonpeak hours to actually clear services or data that is no longer active.

SETTING UP ORCHESTRATOR WORKFLOWS

As the orchestration system is essentially the brains of the cloud management system, it is also the place where any custom business logic and customized workflows are created. The cloud service provider can use the orchestrator to provision simple or multitiered cloud applications, send messages, send out customer invoices, and automatically trigger an alert for any event within the cloud. As future "as a service" products are deployed, the orchestrator is updated with new workflows, scripts, processes, and rules that facilitate automated provisioning, utilization tracking, billing and metering, and operational management. Many cloud management platforms include a service designer tool (through programming and/or a GUI interface) with which the cloud provider or technically skilled customer can create new workflows, single or multiple VM platform applications, network segmentation, and so on.

Often, in a private cloud deployment model, the orchestrator can be used to handle highly customized customer needs. These custom tasks could be to perform multiple-level order approval, approver reminders after a period of time has passed, or customer notification of certain events. You can also program the orchestrator to do non-cloud-specific tasks such as opening a support ticket, gathering statistical data and sending a monthly report, or warning the cloud provider's support personnel well in advance before they run out of available disk storage.

Key Take-Away

Some orchestration systems include a library of preintegrated service designs and connectors to external software systems, hypervisors, network management tools, and additional cloud providers in a hybrid cloud environment.

Creating Reports and Dashboards

A cloud management system provides numerous reports for finance, service availability, performance, and service-level agreement (SLA) adherence. Reports and a *dashboard* displaying metrics can show customers a real-time view of the service status and utilization, which is a tremendously valuable feature for those customers that need more than a monthly written report to monitor statistics and performance metrics. Most public cloud providers give only limited reporting and dashboard views into the cloud service. You can customize private cloud systems to a significantly higher degree to meet customer needs and integrate with internal service management or business intelligence systems.

When an organization goes beyond basic IaaS and SaaS offerings, integrating legacy applications into a single cloud management system will provide huge benefits. You can truly have an "executive dashboard" of all your services and applications with metrics, statuses, and financial information in a single web portal.

These reports and dashboards provide cloud customers with visibility into their services, utilization, performance, and costs. The first generation of clouds and providers rarely provided this visibility, which still causes concern and impedes new customer adoption of cloud computing.

Managing Systems and Services

As the cloud management system handles resource allocation and provisioning of services, it is fully aware of all servers, networks, storage systems, and applications that are available and already deployed. The cloud provider or your internal enterprise support staff will use this information to detect system problems, identify systems with low remaining capacity, or take individual servers offline for maintenance. When one system is turned off, the cloud management system has the ability to move any active customer resources (e.g., virtual machines, storage volumes) to other infrastructure devices in the datacenter so that, in a perfect scenario, nobody notices the maintenance outage.

The systems management tools utilized in large datacenters are commonly used for capacity management, security monitoring and alerting, asset and configuration management, and software distribution and automated updating of applications. In a cloud environment, these traditional tools use much of the same technology but the emphasis is on forecasting, real-time updating of statistics, and automated response to events. Clouds work because of automation, so elimination of human-caused delays and eventual inaccuracies is the new paradigm for systems management.

Earlier in Chapter 2, cloud operations management lessons learned and best practices were discussed. There are many aspects of traditional IT or datacenter operations that change in an on-demand, automated, and elastic cloud environment. Capacity management and continuous careful monitoring of the automated provisioning is significantly more important in a cloud environment than ever before. For full details on system-management tools, techniques, and best practices in a cloud ecosystem, refer to Chapter 2.

Providing Self-Service Control Panels

The cloud management system not only handles customer orders, orchestration, and provisioning functions of the cloud, it also provides a (usually web-based) portal for customers to configure their cloud services. The first generation of cloud providers and private cloud management platforms had only given customers extremely basic service administration capabilities. Almost all cloud management portals make it possible for the customer to order new services, upgrade subscriptions, and terminate services. Depending on privileges as defined in roles-based access controls, some IaaS providers give the customer the ability to restart or reboot IaaS VMs; however, this is significantly less capability that a customer would have if it ran its own on-premises virtualization hypervisor. These limitations are further exacerbated when a cloud provider offers PaaS and SaaS that have more sophisticated software applications, configuration settings, and daily user administrative tasks.

Key Take-Away

There are significant gaps in self-service application administration capabilities in first-generation cloud providers and cloud management systems. Many SaaS-focused providers have long understood this problem, and their customer-facing cloud portals offer excellent self-service control panels for each application and cloud service. Public cloud providers and private cloud management systems are slowly understanding and catching up to this level of application self-service administration capability.

Given that the initial priority for most public cloud providers has been to offer IaaS applications, the lack of fully featured self-service application administration control panels has not been a significant problem. The entire industry and customers agree that platforms (PaaS) and applications (SaaS) will be much more of a focus in the coming years; therefore, the lack of self-service application-specific control panels must be solved. In the meantime, early adopters of SaaS cloud services are forced to rely on submitting service tickets to the cloud provider or internal cloud operations team for routine application administrative tasks. This is a waste of time and money for everyone.

For more details on the future of self-service control panels and next-generation priorities and challenges, refer to Chapter 9.

Software Applications and Packaging

Cloud management systems have varied capabilities to provision and administer industry-leading commercial off-the-shelf (COTS) and custom software products. It is this ability to quickly add applications to the cloud management system—and thus make them available to customers—that differentiates a powerful, robust cloud management system from an average one.

SOFTWARE APPLICATIONS

There are two primary types of applications cloud management systems support: COTS and customer "homegrown" applications.

COTS are widely sold and distributed products that cloud providers might install into their datacenters, using the cloud management platform to manage them all. When customers order one of these SaaS offerings, the management system has usually been preprogrammed with a "module" that knows how to provision, automatically configure, and integrate using APIs with the COTS application. As each software vendor releases new versions in the future, the cloud management platform vendor must also update its integration module or API to keep up. The cloud customer is not aware of these continuous upgrades unless new user interfaces or features appear in the self-service control panels.

It is when a provider wants to integrate a custom homegrown application—or some legacy customer-owned application—into the cloud that you can use or develop an integration module so that the environments can communicate with each other. Maybe the customer has a finance application that it would like deployed to the cloud; in this scenario, the cloud provider will migrate the application and data, but it will also have to utilize a module so that automated provisioning, billing, reporting, and the self-service control panels are functional. The customer simply sees an additional tab or icon on its cloud control panel called, for example, "finance application." For more details on legacy application migration, porting, and redesign options, refer back to "Chapter 4".

By integrating all the custom and COTS applications, the cloud management system gives both the provider and the customer support staff a single management console for all cloud and application configuration and administration. This is very important: without this single unified cloud management console integrating everything, the cloud provider's support personnel would have dozens of different software tools, one for each application, that they would need to use every time they wanted to create a new user or perform routine administrative tasks.

EXTENDING THE SYSTEM VIA APIS

You can use cloud management platforms to access and control the cloud by integrating with third-party applications and software systems through an application programming interface (API). APIs are the means by which cloud management platform can access and initialize commands or tasks into other software applications. Just as with the orchestrator, the cloud provider can create its own programs to do mass import, exports, or other tasks using the API features of the cloud management system. The purpose of an API is to allow integration and exchange of automated commands between multiple applications and, in the case of cloud, the cloud management platform.

In a hybrid cloud environment, APIs are also utilized to integrate with external XaaS providers. The cloud management platform will normally have a library of premade modules that use APIs with multiple cloud providers, applications, and future as-yet-unknown cloud providers and XaaS offerings. Cloud brokering, which is covered in Chapter 8, also relies heavily on APIs between cloud providers.

SOFTWARE PACKAGING/CONFIGURATION MANAGEMENT TOOLS

Cloud management platforms control the overall processes and workflows within a cloud through their automation and orchestration features. However, there are numerous other software packaging and software configuration management tools that you can use, as well. These tools, such as Puppet and Chef, are popular open source software configuration management tools that are commonly used in modern datacenters. Both of these tools have server-based applications with distributed agents on other target computers throughout the chosen network. Systems administrators specify the desired software state (e.g., software applications and patches) for each target server/host machine and the Puppet/Chef software will update each target system automatically based on configurable rules and parameters. Both tools support multiple programming languages and techniques for even more advanced software installations.

Another type of software packaging tool that has gained significant popularity is the open source product called Docker (you can read more about this product in Chapter 9). Docker is an application containerization technique with which you can package and run software programs in a virtualized memory compartment within any server and OS that runs the Docker [Application] Engine. These "Dockerized" applications are in theory portable and would run on any server or operating system without the need to be recompiled.

There are other tools with which you can package applications into self-installing modules that can also be integrated into the orchestration system of a cloud management platform. These tools vary by software vendor, but they can use a combination of sequential scripts, state/image capturing, or programming tools to intelligently install software onto target servers/hosts in the cloud or datacenter. By using these tools, you can greatly simplify and automate the distribution of software and updates across any number of systems—a level of automation that is critical for a cloud or any modern datacenter environment.

It is important to note that although a cloud management platform has its own automation and orchestration system, with workflow, scripting, and service design capabilities, you can easily integrate third-party software tools such as Puppet, Chef, and Docker. There is no need to re-create software installation scripts from these third-party tools into the orchestration; simply make calls out to the appropriate external tool from the orchestrator in the workflow engine.

Cloud Management Platforms: The Build Versus Buy Decision

Depending on the number and complexity of services, cloud providers might decide that developing their own cloud management system is the right way to go. Because this is custom developed, the cloud provider has complete freedom in what features, functionality, and customer interfaces to include. If the cloud provider is only offering a simple cloud service or to a small customer market, developing a cloud management system might not be cost effective.

BUILDING YOUR OWN CLOUD MANAGEMENT SYSTEM

There are two sides of this build-versus-buy decision. Even the simplest cloud management system still needs to have some sort of shopping cart, billing system, reporting system, resource metering system, workflow orchestration, and automated service provisioning. Cloud providers have a significant task ahead of them to create constantly enhance their own cloud management systems to be competitive. Those who do take on the build task themselves often end up spending 2 to 3 times the amount of time and money than they originally planed—and find they are still years behind the competition. The cloud provider will then want to add new applications or services and keep up with future revisions of every software application, resulting in never-ending development costs.

When customers begin to use the cloud management system, the need for additional features, more reporting, and more visibility on status and usage will become apparent. Customers are not shy about sending cloud providers requests for new features and enhancements. In fact, feature and scope creep is so significant that an entire section of this book covers this topic in Chapter 3. Multiply this across dozens or hundreds, or thousands of customers, and cloud providers quickly realize that their homegrown cloud management systems are insufficient. It might not be as modular as desired for easy upgrade; it might not scale up as intended; the customer interface may not be as intuitive as expected; or performance may be dragging down the user experience. Adding new service offerings to the homegrown cloud management platform now takes longer than the deployment of the new servers and applications that customers actually use.

Ultimately, most cloud providers end up redeveloping some or all of their cloud management systems within the first two years of becoming a provider. The amount of money spent developing a homegrown system is only surpassed by the amount of time it takes to maintain and continuously improve it. Lessons learned have proven that a homegrown cloud management system is a long and painful road. Cloud providers should seriously consider using a commercial platform that already has the needed basic functionality and a library of premade modules for integrating with server farms, VM hypervisors, SANs, software-defined networking, and COTS applications. Most important, the software vendor who creates and sells the cloud management platform also maintains its code, provides all future upgrades, new application integrations, and supports its system. You get to run your cloud and service your customers instead of dealing with the distraction of software development and maintenance.

Key Take-Away

The few companies that make money developing their own cloud management platform actually resell their system to other providers—everyone else who develops their own cloud management system wastes millions of dollars trying to build and continuously improve their homegrown cloud management systems.

BUYING A CLOUD MANAGEMENT SYSTEM

The only company that makes money and is successful in the cloud management software tool industry is one that creates and resells it; you don't make money building your own system just for your own cloud. This lesson has been learned again and again, particularly in large datacenters and government organizations that, for various reasons, believed they would "do it better themselves." History has shown that most of these attempts fail, cost exponentially more than expected, and result in a complete redevelopment or eventual purchase of a commercial cloud management product after years of frustration.

The exception to this "don't build your own rule" is for extremely large public cloud providers such as Amazon, Microsoft, and Google, all of whom have the investment capability, internal developers, and massive growth plans to justify using their own cloud management platform. This being said, even these large providers end up starting with a very basic, unintuitive customer experience that limits customer adoption and satisfaction initially. These large providers spend millions of dollars continuously improving their cloud platforms—eventually maturing to a level of competitive features and hopefully keeping up with competitors who are continuously improving, as well.

As a private cloud provider, you should focus on your cloud services and your customers rather than spending all your money, time, and focus building and managing your own cloud management tool. Just as cloud providers sell the cloud by telling customers to focus on their customers' needs and not commodity IT, the cloud providers should heed their own advice and focus on being a cloud provider, not a software development shop.

There are many cloud management software systems available for purchase. Of the major vendors and open source options, there is a considerable variance in features and maturity. Later in this chapter, "Commercial Cloud Management Platforms" on page 283 presents a summary of available cloud management platforms and software providers.

PURCHASING AND UPGRADING A CLOUD MANAGEMENT SYSTEM

When evaluating and purchasing a cloud management system, some software vendors will sell you a license for their product with an initial up-front price, and then charge a percentage of that cost each year for support, maintenance, and free upgrades.

These upgrades aren't really free given that you are paying the annual maintenance fees; however, the huge benefit to this approach is that you don't need to worry about continuously developing updates for your cloud management system. As the software manufacturers release new versions of your hosted COTS applications, the cloud portal vendor will provide you with its latest version. There is usually a two to four-month gap from when a major COTS product is updated and the cloud management vendor releasing its corresponding new version. You aren't in the business of constantly keeping up your cloud control panels updated with every new COTS release. As a provider, you will need to upgrade your COTS application servers in your server farm, but at least the cloud management system upgrade will be done for you.

Key Take-Away

The first time you go through a major software application upgrade, you will truly realize the benefits of having purchased your cloud management system and support from a third party.

When purchasing your cloud management system, some software vendors have an alternative licensing model by which they will charge a smaller up-front fee in lieu of pay-as-you-go charges for each user, VM, or other unit of measure depending on what services you have enabled. This makes it possible for the provider to start small with just a few customers and pay only the low licensing fees each month. As you grow in users and revenue, so do the fees you pay to the cloud management software vendor; this is essentially a shared-growth model wherein both parties are incentivized to maintain a stable system and increase customer count. I highly recommend this model for small but growing cloud providers to reduce up-front capital expenses.

For private cloud deployments within an organization that has a relatively fixed number of users, you might get a better "bang for the buck" by purchasing the cloud management system outright and only paying ongoing maintenance fees.

COMMERCIAL CLOUD MANAGEMENT PLATFORMS

With the industry's newfound understanding that the cloud management platform is the core of any public or private cloud, the software companies providing these platforms are becoming better known. For most public cloud providers, the underlying cloud management platform is more likely a self-developed tool with possibly some COTS tools that providers often do not announce publicly. The private cloud management tools are where the competition is fierce and where the management platform that you choose effects just about every aspect of the customer experience, services offered, billing, operating procedures, flexibility, and cost of the service.

There are several industry-leading private cloud management platforms available. There have been numerous acquisitions in this industry—many by systems integrators—that further illustrates the importance and competitiveness of these cloud management platforms.

In the following subsections, I describe the industry-leading private cloud management platforms and providers (note that many of these companies also provide public or other cloud-related services that are described in Chapter 9); the following list is strictly for cloud management software platforms:

VMware

VMware's cloud management platform is called vRealize Suite. This suite includes multiple software components for private and hybrid cloud management. The vRealize Suite integrates with VMware's well-known hypervisor vSphere and the vCloud Suite for internal datacenter and infrastructure management. Given VMware's popularity and long history in the server virtualization industry, it is a common choice for private clouds as the VM hypervisor.

Microsoft

Microsoft's private cloud management platform is called Microsoft Azure Pack. This system integrates with on-premises Microsoft System Center and Windows Servers in your datacenter. Microsoft also has its own hypervisor server virtualization technology (Hyper-V) through which it can provide a complete end-to-end cloud software platform, from hypervisor to cloud management system, to operating systems and applications. Microsoft also has a public cloud service also named Azure (described in Chapter 5) which can integrate with this private cloud Azure Pack to provide hybrid capabilities.

Hewlett-Packard

Hewlett-Packard's suite of cloud management software components include Cloud Service Automation, Operations Orchestration, and Server Automation. These software components are also available as an integrated platform called HP Helion CloudSystem that includes OpenStack, supports multiple hypervisors, and manages any combination of private, public, and hybrid cloud providers. Hewlett-Packard also offers a suite of cloud application development, database automation, security, and datacenter service operations tools.

BMC Software

BMC's cloud management platform is called Cloud Lifecycle Management. This system was originally based upon an industry-leading IT service-request management system called Remedy. BMC has its own automation, orchestration, and library of integration modules to connect to its own suite of datacenter operations tools and many third-party applications, hypervisors, and cloud providers.

Citrix

Citrix's cloud management platform is called CloudPlatform. This system is powered by Apache CloudStack, the open source cloud platform Citrix open sourced after purchasing from Cloud.com. CloudPlatform managed private, public and hybrid cloud environment and supports multiple hypervisor. Citrix also has its own hypervisor call Citrix XenServer.

Computer Sciences Corporation (CSC)

CSC's cloud management platform is called ServiceMesh. This system provides workflow, policy, and governance–focused IT service-management deployed in a private cloud. The system is designed for flexibility in automated business processes of a wide range of IT services including integration to cloud-centric hypervisors, applications, and third-party PaaS and SaaS providers.

Parallels

Parallels' cloud management platform is called Parallels Automation. This system was originally a SaaS-focused automation and self-service control panel system, but it now manages IaaS aoolications with multiple hypervisor support. Parallels manages private, public, and hybrid clouds and is used by many Internet, telecommunications and cloud service providers. Parallels also has a hypervisor platform called Parallels Cloud Server.

RedHat

RedHat's cloud management platform is called CloudForms. This system is based on its acquisition of ManageIQ's Enterprise Virtualization Manager and is focused on management of internal infrastructure servers and virtual machines with a mature self-service administration portal. RedHat has also committed to using OpenStack so that it can continue to mature and evolve its private and hybrid cloud platforms and integration to its industry-leading Linux platform.

RightScale

RightScale's cloud management platform is called Cloud Portfolio Management (CPM). This system provides a single "pane of glass" to manage and govern cloud services across private or multiple public cloud service providers.

There are many cloud management platform vendors and software systems that are not included in this book. There are simply too many mid-level and up-and-coming platforms to include so I have attempted to cover the most significant and industry-leading vendors. It is safe to say that I've more than covered all the "industry leader" cloud management platforms that appear in the top two industry analyst publications.

Open Source Cloud Platforms and Industry Standards

There are several open source cloud management platforms forming and continuously improving in the industry—OpenStack and CloudStack being the two most significant in the industry. Some of these cloud management platforms have broad industry support but might lag behind in terms of the features and functionality provided by commercial cloud management platforms. Organizations that want to evaluate or deploy this class of cloud management system should consider the pros and cons of using open source versus commercially supported software platforms. Open source's largest benefit is avoiding software vendor lock-in; however, the reality is that some of the best cloud management platforms in the industry are either proprietary or a combination of open source and proprietary—evaluate and choose carefully.

Following are two widely used open source cloud management platforms:

OpenStack

OpenStack is an open source project with the largest community, code contributors, and cloud provider and system integrator involvement. OpenStack's main goal is to support interoperability between cloud services while enabling enterprises to create Amazon-like cloud services. OpenStack is a combination of modules that you can use to build, host, and operate your own cloud. OpenStack modules are available to provide IaaS VMs, object and block storage, networking, identity, and many other services. There is an OpenStack module for cloud management automation and orchestration called Heat and another module called Horizon that is a customer-facing self-service configuration portal. Being an open source project, all developed source code is submitted to the OpenStack committee, with the combined code being released to the public free of charge. Notable founders and adopters of OpenStack include RackSpace, NASA, Hewlett-Packard, and IBM—each adding to and customizing OpenStack for their customer deployments and integration into other cloud management platforms and providers. Beyond a cloud management platform, OpenStack is also seen as an industry standard for application interfaces, interoperability between cloud providers, and eventually will at least influence software-defined networking and datacenters in the future. Given the quantity and well-known industry companies that have committed to OpenStack, it is expected to dominate as the industry open source for cloud and API integration between clouds.

CloudStack

CloudStack is largely considered the primary competitor to OpenStack. CloudStack was originally developed by Cloud.com, which was purchased by Citrix, and later released to the Apache Incubator program. Citrix is still involved in the open source platform, but the Apache Software Foundation now governs CloudStack. Key features of CloudStack include an easier, streamlined deployment, scalability, and multiple hypervisor support (Citrix Xen, Oracle VM, VMware, and KVM). CloudStack has fewer sponsors and corporations providing code and support compared to OpenStack.

The Organization for the Advancement of Structured Information Standards (OASIS) Topology and Orchestration Specification for Cloud Applications (TOSCA) (*http://bit.ly/1DesndR*) is an industry-standards organization notable for creating both cloud portability standards and orchestration standards. TOSCA is not a full cloud platform like OpenStack or CloudStack but is instead a standard for cloud management platforms. The TOSCA standard provides an interoperable description of application and infrastructure cloud services and the operations of these services. As of this writing, TOSCA is continuously evolving, with version 2.0 in development. Several cloud management platform software vendors as well as open source cloud platforms are already planning to include TOSCA support in their software systems.

CONFIGURATION AUTOMATION TOOLS

There is a class of cloud automation and configuration platforms that focus on the creation of provisioning packages (known as *recipes*) and automated software configuration. This class of configuration automation tool does not normally have the service catalogs, unified billing, resource utilization tracking, and overall cloud management features those in the products just described. These tools often specialize in scripted execution of VM, OS, and software—using a full cloud management platform to kick-off or initiate these automated configuration tools.

There are too many similar automation tools available as open source or commercial software to cover in this book. Notable open source configuration automation tools in the industry include the following:

Puppet

This tool provides both a command-line and web user interface for managing automated configuration scripts. Puppet uses its own programming language, which is based on Ruby (native Ruby is also supported) and requires programmatic expertise. Puppet uses a modeling approach to configure automated provisioning recipes and a robust push capability to update existing servers.

Chef

This tool is similar to Puppet in that it uses programmed scripts or recipes to automate the deployment and updating of servers, OSs, and software. Chef uses the Git programming language that is sometimes preferred by IT teams that have significant programming experience, which affords extremely detailed and customized scripts.

Salt

Salt is similar to Puppet and Chef in its ability to configure automated scripts or recipes for deploying software. You can create customized scripts or modules by using Python or PyDSL programming languages or you can download premade modules. Salt's biggest advantage is in scalability and resiliency through the optional use of multiple master, distribution servers, and minion remote agents.

Git

Git is a popular software developer distribution control system with programmable workflows. Git is commonly used to automate the deployment of applications or websites to the cloud via Linux commands. GitHub is a web-based service for Git users and developers. Whereas Git is strictly a command-line tool, GitHub provides a graphical interface for desktop or mobile integration, code sharing, collaboration, task management, and bug tracking.

Docker

Docker is an open source software system and development community that is focused on the automated deployment of applications by using software containers. Using Docker's application containerization technique, you can package and run software programs in a virtualized memory compartment within any server and OS that runs the Docker [Application] Engine. You can use Docker containers within most private clouds as well as many of the industry's most popular public cloud environments.

Cloudify

This is an open source cloud orchestration tool for automated deployment and updating of servers, OSs, and software. Each Cloudify recipe describes an application blueprint that includes the detailed instructions for installing and managing applications, including subcomponents and dependencies. Cloudify follows the TOSCA standard for cloud automation.

Cloud Management Best Practices

Based on lessons learned and experience from across the cloud industry, you should consider the following best practices for your organization's planning.

CLOUD MANAGEMENT PLATFORM

All cloud providers and operators of a private cloud utilize a cloud management system that provides a customer ordering portal, subscription management, automation provisioning, billing and resource utilization tracking, and management of the cloud. Here's some recommendations for you:

- Use the full capabilities of the cloud management platform's orchestration system. Do not rely on legacy sequential scripts for automation; instead, use orchestration-based workflows and service designs.

- Utilize third-party automated software installation packaging tools along with the orchestration system for maximum flexibility, but ensure that the orchestrator is the primary logic engine/workflow tool.

- When selecting or building a private cloud, evaluating and selecting the cloud management platform is one of the most critical decisions. The features, functionality, and vendor support (including future updates and new features) of the cloud management system will have an impact on every aspect of how a private cloud is managed, the user experience, and the time and cost of releasing initial and new service catalog items.

- If your organization is planning to use a private cloud and one or more public cloud providers, consider implementing a hybrid cloud management platform rather than just a private management system. For full details on hybrid cloud and management platforms, refer to Chapter 8.

- The following are the features to look for in a cloud management platform:

  — Usability and customization capabilities of the consumer-facing portal

  — Ability to create, manage, and display multiple categories and types of cloud services through a service catalog

  — Ability to see pricing, optional services and pricing, terms and conditions, and renewal settings for all cloud services through a shopping cart or order checkout process.

— Customizable order-approval workflow process

— Consumer-visible status dashboards and reports on utilization, billing, and service status

— Ability to manage subscribed cloud services (i.e., perform service restart, stop, pause, and add new capacity) via the cloud portal

- Preintegrated support for multiple hypervisors, external cloud service providers, internal service ticketing system integration, integration with security and network/systems monitoring software.

- Most cloud management platforms have some form of on-demand reporting and statistics dashboard available for cloud consumers. Cloud operators and consumers will quickly want more and more real-time dashboards, usage statistics, trending/forecasting, and so on. Expect customer requests to outpace development efforts initially, so manage expectations and plan enhancements for future portal releases.

- There is a trend in the industry by many service-ticketing software vendors to create cloud XaaS items in their service-ticketing system and claiming they are a cloud management platform. Most of the backend architectures of these products are not conducive to the cloud and are just IT service-desk ticketing and workflow systems. These systems can make API calls into hypervisors and other cloud services, but the architecture, functionality, and integrations are nowhere near the level of a true cloud management platform. Be very detailed and careful in evaluating service-desk, IT service delivery, and other platforms that were originally designed and intended as IT service management and support ticketing systems.

BUILDING VERSUS BUYING A CLOUD MANAGEMENT PLATFORM

Cloud management platforms are very complex and expensive to design, develop, support, and then continuously upgrade with new features and integration with the latest cloud technologies. Here are some considerations:

- Even large-scale cloud providers rarely build their own cloud management platforms. When building your own private cloud, don't build your own cloud management platform, because the cost and effort is extensive and will likely draw your focus away from your core mission.

- Although you can certainly customize your private cloud management platform to suit your cloud operations and your customers, remember not to go too far with the customizations to the point where your system is now so unique that the original software manufacturer can no longer apply new features and upgrades to your cloud platform.

HYBRID CLOUD

A theme and trend mentioned throughout this book is that most private clouds will eventually use one or more third-party public cloud services, so hybrid clouds will soon be the norm. Here are some considerations:

- When starting with a public cloud provider, you must use its cloud management platform and that platform's inherent capabilities. If you later deploy a private cloud, you will need to deploy your own private cloud management platform and manage your two clouds individually. If you begin first with hybrid cloud management platform, you can use the hybrid platform's capability to integrate with and effectively hide the public cloud management systems—using your private/hybrid cloud platform for a single management and customer experience.

- When evaluating and selecting a private or hybrid cloud management platform, look for preintegrated features and integrations with legacy datacenter hypervisors, networks, storage systems, and support for third-party cloud providers. This means that the external cloud provider's capability is readily supported when you are ready to use those features.

- Remember that hybrid clouds can involve any combination of private, public, community, or legacy enterprise IT, regardless of where the data, applications, and server farms are hosted (e.g., on premises, at a provider, or at a leased colocation facility).

- If you use a public cloud provider's management platform and self-service portal, the provider might offer some hybrid capabilities to integrate back to internal enterprise IT applications, directory services, and data; however, you might be very limited in flexibility and management. In most scenarios, you are better off starting with a private/hybrid cloud management system that extends outward to one or more public cloud provider(s)—giving you the most flexibility, customization, and choice of providers and XaaS.

OPEN SOURCE

Just as occurred in the IT industry over the past 30 years, proprietary platforms and services often lead the market until the eventual need for standards and interoperability becomes so paramount that open source platforms become the norm. Cloud services and management platforms are now at this stage of evolution, and now nonproprietary open source cloud services and platforms are more desirable, cheaper, and offer more integration capabilities with other applications, cloud providers, and legacy enterprise IT. Here's more information:

- Using an open source cloud management platform has some unique implications:

    — Open source platforms do not always have as many features or mature as quickly as a COTS system, especially during initial project startup years. This is where some software vendors offer their own version or distributions of the open source platform—adding additional capabilities or enhancements above and beyond the open source application.

    — Open source has the benefit of reducing software vendor lock-in

    — Some organizations contribute a significant amount of code and suggested standards, but do not always get their ideas adopted as the part of the new software release. Any enhancements a software vendor wants to add to the open source system capability will need to be retested and modified every time a new software revision is released to ensure compatibility—this can be a costly and never-ending endeavor.

    — Open source often becomes (officially or de facto) the industry standard for APIs and cross-vendor integration

- Systems integrators and cloud service providers that use open source systems might find it difficult to differentiate their capabilities and features from other competitors who use the same open standard (or even end customers with their own deployment of the open source platform).

- Customers often use open source to avoid lock-in to any single vendor's cloud management platform and API standards. Open source platforms are also easier to evaluate for security purposes, given that the source development code is available to the public. Of course, some could also argue that this open source code also helps hackers identify potential weaknesses in security, but this is usually mitigated by a large community of open source testers.

Hybrid and Cloud Brokering

Key topics in this chapter:

- What is a cloud broker

- Key hybrid and brokering terminology

- Hybrid cloud versus cloud broker

- Selecting a cloud broker

- Arbitration and selection of service providers:

- Spanning multiple cloud providers

- Systems portability and dynamic allocation to providers

- Industry standards and the future

- The challenges of cloud brokering

- The future of cloud brokering

- Hybrid and cloud brokering best practices

The evolution of cloud computing has been rapid, focusing first on basic Infrastructure as a Service (IaaS) virtual machines and then Platform as a Service (PaaS) and Software as a Service (SaaS). Leading public cloud providers are now well established, whereas enterprise organizations still work on deploying private and hybrid clouds and evaluating which legacy applications to migrate. Some organizations are already going beyond private hybrid cloud and beginning to consider cloud brokering. As of this writing, there are no true cloud brokers in the industry, but you can expect to see customer adoption and even some public-style cloud brokers in the coming years. In this chapter, I explain what a cloud broker's role is and the technological challenges it must overcome.

What Is a Cloud Broker

Cloud brokering refers to an organization that serves as a centralized coordinator of cloud services for other organizations, departments, or subagencies. Many IT departments already serve as an IT broker today—providing IT services for their overall organization or procuring or outsourcing the required services to a third party to meet the needs of internal customers within the enterprise organization. A cloud broker is a similar role, taking requirements or orders via an online service catalog and then determining which of multiple cloud providers will receive the provisioning request.

As of this writing, there are no public cloud broker service providers in the industry. Cloud brokering is not something you can purchase from a public cloud provider. Brokering is normally deployed by installing a cloud management system (with specialized brokering capabilities) within an enterprise datacenter or leased facility. There are some specialized systems integrators that concentrate on cloud brokering that are planning to offer a managed community cloud broker service; however, the level of complexity and customization required per tenant or customer is very challenging. This is why there are no "public" cloud broker service providers in the industry.

The National Institute for Standards and Technology (NIST) defines a cloud broker as "An entity that manages the use, performance, and delivery of cloud services, and negotiates relationships between Cloud Providers and Cloud Consumers." The "entity" in this definition refers to you as an IT organization serving in the broker role for the rest of your users or as a commercial cloud broker which, as I will discuss later, there really are none in the industry at this time.

Following is a summary of the six specific areas in which the cloud broker plays an important role:

Service catalog
> Provide a consolidated service catalog for customer ordering of all downstream cloud provider Anything as a Service (XaaS) offerings

Workflow
> Facilitate ordering processes such as approvals and notifications within consumer organizations

Provisioning application programming interfaces (APIs)
> Manage service provisioning by using API calls to downstream cloud providers

Resource management
> Manage all service costs, resource metering, billing or chargeback—consolidated across all cloud providers

Tracking status
> Track completion and success of provisioning and availability of services by using APIs with each cloud provider

Reporting
> Collect and aggregate all system statuses, statistics, and service-level agreement (SLA) dashboards from downstream XaaS cloud providers into a centralized portal hosted by the broker

Although NIST defines two separate roles for broker—business and technical (NIST Special Publication 500-299)—I have combined these roles for clarity and simplification. Although the broker industry is very new, early adopters and broker providers are finding that a combined broker role is more effective, offers better multiprovider integration, and provides a more unified customer experience.

In a cloud broker environment, the simplified layers of cloud management, described earlier in Chapter 7, become more complex because there is now the expectation of supporting one or more downstream cloud service providers. Figure 8-1 presents a diagram of a cloud broker functional management structure. The cloud broker performs the functions within the boxes at the top and bottom, whereas one or more downstream service providers performs the functions contained in the box in the middle. The box on the bottom, operations and management, is really an encompassing function also performed by the cloud broker.

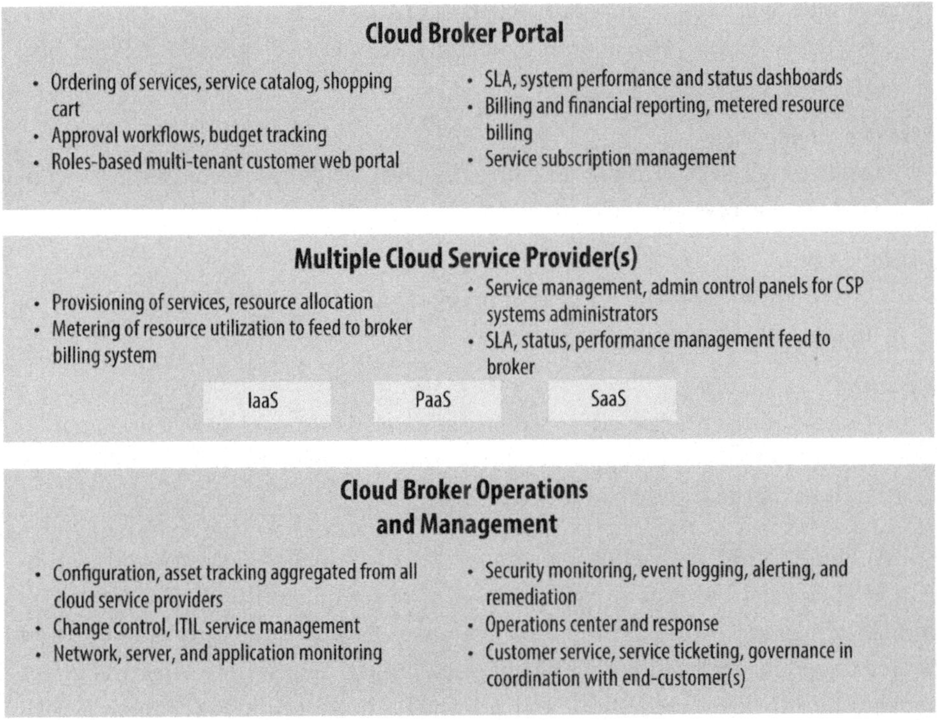

Cloud Broker Portal

- Ordering of services, service catalog, shopping cart
- Approval workflows, budget tracking
- Roles-based multi-tenant customer web portal

- SLA, system performance and status dashboards
- Billing and financial reporting, metered resource billing
- Service subscription management

Multiple Cloud Service Provider(s)

- Provisioning of services, resource allocation
- Metering of resource utilization to feed to broker billing system

- Service management, admin control panels for CSP systems administrators
- SLA, status, performance management feed to broker

| IaaS | PaaS | SaaS |

Cloud Broker Operations and Management

- Configuration, asset tracking aggregated from all cloud service providers
- Change control, ITIL service management
- Network, server, and application monitoring

- Security monitoring, event logging, alerting, and remediation
- Operations center and response
- Customer service, service ticketing, governance in coordination with end-customer(s)

Figure 8-1. Cloud broker management functions

The cloud broker must provide APIs and standards so that each XaaS cloud service provider can easily integrate with the overall cloud brokering system. Finally, the cloud broker normally performs some level of overall systems management (shown in the box on the right in Figure 8-1) to at least aggregate system status and performance metrics from the downstream XaaS cloud providers. Individual cloud providers also perform their own internal network and systems-operations management functions at a more detailed level within their own data-centers and server farms (similar to the cloud management functions and architecture shown in Chapter 7).

Key Hybrid and Brokering Terminology

NIST defines three common industry terms that define the processes and functions that a cloud broker must perform in order to have full integration with one or more third-party cloud providers. While I use the NIST terms, I have provided you my definitions and descriptions:

Aggregation

Service aggregation involves the integration and consolidation of data across multiple cloud services. Service catalogs, statistics, resource usage, billing, and service-level management across multiple cloud services and providers is combined into a single management interface and customer experience. The end consumer of the cloud might not be aware that multiple services and/or multiple cloud providers are being used.

The aggregation of IT services is not a new concept. The aggregation of cloud services across multiple public and private cloud providers and XaaS *is* a new approach used in hybrid clouds. The cloud management system must include aggregation processes and technology across multiple cloud providers to facilitate the hybrid cloud.

There are no industry standards (yet) that readily enable each cloud provider to share their utilization, service catalog, performance, SLA, error/event, or security information with other providers or cloud management platforms. Given the lack of industry standards, aggregation requires implementing a common software tool and data exchange technique between the cloud management platform and all downstream cloud providers. Most hybrid cloud management systems have some form of aggregation in place, but we will see significant improvements in this area with the next-generation clouds. The cloud management platform collects data from all connected cloud providers and presents it in a consolidated fashion via a centralized portal. This aggregation of data provides numerous other reporting capabilities such as overall system status dashboards, system and event tracking, and analytical data for use in service arbitration decisions.

Arbitration

Service arbitrage is the process of determining the best cloud service provider for each workload. As orders for cloud services are placed, usually through a service catalog, a combination of business logic and technical processes determine which cloud provider is the best match to the requirement. Arbitration decisions can be based on many criteria such as provider pricing, SLA guarantee, and geographic location for data sovereignty, or they can be based simply on customer preference. Depending on the decision logic, the broker cloud management platform can provision any given XaaS to the selected cloud provider or span the XaaS offering across multiple cloud providers.

Automated arbitration of services provides a best-fit recommendation to the customer (or cloud operator) as to which cloud provider or XaaS best meets static or policy-driven requirements. When a customer orders a cloud service, the arbitration-logic engine (part of cloud management platform) compares all available cloud providers to present the customer with a list of recommended or ranked services. The arbitration logic can be based on static (hardcoded) rules or on customer policies such as country location, required SLAs, or pricing. More advanced arbitration logic can use historical analytics data to calculate reliability and availability statistics, performance, or other dynamic metrics to determine the recommended cloud provider. In some cases, the cloud management system will give the customer the option to override or manually select the provider.

Upon selection of the cloud provider, the cloud management platform performs a series of background commands to one or more cloud providers—provisioning the ordered cloud services and handling the tracking notifications that come back from each cloud provider's cloud management and automation system. This type of automated provisioning is very complicated when a single application or XaaS is configured to span multiple cloud providers. For example, configuring web services on one provider with database and application running on another provider—all done seamlessly to the customer but divided up between providers for best performance, flexibility, redundancy, elasticity, cost, and so on.

The arbitration of services, as described here, has focused on hybrid cloud; however, arbitration is a critical feature that will differentiate cloud brokers.

Intermediation

Service intermediation is a technique by which the cloud management system (or provider) centrally controls a specific service that is then distributed to multiple cloud service providers. Key examples of intermediated services include identity management, utilization and performance reporting, and security, with all cloud providers agreeing to use an integrated common service standard so that all providers and systems can easily exchange data.

Intermediation is the means by which the primary cloud management platform or provider can create a standard and manage the methods for any application or service that spans all subordinate cloud providers. Identity management or user authentication is one primary example whereby the primary cloud provider (hybrid cloud or broker) controls and publishes standards and a single system that all cloud providers can agree to use. This intermediation affords true interoperability and exchange of information between cloud providers so that the hybrid or broker provider can have visibility and collect data from all downstream XaaS providers. Without this intermediation, each cloud provider would run its own version or choice of monitoring, provisioning, security, and operational management tools that wouldn't communicate with other providers or up to the hybrid or broker cloud provider.

Just as with aggregation, there are few industry standards upon which each cloud provider can agree and implement. One standard that is already in place for identity and authentication is Security Assertion Markup Language (SAML). In future cloud deployments, we will see more hybrid clouds, cloud brokers, and integration between cloud providers, so intermediation might not be specifically named as a feature, but it will be a critical background technology.

These three NIST-based terms are business processes and technical methods used to perform cloud brokering. A private cloud management platform and a hybrid cloud would utilize these same techniques to provision services to multiple cloud providers—the difference between hybrid clouds and cloud brokering is less technical and more process-, governance-, and role of the IT provider-based. These differences are described in the following section.

Hybrid Cloud Versus Cloud Broker

Just as in a private or hybrid cloud, the cloud management system is used in a broker scenario to provide customers a service catalog for ordering services and an automated orchestration system for provisioning workloads to multiple cloud service providers. Because cloud brokering by definition involves a variety of cloud service options from multiple cloud providers, the cloud management system must be capable of multiprovider orchestration. This also means that the cloud management system contains the necessary APIs that with which it can communicate and provision workloads for each cloud provider (e.g., Amazon or Microsoft public clouds). These specialized versions of cloud management platforms are called cloud brokering management systems. Cloud brokering management systems have every feature and capability as a "regular" cloud management system described in Chapter 7 but with additional capabilities specialized for managing cloud services across multiple cloud providers.

Key Take-Away

Cloud brokering management systems have every feature and capability as a "regular" cloud management system with additional capabilities specialized for managing services across multiple cloud providers.

Although a hybrid cloud is usually based on a private cloud as the core infrastructure, you can deploy a cloud broker management system without a private cloud involved, depending on your business needs and use case. For example, you can compare a cloud broker to the Expedia online travel service, which functions as a marketplace for numerous suppliers.

Though the cloud brokering industry is not yet mature, there are already some early examples of differences between hybrid clouds and cloud brokering:

- Cloud brokering management platforms have a more significant focus on service arbitration across numerous providers, whereas a hybrid cloud might only have limited provisioning capabilities (e.g., basic VMs only) to one or two third-party cloud providers.

- A cloud broker utilizes advanced dynamic-arbitration logic engines to determine the best cloud provider for any given customer order. These advanced arbitration services can use performance, price, analytics, geography, and customer preference data to automatically recommend which cloud provider should be used for any given XaaS workload. A hybrid cloud might have only basic sequential scripting and static hardcoded rules or policies with much less sophistication in the arbitration logic.

- A hybrid cloud will have its authentication, directory services, management, security, and monitoring tools and standards established based on the private cloud. A cloud broker environment has far more complexity and quantity of providers and management tools that the broker needs to establish as well as published APIs to each cloud provider, while managing intermediated services.

- A cloud broker might establish and maintain contracts directly with service providers and effectively resell services to end-user customers; whereby in a hybrid cloud, only the private cloud infrastructure owner chooses and establishes agreements with service providers.

The NIST Cloud Broker Architecture

The NIST Cloud Reference Conceptual Model shown in Figure 8-2 articulates the roles of a cloud broker, auditor, carrier, and provider. This diagram, when released by NIST, was one of the first to document the specific role of cloud broker.

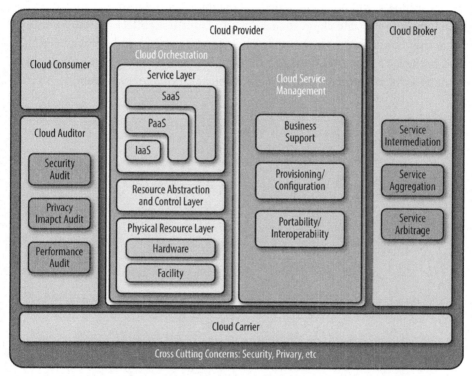

Figure 8-2. The NIST cloud reference model (Source: NIST, www.csrc.nist.gov/groups/SNS/ cloud-computing/index.html)

In Figure 8-2, notice the core functions (both business process and technical methodology) are intermediation, aggregation, and arbitrage, as I detailed earlier. In the center of the figure is the cloud provider but what might not be clear in this NIST model is that there would normally be multiple cloud providers in a cloud broker ecosystem. Within the cloud provider functions (shown in the large center box) are all of the XaaS each cloud provider offers to cloud consumers as well as the provider's computing infrastructure and the internal cloud management system. The cloud auditor is another role that could be used as part of the cloud broker service or executed by a third party to oversee and audit the overall service governance.

Cloud Broker Functional Architecture

To better explain the functions that the cloud broker provides, I have created Figure 8-3 which presents a more detailed model showing all of the primary tasks, workflows, and business logic. The diagram is similar to that shown earlier in Chapter 7 for private cloud management platform architecture, but is unique in that this model supports multiple XaaS cloud service providers managed by a cloud broker. This is a vendor-agnostic sample cloud broker architecture—there are many ways to portray this information and at varying levels of detail.

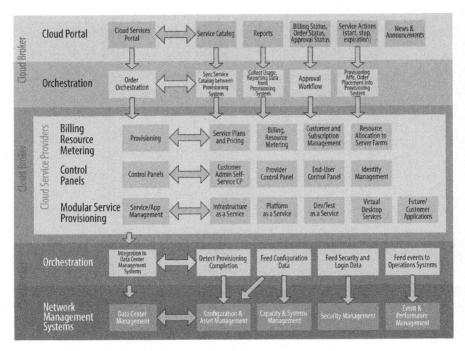

Figure 8-3. Notional cloud broker functional architecture

Figure 8-3 shows five layers of functionality for a cloud broker; however, the center layer (labeled "Cloud Service Providers") represents services and functions provided by each downstream integrated XaaS cloud provider—this is equivalent to the Cloud Provider box in the NIST model shown earlier in Figure 8-2. The key functions of the broker are all focused on the centralized portal concept, whereby consumers of the cloud can place orders, provision services to one or more cloud providers, track all billing, SLAs, reporting, assets, configurations, and operations monitoring. The cloud broker initiates service provisioning and collects data from all of the downstream cloud providers; however, the broker is not involved in the day-to-day communications between consumers and the cloud provider's computer networks. The broker provides the cloud management systems and interoperability between all providers as well as keeping up with enhancements and future revisions of each downstream XaaS provider (and their API).

THE CLOUD PORTAL LAYER

The Cloud Portal Layer (see the illustration that follows) provides the primary web-based interface with which customers can order services, view reports, and review billing information. Customer executives and project owners use this portal to initially procure cloud services and see the status of their ongoing services.

Figure 8-4. The cloud portal is the primary interface with cloud consumers. Features vary depending on the cloud provider or brand of cloud management platform but the most important functions of the cloud portal are the service catalog, billing, and service actions. Other functions, such as reporting, and notifications/announcements are optional and may or may not be enabled depending on the needs of the cloud provider or enterprise private cloud.

Here's what you can find in the portal:

Service catalog

The service catalog provides customers with a list and description of available cloud services and pricing for all available options. The services available in the catalog are an aggregation of all downstream integrated XaaS cloud providers. Upon choosing one or more services, the customer processes the order by selecting from one or more preestablished funding sources such as purchase orders, task orders, or encumbered funding documents.

In this architecture, the billing and provisioning system contains the pricing for each service catalog item, each optional service, and the price for every resource, such as virtual machines (VMs), memory, storage, and user licenses. The billing and provisioning system calculates the bills based on fixed pricing per service or variable pricing based on actual resource utilization. The invoices or bills can be sent to the customer by the orchestration system or from within the billing system, depending on customer requirements and the capabilities of the selected cloud management system. The cloud portal displays only a viewable report of the billing data, invoice history, utilization, or other ad hoc reports.

The primary purpose of the service catalog is to display the descriptions of each cloud service along with pricing. The descriptions and actual pricing of each service item available to customers can be programmed into the cloud portal itself, but the NIST Cloud Reference Conceptual Model calls for this data to be held within the provisioning and billing system. The orchestration system synchronizes all of this data into the service catalog so that it only needs to be configured and managed in one place. The advantage of holding the descriptions and service pricing within the billing system layer is that it can better handle all pro-rating, billing periods, and variable-priced metered-resource charges. Because this data must be tightly integrated with the provisioning and metered-resource systems, the architecture calls for the service catalog data to be pulled from the billing system and synchronized up into the service catalog.

To maintain a consistent ordering and tracking process for all services and across all customers, even manual orders placed by the provider on behalf of a customer should still be performed within the cloud portal. Manual orders placed outside of the cloud portal might not be tracked, billed, and shown to the customers correctly.

Billing

As services are consumed and billing occurs, the customer can track all invoices (or chargeback reports) and remaining budget balances via the portal. In an environment that has multiple downstream XaaS cloud providers with a central cloud broker, billing might occur between each provider and the customer directly, without the broker's involvement. The cloud broker provides a series of reports and dashboard views for customers to see real-time system status, utilization, and performance information of all aggregated downstream providers. This provides the customer with a centralized cloud management system managed by the broker, although each downstream provider is still ultimately responsible for meeting its SLAs, contractual obligations, and reporting statistics up to the cloud broker's dashboard. Within enterprise organizations, billing and invoicing might not be required; however, chargeback accounting for the cost of services can still be calculated to determine utilization by department. This is often useful for planning and budgeting purposes even if your organization does not directly charge for your brokered cloud services.

The billing system is heavily reliant upon the resources ordered and consumed based on utilization; therefore, this reference architecture calls for the billing to be generated as part of the provisioning and metered resource tracking layers at the XaaS cloud provider level. The invoices or billing data is then captured by the orchestration system, and sent to the cloud portal system for viewing by customers.

It is important to understand that billing is an integrated part of each cloud provider's provisioning system and cannot easily be separated. The integration of billing within each XaaS cloud provider's system makes it possible to track both fixed-price and variable-priced services. Variable pricing occurs for any service that is configured to allow metered pricing based on storage, processors, or other resource utilization per billing period. Variable pricing can also occur, for example, when a customer upgrades its services in the middle of a billing period, and the price is pro-rated automatically by the system. To accommodate all of the possible scenarios, this architecture calls for the billing system to be very tightly integrated with the provisioning system. The resulting invoices or actual bills generated can be linked to the cloud broker for reporting purposes, or directly billed from the cloud service provider to the customer, depending on the type of contract.

Service actions

Service actions, within the cloud portal, are where the cloud customer can view or change an existing service subscription. A subscription might be one or more VMs or a particular application that has been ordered through the service catalog. After a subscription is active, customers can go into the cloud portal and add or change the subscription, adding additional VMs for example.

In addition to adding or removing services within a subscription, the cloud portal allows customers to pause, restart, or terminate a subscription. Terminating a subscription stops all billing, and all computing resources are cleared. Pausing a subscription simply stops the computing resources or applications but does not delete the data. This allows the customer to restart the subscription and compute resources whenever it needs them again. Depending on the cloud provider and portal capabilities, there might be other features within the subscription that can be turned on, such as taking VM snapshots, restoring a snapshot, rebooting a VM, and adding additional disk space.

THE ORCHESTRATION LAYER

The orchestration layer (see Figure 8-5) provides all logic, workflow, and integration between other layers of the cloud architecture. By using orchestration for most of the customization to meet customer needs, the higher and lower layers can be independently managed and upgraded. The orchestration system contains customized code and scripts and has the ability to interface and interact with multiple downstream XaaS cloud provider-provisioning systems. The layers architecture, and specifically the orchestration layer, is intended to hide the complexity of potentially dozens of private, public, hybrid, internal, and future unknown clouds, providers, and provisioning systems. The customer-facing cloud portal and other layers of the architecture should not experience any impact or need changing when a new provisioning engine is added or when something is changed, upgraded, or removed.

Figure 8-5. The primary functions within the orchestration layer include synchronization (aggregation) of the service catalog and reports that are pulled from all of the cloud service providers. This level of orchestration also handles any approval workflows of orders the customers place via the cloud portal layer. After an order is fully approved, the orchestrator uses API calls to initiate the appropriate cloud provider and the provisioning of cloud services—this includes the arbitration logic.

Approval workflow

Depending on the customer's preference, the cloud portal layer sends all customer orders to the orchestration layer to handle workflow approval rules. All new orders trigger an email to one or more predefined approvers within the customer's organization; the approvers then click the link contained within the email to launch the cloud portal and approve or deny orders. Upon approval, the orchestration system sends the necessary commands into the provisioning and billing system to launch the new service.

You can create or customize more complex workflows within the orchestration system without without affecting the higher level cloud portal or provisioning systems. This can include multilevel approval workflows, timed reminders of pending approvals, and inclusion of additional customer roles (e.g., procurement).

Ordering

The orchestration system receives the request from the cloud portal system whenever a new service is ordered, terminated, or changed. It contains the necessary coding and scripts to call APIs within the lower-layer provisioning and billing systems. In a broker environment with multiple downstream XaaS cloud service providers, new orders and requests are transmitted via standardized API calls to the downstream provider's internal cloud management system. The orchestration system also detects the completion of the provisioning process to complete the overall workflow. These completion tasks include updating configuration, asset, and management systems, as well as updates back to the cloud portal status, reports, and dashboards.

Service catalog synchronization

The orchestration system pulls all current and changed services offering descriptions and pricing from downstream XaaS cloud providers and then sends this information to the broker-managed centralized service catalog, keeping it perpetually up to date. This synchronization can be scheduled to occur on a recurring basis, or whenever a change is detected; this is part of the API specification between the cloud broker and each downstream provider.

Billing and reporting synchronization

The Orchestration system captures billing, service, and resource utilization from the provisioning layer (and downstream service providers) and updates this information in the cloud portal for customers to view. The primary goal is to show customers their account balances and utilization, even if the actual billing is sent directly from each XaaS cloud provider; this arrangement depends on the governing contracts.

Centralized programming logic (including arbitration)

The Orchestration system is the primary location for all custom coding and scripts within the cloud architecture. The purpose of this is to keep the other components of the system as stock as possible, to allow for a wide selection of software options in each layer, aid in the ability to independently upgrade software with each layer, and centralize the "brains" and workflows of the overall system into the Orchestration system.

Within this centralized orchestration engine is where arbitration logic occurs. As described earlier, the cloud broker must determine which cloud provider is the best fit for each service catalog order. Sometimes, the cloud provider has already been chosen based on customer preference or based on a intentional hardcoded service catalog item that specifically indicated the cloud provider by name/brand. In an ideal dynamic scenario, the arbitration will use pricing, SLA terms, past performance, latency measurements, geographic location, or other metrics—or customer preferences—to make an automated decision on which cloud provider to send each service catalog order.

Integration with downstream XaaS cloud service providers

The orchestration layer, or modules within this layer, contains standardized API calls by which it integrates one or more downstream XaaS cloud service providers. The cloud broker assumes that there will be multiple cloud service providers contracted by the customer, with future as-yet-unknown providers to be integrated. Most cloud providers utilize different APIs (proprietary or industry-standard), so the orchestrator has a library of modules to support each provider and any unique capabilities of each.

THE PROVISIONING LAYER

The provisioning layer in this architecture provides three distinct functions that, depending on the selected cloud management system, can be separate software products. In a brokered cloud ecosystem, each downstream XaaS cloud service provider has its own cloud management tools that perform these or similar functions within its environments, interacting with the cloud broker at both higher and lower layers of this functional architecture.

These three functions are order processing and billing, control panels, and provisioning. It is preferred that all three of these functions be highly integrated or part of the same software system; otherwise, the level of complexity and integration that must be done can take millions of development dollars and years to complete. This is the most-often overestimated problem in the cloud management industry at this time, so preintegration of these functions is critical to success. In a cloud brokering model in which there are multiple XaaS cloud service providers, each of these providers has its own cloud management system, similar to the functions shown in Figure 8-6.

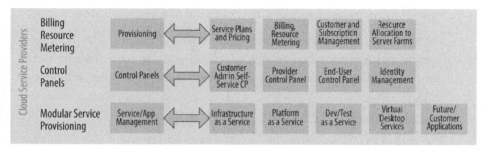

Figure 8-6. Provisioning layer (cloud service providers)

This layer is specific to each individual cloud service provider. The previous cloud portal and orchestration layers were hosted and operated by the cloud broker, which fed customer orders and provisioning requests, via APIs, into each layer—this is the cloud management system that each cloud provider owns and operates. Every cloud provider will have its own unique cloud management system, but to communicate with the broker, only the agreed-upon APIs can be used.

Many of the functions within this layer, and described in the list that follows, are similar to functions that the cloud broker performs, but again, these are very specific to the cloud provider and are also specific to the XaaS or applications that the cloud provider is hosting:

Order processing and billing

This functional area handles the definition and management of customers, subscriptions, and one or more cloud services ordered within each subscription. As customers place orders for services at the cloud broker level, these orders are then passed into this layer for the cloud provider to now process the order, start billing, and provision the actual compute and applications resources.

Depending on the cloud service that was ordered and the contract terms between the broker, provider, and customer, the billing might be a fixed price per billing period or variably priced, based on actual usage. The billing functional area handles all calculation of pro-rated billing, resource utilization metering, and generating an invoice at the end of each period. You can configure billing periods to be daily, weekly, monthly, quarterly, or yearly, and automatically renew until the customer cancels a subscription. During the initial order, the customer can also select a specific "end date" for its service from the service catalog, instead of a perpetual subscription.

The broker's orchestration system synchronizes all billing activity, invoice history, and account balances with the cloud portal system. This hides the complexity of individual downstream cloud service provider billing systems.

Control panels

The control panel functionality provides both the provider and customers with multiple configurable roles-based access to a web portal. Through the portal or control panel, the provider or customer systems administrators—depending on their assigned role—can perform administrative tasks on their cloud services. This can include managing VMs, email mailboxes, user accounts, and wireless mobile devices. All infrastructure, software, platform, workplace, and even customer-owned applications hosted in the cloud are managed through this single control panel. Providing customers with the ability to manage their account and applications greatly reduces the number of support tickets that would otherwise need to be handled by the cloud provider.

This self-service control panel is a critical area that needs to be carefully evaluated when selecting control panel software; many cloud management systems and vendors provide little or no self-service administrative functionality. For every application or function that needs to be configured, the control panel should provide that ability to the customer. Without this detailed level of control, the customer would need to submit support tickets for routine administrative chores, costing a great deal in labor and time and going against the basic principles of an automated, on-demand, cloud service.

There is also an end-user control panel role. You can configure this to provide end users with limited abilities to update such things as their names, mailing addresses, and email account settings. You can turn off this end-user control panel functionality if the customer doesn't want it.

In a cloud broker environment, there could be multiple control panels hosted by one or more of the downstream XaaS cloud service providers.

Because there are multiple providers, the control panels for day-to-day administration are unique to each provider's service offering. It is often unrealistic for the cloud broker to re-create all of the control panel functionality for each downstream provider; hence the likelihood of multiple self-service control panels. One method for achieving a truly integrated, single self-service control panel is to purchase all of the XaaS offerings from the same downstream provider as well as those of the broker.

Provisioning and application management

This functional area (see Figure 8-7) is where the interaction with the actual server farms and applications occurs. The provisioning system uses the APIs to call into each application to create, for example, new VMs, user mailboxes, Blackberry accounts, or Microsoft SharePoint sites. There are typically multiple modules within the provisioning system that the cloud software vendor has preconfigured for many of the top commercial off-the-shelf (COTS) products. The software vendor maintains this code and future upgrades as each COTS manufacturer releases new revisions. Because of this modular approach, upgraded modules do not break any other functional areas or layer in this architecture.

Beyond just COTS applications, the provisioning system must be extensible to create modules for customer-unique applications, other cloud providers' software systems, and future applications that might need to be integrated. With all of these systems plugged into the overall provisioning system—and, by extension, the control panels—both the provider and customers benefit from managing everything from a single cloud management system. All applications and services utilize the overall billing, resource metering, reporting, and service catalog systems.

In a cloud broker environment, these API calls would communicate provisioning requests to downstream XaaS providers rather than remain within a single cloud broker's management system.

Figure 8-7. Orchestration layer

Integration with systems management

> The orchestration system integrates with the systems management layer. The orchestration system updates the asset, configuration, and management system databases each time a new customer or service is ordered and provisioning is completed. This keeps the network, security, and application monitoring and management functions always updated with the latest VMs, applications, customers, and users that have been brought online.

THE SYSTEMS MANAGEMENT LAYER

The systems management layer consists of all the network, server, security, and application management tools (Figure 8-8).

Figure 8-8. Systems management layer

> In a cloud broker environment, each individual cloud service provider has its own systems-management layer. Each is also responsible for providing status, performance, billing, and other information to the cloud broker through standardized APIs—this is the aggregation function that the broker performs. The cloud broker provides at least an overall view of the cloud environment, system status, performance metrics, and SLAs. Here are some areas in this layer:

Datacenter management

> This functional area contains numerous datacenter management systems such as power, HVAC, physical security, power distribution units, communications circuits, and anything else related to the physical datacenters, including redundancy and ongoing management of these facilities.

Configuration and asset management

> This functional area holds the configuration information for every physical or virtual server, application, and other computer or software asset in the datacenter. Specifically, in a cloud environment, the automated provisioning of VMs, storage allocation, and applications mean that these configuration and asset databases should be updated in as close to real time as possible. Equally important is the automated updating of these databases

whenever a system or application is changed or disabled. This reference architecture calls for a fully automated update to these systems, handled by the orchestration system. This information is also available to customers via the cloud portal system for reporting; customers want visibility into their cloud environment, so an accurate and up-to-date asset and configuration database is a must to provide this transparency.

Security management

Similar to configuration and asset management, the automated updating of the security systems is critical. There should be little or no delay from the point at which a new VM is ordered and launched until an initial security scan is performed. The VM should also become part of the overall network as a fully monitored node. Disabling users and service termination must also be synchronized across the cloud in as near real time as possible.

Event and performance management

This functional area handles the monitoring of the network, servers, and applications for both status and troubleshooting purposes but also for performance management. By managing the performance of VMs and applications running in the cloud, customers can be automatically informed when a VM or application is reaching its maximum processor or memory thresholds. Depending on the service offering that the customer orders, the cloud system can automatically increase resources for the VM or just advise the customer of the recommended upgrade in services.

Although individual cloud service providers perform their own datacenter, network, security, event, and performance management, it is the broker's responsibility to aggregate all of this data. Cloud consumers are not aware of, nor have the ability to access, each individual cloud provider's data, so the aggregation, reporting, and dashboard views provided by the broker are critical for customers to have visibility into the overall cloud ecosystem.

Governance

Governance is a significant part of a successful cloud brokering solution. There are several standards, processes, and coordinating activities that either the cloud broker or the end customer must perform. Often, large organizations and government customers need and want to be the centralized IT provider of cloud services to their departments or subagencies; therefore, these agencies need to take on many of the governance functions. I caution large customers who do not have the necessary personnel, expertise, or desire to take on this level of governance to consider assigning this responsibility to an experienced third-party contractor.

Specific essential governance functions include the following:

Security accreditation

The accreditation of the cloud broker and downstream XaaS providers can be performed by the customer or a third-party independent organization, but the standards that need to be met must come from the customer or parent organization in coordination with the cloud broker, given that the broker ultimately has responsibilities to ensure security, operations, monitoring, and reporting.

Operational procedures

As the normal operation of server farms, storage, network, and applications will be transferred to the cloud broker and XaaS providers, the level of involvement by the end consumers or organizations will significantly change. The customer must determine what level of interaction in network, security, and operational monitoring and events it wants to assume so that the cloud broker can provide this level of visibility into the unified portal.

Contracts and procurement

How cloud services will be acquired contractually through the procurement process is something the customer or parent organization must determine. The cloud broker can provide a service catalog and workflow process, but this needs to be customized and approved by the customer to meet regulatory or internal standards. The customer must also determine if the broker is contractually or legally liable for all downstream XaaS providers (essentially making the broker a reseller of the other provider services) or if the customer will contract with each downstream XaaS provider themselves; therefore the broker is only a coordinator and aggregator rather than fully responsible for subordinate providers.

SLAs

The customer should specify the SLA to be met by the cloud broker and downstream XaaS providers. Normally, these SLA standards are published and part of the contractual obligations as each cloud provider is evaluated.

Set an SLA standard so that individual procurements or subagencies that purchase services do not individually set or attempt to control individual SLAs. Having multiple levels of service is possible, but individual SLAs for every subagency or consumer can become difficult to manage.

Who exactly tracks and enforces the SLA can vary depending on whether you, the customer, have chosen and established contracts with each XaaS cloud provider or if you have left it to a hired cloud broker to form those contractual relationships. If you hire a managed cloud broker as a service provider, it is often best to allow the broker to negotiate its own contracts and enforce all terms and SLAs with each downstream XaaS provider. You as the customer can influence which XaaS cloud providers are chosen, but if you maintain the contract to these XaaS providers, the broker has no legal authority to enforce the SLA on your behalf.

Selection of XaaS cloud providers

Normally, you as the customer evaluate and select the managed cloud broker service provider or contract with a systems integrator to implement a broker capability within your organization. Then, evaluating and selecting each downstream XaaS cloud service provider can be done by either party —the selected broker or you, the customer. If you are hiring a managed broker service, you might want to allow the broker to take responsibility to select their cloud providers (essentially, their business partners that they then manage and coordinate). If you are operating your own cloud-brokering system, you might want to select the cloud service providers, in which case you directly negotiate the contracts and service terms with each provider as well as own the ongoing business relationship.

Data Portability

Customers considering cloud brokers normally ask for the ability to move data from one XaaS provider to another. Maybe the individual provider is not meeting the desired SLA, has had technical difficulties, or has changed terms or pricing; all things from which the consuming organization wants to be protected. Although they might not have worded the requirement this way, the real need is for data and system portability—the ability to move applications and data from one provider to another.

Complete and automated portability between providers has traditionally been difficult; this is both a technical and a business challenge at a time when the industry had few standards and proven methodologies. More recently, several industry standards—with the blessing and inclusion in NIST publications—are now beginning to be widely accepted and implemented.

Standards for IaaS application interoperability, VM, and data portability come from the Open Cloud Computing Interface (OCCI) specification, which was established by the Distributed Management Task Force (DMTF). The VM portability specification Open Virtualization Format (OVF) from DMTF is still progressing as a leading pseudo standard. The Topology Orchestration Service for Applications (TOSCA) from OASIS is also maturing standards relating to IaaS and PaaS for portability of workloads—this is arguably the industry's leading standards organization working on true automated lifecycle management and portability of services between cloud providers.

Moving the more advanced PaaS and SaaS platforms and applications represents a more significant challenge than just moving basic VMs. Data hosted at one provider might need to be converted into a different database format, re-indexed, or adopt a new data structure, for example. The ultimate objective would be fully automated portability of systems *and* data between cloud providers, acheiving true interpretability, arbitration, and dynamic workload distribution across multiple cloud providers—this is the standard toward which TOSCA is working.

Key Take-Away

The ability for a cloud consumer, or even a cloud broker, to just "push a button" and automatically port applications and data to another provider is difficult at this time. The broker is the party in the cloud ecosystem with the incentive, mandate, and ability to be the interoperability enabler between providers. Upcoming industry standards such as TOSCA will greatly accelerate the capability for automated portability between providers.

Some industry groups are attempting to become *the* standard for cloud-based portability and interoperability, but we are still a long way from having cloud providers all adopt the same standards, much less agree with one another on true interoperability. Some of the current "open" cloud standards are still not fully complete in capabilities, to say nothing of ubiquitous acceptance. There are also numerous software companies with new or soon-to-be-released products that aim to improve workload portability between cloud providers. I predict this specialized category of software will be a fast moving hot topic in the next two to three years. My concern with the current software tools proclaiming to have solved this problem is that they are very specific solutions that might claim to be open source or universally useful, but in reality, they require their brand of software application engine be utilized on both the source and destination cloud providers, which is really not an agnostic industry-wide solution to the problem.

A technique that is recently gaining popularity is application containers (discussed in Chapter 4). Using application containers, portability is achieved by moving the containers (such as the open source product Docker) from one VM to another—even across cloud providers. As long as both the source and destination compute resource is running the Docker application engine, the container will run the same application on the new system, without being recompiled or modified. This doesn't necessarily move the associated application data, but there are many other techniques for porting this between systems or providers. This is just one technique to show an example; however, there are significant limitations (not to mention each application container requires that you use only that software vendor's underlying application engine), so application containers is not going to resolve the industry-wide portability concern.

One way to get a level of portability between cloud providers today is to use the cloud broker to do the heavy lifting. The broker will utilize a combination of available industry standards as they become available as well as custom programming to try to integrate with the multiple downstream cloud providers. This can be as simple as porting a VM image between providers, to complex multilevel applications and databases, which requires more significant programming of the migration technique. Truly, the broker is the only party in the cloud ecosystem with the incentive, mandate, and ability to be the interoperability enabler between providers. Asking downstream providers to "work together," or wait for sufficient standards to mature is not a plan for success. Even when standards do come along, become mature, and are widely adopted, they will be able to handle only simple tasks such as file and VM portability. Complex application stacks will never be as easy as "push a button" without significant custom programming by the broker—for every porting request.

Evaluating and Selecting a Cloud Broker

As I mentioned earlier, there are no public cloud broker service providers in the industry at this time. Existing public cloud providers are focused on keeping customers managed within their domain of service offerings and have no financial incentive to make it easy to integrate (or broker) with other cloud providers. Brokering is deployed by installing a cloud broker management system within your own datacenter or leased facility. There are some specialized systems integrators that concentrate on cloud brokering that are planning to offer a managed-community cloud broker service; however, the level of complexity and customization required per tenant or customer is very challenging.

There are a few large commercial and government organizations that have begun to deploy a full cloud brokering system, and they, too, are encountering significant challenges in business processes, technical processes, and industry standards. Many of these are explained throughout this chapter.

Key Take-Away

There are no true commercial cloud broker offerings in the industry at this time. Early cloud brokering attempts by some commercial and government organizations are encountering challenges in business process, technical methodology, and limited industry standards for multiprovider integration and portability.

As you begin to assess your potential use case for cloud brokering and evaluating cloud management platforms, here are some basic capabilities by which you should evaluate a potential cloud broker platform or provider:

- Extensibility of the system through standards and APIs so that multiple independent cloud providers can easily integrate their offerings. Open standards such as OpenStack might be a good start for provisioning and integration using APIs, but it still lacks many of the advanced cloud brokering capabilities, multiprovider billing, security, and operational management.

- Dashboards and reporting systems that centralize all customer views and data from the downstream cloud providers.

- An aggregated billing and metering system to provide a single system of tracking usage and costs across all downstream cloud providers.

- An aggregated service catalog by which customers can easily order all services from any provider from a single interface.

- An approval workflow system that routes all customer orders to one or more designated approvers within the customer's organization before money is spent.

And here are some questions you need to answer before making your decision:

- Has the cloud broker already created a library of preintegrated modules for the top industry cloud providers? This option could provide better integration and faster deployment of your cloud service, because the broker has already done the integration, coordination, and licensing to other third-party providers.

- Does the cloud broker utilize any existing cloud service interoperability standards, and what is its plan to keep up with open standards, participate in industry standards creation, and update its systems to remain compatible with proprietary cloud provider APIs?

- Will the cloud broker contract directly with your organization or government agency? Is the broker management platform hosted by the provider, or can it be implemented at the customer's premises if desired? Must I, as the customer, manage the cloud broker management system and providers or is this available as a managed service offering?

- Can the broker provide assistance evaluating and integrating new downstream cloud providers? Will the cloud broker be capable of configuring some data portability or interoperability between downstream cloud providers to compensate for today's lack of sufficient interoperability standards?

This last question brings up a key consideration: should the cloud broker you select also be allowed to bid on or function as one of the downstream XaaS cloud providers? Some cloud service providers or cloud broker management software vendors are also XaaS cloud providers. Given their expertise in this particular type of multiprovider service ecosystem, this might represent an advantage to you as a customer. Some organizations might consider this an unfair advantage, whereas others will realize that there is a benefit to having some services operated by the same provider, such as better integration, faster deployment of new services and enhancements, and more consistent portal interface and self-service capabilities.

Challenges of Cloud Brokering

I've stated before that cloud computing as an industry still in its adolescence. Extending that metaphor, cloud brokering is in the infancy phase. As of this writing, there are no commercial cloud brokers in the industry, but many large commercial and government agencies are planning and piloting systems—learning how to best create, contract with, or become a cloud broker.

Some of the challenges of cloud brokering that the industry has learned include the following:

- Each downstream XaaS cloud service provider uses an internal cloud management system, service catalog, orchestration, provisioning, reporting, operations systems and processes. The broker must determine which functions need to be integrated and aggregated at the broker level, which functions are best left to each cloud provider, and how or what to present in a unified customer experience. Terms like aggregation and intermediation are used in the industry, but few detailed use cases and real-world examples exist.

- How will the broker show multiple XaaS providers offering similar services, and how are unique offerings distinguished to the end consumer? Depending on the contractual relationship between the broker, customer, and each XaaS provider, the broker might not be responsible for marketing each downstream XaaS, so there is a level at which each individual XaaS provider must interact with the broker as well as the consumer. If the broker is fully responsible for all brokered services and each XaaS provider, the customer might never see, know about, or need to work with individual XaaS providers.

- The largest cloud service providers offer multiple deployment models, public, private, and virtual private, but some cannot or refuse to comply with certain government standards (such as financial audit or unique compliance regulations) and therefore partner or sell through other vendors. The broker must coordinate with multiple types of cloud providers and resellers, and even legacy customer datacenters that must be integrated into the cloud broker system.

- The investment and technical sophistication required to become a true broker is significant. The broker must have the investment, expertise, and a library of preintegrated XaaS connectors to downstream providers. There will likely be only a few dominant mature cloud brokers in the industry—others being systems integrators deploying brokering platform software for individual or dedicated customers. Brokers must also spend a significant amount of time and money maintaining and monitoring their integration and connections to each XaaS provider as new features are enabled, new providers join, and integration APIs mature in the future.

- Meeting customer requirements to customize is also a challenge because the broker has a necessary goal to use the same integration and connector tools for multiple customers and XaaS providers. A custom, unique broker system for a single customer is always possible but will often be cost prohibitive to the end consumer.

- Brokering is the newest role in cloud computing. No mature models or providers are on the market yet, so there will be a limited number of cloud-broker management platforms, and tens of millions of dollars invested by a broker just to create an initial offering.

- Many large commercial and government organizations have solicited requests for information or proposals seeking cloud brokering, but few of these show a true understanding of brokering. Many of these RFI/RFPs ask multiple competing cloud providers to "just get along" without standards or ask systems integrators to build a cloud broker platform costing tens of millions of dollars with little or no commitment by the customer, which represents huge, often unreasonable, risk to the systems integrator.

- The ability to provide a customer-owned and operated cloud broker solution versus that of a vendor has both initial investment and ongoing management cost considerations. Some cloud brokers can only be the host and operator and do not want to develop code or manage on-premises implementations for customers.

- There is no "move" button to automatically migrate data and services between cloud providers. The type of XaaS matters; moving a VM is relatively easy, but moving applications, data structures, and networking is not easily automated. Lack of portability standards means the broker might need to create a combination of open source and proprietary code to facilitate service migration between downstream XaaS providers. As open source systems or industry standards mature, brokers will need to constantly adjust their systems.

- Should the cloud broker invest in the creation of a library of preintegrated service connectors to downstream XaaS providers? Or, should it allow customers to pick their own XaaS provider and try to integrate these independent providers, one at a time, using industry standards if they exist or the proprietary API that each XaaS provider uses?

- Customers concerned with vendor lock-in at the cloud service provider level can look to a cloud broker model. Customer lock-in at the cloud broker level is still a concern, but early analysis indicates that trying to use multiple cloud brokers will present significant (possibly insurmountable at this time) issues —a single, well-chosen cloud broker service or an internally deployed broker software platform is recommended.

- Procurement challenges:

  — Will the customer procure a single broker service and then multiple XaaS cloud providers through a single contract with broker or multiple contracts to each of the downstream XaaS providers?

  — Is there a procurement process (e.g., a purchase order) for every micro-transaction purchased in a cloud service catalog? How can each transaction from the service catalog be actively or passively approved without contract or procurement personnel involved on every order?

  — How are variable-service costs (e.g., expanding storage and VMs) handled? Alternatively, do you fix costs, and therefore disable automatic expansion?

  — How will chargebacks to consuming subagencies be tracked? Will subagencies submit their own procurements, or submit to a parent organization before going to cloud provider or broker?

- Contractual issues:

  — Should procurements of XaaS to cloud providers go through the broker? Alternatively, if contracts are issued to multiple downstream XaaS cloud service providers, it becomes more difficult to ensure integration and avoid unique characteristics.

  — Is the broker allowed to also provide one or more of the XaaS cloud services, or is it prohibited from also being a cloud service provider?

    — A broker is more likely to have better integration and faster deployment of XaaS compared to a third-party provider that has to integrate with the broker's system

— A broker might need to provide interoperability, portability, and advisory services to the customer as a function of being the broker, so a conflict of interest is possible; this broker might not be allowed to provide all XaaS

- Security accreditation:

  — Will consumers of cloud services accept the security accreditation of the parent organization? Will a government standard for cloud security such as FedRAMP apply and be sufficient for cloud brokering technologies and broker/provider relationships?

  — Can traditional security processes change to precertify VM and platform templates so that they can be automatically deployed 24-7-365 without human intervention?

  — What level of visibility, monitoring and shared management is possible between the customer and broker all the way down to the individual cloud service providers?

  — Will multiple levels of security, particularly in government clouds, be allowed? Can the same cloud broker system provision and manage XaaS at multiple levels within FISMA and DIACAP?

- SLAs:

  — How will SLAs be established?

  — How are they managed, aggregated, and reported across multiple cloud providers?

  — Who enforces the SLAs: a hired cloud broker or the end customer?

  — Will consuming agencies agree to use the same SLAs that are essentially prenegotiated with the cloud service providers of XaaS?

The Future of Hybrid and Cloud Brokering

Hybrid clouds will become the most common form of cloud model in the industry. Customers of the cloud already want combinations of public, private, and legacy datacenter cloud enablement, so eventually the hybrid cloud will be the norm. Techniques for hybrid clouds and cloud brokering are very similar, differing primarily in the role, governance, arbitration, and level of integration between clouds and enterprise datacenters.

Key Take-Away

Techniques for hybrid clouds and cloud brokering are very similar, differing primarily in the role, governance, arbitration, and level of integration between clouds and enterprise datacenters.

Hybrid cloud will soon become the so prevalent in private and public clouds —with optional integration back to on-premises datacenters—that the line between internal private clouds, public cloud providers, and legacy datacenters is already blurring. Although there are clear technical, operational, and governance differences with the cloud broker role, this, too, will merge into the hybrid cloud model as currently defined.

As hybrid clouds and the cloud broker role matures over the next two to five years, here are some key areas that will evolve and become more sophisticated:

Portability

Significant new standards need to be created, vetted, tested, and matured over the next few years to enable true system and data portability between multiple cloud providers. Along with improved standards, the sophistication and automated movement of XaaS workloads and data between cloud providers will evolve. Future hybrid clouds and brokers will be able to shift services between datacenters and cloud providers to achieve maximum availability, scalability, and lowest cost—all of this with zero outages or customer impact.

API standards

Standards by which a cloud broker and multiple downstream cloud providers integrate will need significant improvement. Currently, there are some standards or open source systems such as OpenStack, but none of these completely cover every aspect of provisioning, reporting, portability, and operational management standard APIs. As APIs and portability standards are created and eventually adopted by cloud brokers and XaaS cloud service providers, hybrid and cloud brokers must continuously update their software systems.

Preintegration of XaaS providers

Many hybrid providers and cloud brokers will not wait until contracted by a customer to begin creating a library of preintegrated connectors to downstream XaaS providers. The larger cloud brokers will proactively create relationships (e.g., resell or white label) multiple downstream XaaS providers. As stated earlier, many public cloud providers will also launch hybrid services to improve integration back to existing enterprise datacenters.

Software-defined datacenters and networking

Achieving true dynamic arbitration and portability of services between cloud providers will require more adoption and maturity in the areas of virtual networking, IP addressing, DNS, and virtual local area networks (such as software-defined datacenters and software-defined networks). If the broker controls all aspects of the virtual networking and addressing, moving cloud services from one provider to another can be performed without affecting the customers—this is the ultimate goal but not a reality today.

Dynamic arbitration logic

Future cloud brokering technology, services, and cloud management systems will shift from today's mostly static-rules logic to more dynamic learning engines for arbitration. This means that statistics on utilization, performance, SLAs, network latency, and even security and pricing factors will be continuously analyzed to determine which of many XaaS cloud providers should be used for any given workload. This dynamic method of automated decision making can still have some customer-provided influence, policies, or choices within the calculations with regard to which cloud providers to provision cloud services. Providers that are faster, cheaper, and more reliable will receive more new customers and workload; automatically moving workloads between providers with little or no customer service disruption. Cloud brokers will be able to utilize this advanced dynamic arbitration logic and portability to shift workloads in order to ensure SLA adherence, performance, reliability, and price. Imagine the cloud broker automatically selecting and shifting workloads between multiple providers almost as automated as a network traffic load balancer.

Hybrid and Cloud Brokering Best Practices

Based on lessons learned and experience from across the cloud industry, you should consider the following best practices for your organization's planning.

HYBRID VERSUS BROKERING

Many organizations misuse the term "brokering." Hybrid clouds typically begin with a private cloud for most services, automation, and operations with the added ability to provision to one or more XaaS public cloud service providers. Brokering is an IT service marketplace provider role, which uses more advanced aggregation, arbitration, and intermediation technologies across numerous XaaS cloud providers, often without a private cloud infrastructure. Specific differentiators between hybrid clouds and cloud brokering include:

- Techniques for hybrid clouds and cloud brokering are very similar, differing primarily in the role, governance, arbitration, and level of integration between clouds and enterprise datacenters.

- Cloud brokering management platforms have a more significant focus on service arbitration across numerous providers, whereas a hybrid cloud might only have limited statically scripted provisioning capabilities to one or two third-party cloud providers.

- A cloud broker utilizes advanced dynamic-arbitration logic engines to determine the best cloud provider for any given customer order. These advanced arbitration services can use performance, price, analytics, geography, and customer preference data to automatically recommend which cloud provider should be used for any given XaaS workload. A hybrid cloud might have only basic and static, hardcoded rules or policies with much less sophistication in the arbitration logic.

- A hybrid cloud will have its authentication, directory services, management, security, and monitoring tools and standards established based on the private cloud operator. A cloud broker environment has far more complexity and quantity of providers and management tools that the broker needs to establish as well as publish APIs to each cloud provider, while managing and aggregating these intermediated services.

BROKERING ROLE

Determine if your organization wants to own and operate the brokering process and technology, or if you want to outsource this to a cloud brokering service provider. You'll need to consider the following:

- Organizations that want to function as the broker must perform the governance, set standards, coordinate procurements, promote and support client-organizations, and continuously upgrade the cloud brokering platform software. Organizations also evaluate, select, and contract with each downstream XaaS cloud provider based on end-user needs.

- Outsourcing the cloud brokering management requires much less involvement and operations by the customers and consumers of the cloud services. The cloud broker handles all integration and contracts with each downstream provider. The cloud broker manages the entire environment with some input from the customer on desired policies and governance issues.

HYBRID AND CLOUD BROKERING PLATFORMS

You should evaluate a potential hybrid or cloud broker platform or provider using the following criteria:

- Extensibility of the system through standards and APIs so that multiple independent cloud providers can easily integrate their offerings. Open standards such as OpenStack might be a good start for provisioning and integration using APIs, but it still lacks many of the advanced cloud brokering capabilities, multiprovider billing, security, and operational management.

- Dashboards and reporting systems that centralize all customer views and data from the downstream cloud providers.

- A billing and metering system to provide a single system of tracking usage and costs across all downstream cloud providers.

- A service catalog by which customers can easily order all services from a single interface.

- An approval workflow system that routes all customer orders to one or more designated approvers within the customer's organization before money is spent.

And here are some questions you need to answer before making your decision:

- Has the cloud broker already created preintegrated API modules with popular downstream cloud service providers? This option could provide better integration and faster deployment of your cloud service, because the broker has already done the integration, coordination, and licensing to other third-party providers.
- Does the cloud broker utilize any existing cloud service interoperability standards, and what is its plan to keep up with standards, participate in standards creation, and update its systems to remain open or proprietary?
- Will the cloud broker contract directly with your organization or government agency? Is the broker management platform hosted solely by the provider, or can it be implemented at the customer's premises if desired? A cloud broker might also have designed its cloud management system to only be deployed and run from the cloud provider's network, not a dedicated on-premises installation at a customer-specified facility.
- Can the broker provide assistance evaluating and integrating new downstream cloud providers? Will the cloud broker be capable of configuring some data portability or interoperability between downstream cloud providers to compensate for today's lack of sufficient interoperability standards?

BROKER GOVERNANCE

Understand that governance is a significant part of a successful cloud brokering solution:

- The cloud broker management platform can be hosted by a provider, or implemented at a customer-specified facility.
- There are several standards, processes, and coordinating activities that the cloud broker or the end customer must perform. Often, large organizations

and government customers need and want to be the centralized IT provider of cloud to their subagencies or consumers; therefore, these agencies need to take on many of the governance functions.

- Specific governance functions that need to be performed include security accreditation, operational procedures, contracts and procurement, SLAs, and selection of XaaS cloud service providers.

SERVICE PORTABILITY

Customers need to understand that porting of cloud services or data from one provider to another is not as simple as "pushing a button."

- The process and technology standards are not mature enough in the industry to make porting an automated process. A cloud brokering provider is best suited to establish the necessary integration APIs and processes to facilitate portability—potentially charging customers for the migration as there is still some level of manual configuration and testing/QA required.

- In an ideal scenario—possibly sometime in the future—a cloud broker could move VMs or other application workloads between XaaS providers with zero downtime or customer impact. This future capability requires significant maturity of industry standards and software-defined networking to automate the porting.

Industry Trends and the Future of Cloud Computing

Key topics in this chapter:

- Analysis of industry trends
- Evolution from IaaS to PaaS applications
- Convergence of IaaS and SaaS providers
- Trends leading from private to hybrid clouds
- The future of cloud computing:

  — Hybrid clouds and cloud brokering

  — Application transformation: fully multithreaded, multiprovider, dynamically scalable applications

  — Self-service administration: consolidated application control panels

  — Software-defined datacenters

  — Big Data and analytics

  — The Internet of Things

The cloud computing industry has matured quickly in its initial years, and certainly since the term "cloud" was first coined. As the pace of computers and information technology in general continues to accelerate. The cloud industry has clearly gone through its infancy and is in what I would call the adolescent stage. This book has focused on providing lessons learned during these early years, and now we look to the next generation of cloud computing.

In this chapter, I first discuss some important industry trends, some of which are lessons learned by cloud providers and early-adopter customers. Then I will discuss the technologies, trends, and forecasts for the next-generation clouds. By understanding these trends and technologies, you and your organization can improve your cloud transition, better comprehend the current cloud industry, and build a more flexible future-ready enterprise cloud.

An Analysis of Industry Trends

As I've discussed throughout this book, cloud computing can be considered as the modern incarnation of legacy datacenters embodying a new style of IT operations, procurement, and management. The concepts of virtualization, rapid provisioning, pay-as-you-go, and elasticity are no longer new concepts; they are now common benefits and techniques employed by public cloud providers and operators of private clouds. To determine where the industry is headed and the future of cloud computing, it is important to evaluate the latest trends.

PUBLIC CLOUD PROVIDERS

Most of the major public cloud providers such as Amazon AWS originally focused on providing Infrastructure as a Service (IaaS), virtual machines (VMs), and web hosting and content delivery network (CDN) services. Then, these providers began to add Platform as a Service (PaaS) and Software as a Service (SaaS) offerings. IaaS is now so commonplace that every public cloud provider is expected to have this capability, and price is one of the few differentiators between competitors.

SAAS PROVIDERS

A mere five years ago in 2010, cloud providers with a SaaS focus were called application service providers (ASPs). These cloud service providers and software-management platforms are quickly expanding into PaaS and IaaS applications, seemingly taking the opposite approach used by Amazon, which started out with IaaS and then moved to PaaS. These SaaS providers have the advantage of mature and feature-rich self-service application control panels, but they do not have the size, scalability, and investment funding that the big IaaS public cloud providers enjoy.

THE CONVERGENCE OF THE IAAS AND SAAS INDUSTRIES

The primarily larger IaaS-focused providers and the often-smaller SaaS providers surprisingly have not merged or had any significant rounds of acquisitions yet. Providers such as Microsoft have a significant internal portfolio of both SaaS, IaaS, and PaaS technologies that it is transforming into cloud offerings. Using Microsoft again as the example, it started with the SaaS-based Office 365, and then later launched its Azure cloud service, which includes IaaS and PaaS offerings based on its Hyper-V, SQL, and other platforms. Microsoft has yet to combine some of its SaaS offerings (such as Office 365) with its Azure public cloud in an integrated unified interface. Google also began with mostly SaaS applications (such as Google Apps). More recently, it has added IaaS offerings via the launch of Google Compute, but the Google Apps SaaS offering is still a separate product. Throughout the industry, you can expect to see more SaaS and PaaS products offered by traditional IaaS providers, and numerous acquisitions of small SaaS providers by the industry giants—particularly because competitive pricing for basic IaaS applications continues to drop, whereas PaaS and SaaS is projected to be profitable in the long term.

SYSTEMS INTEGRATORS

IT systems integrators have mostly skipped the public cloud business and focused more on customizable and secure private clouds—often built as dedicated enterprise clouds for mostly larger customers and public sector government agencies. Hewlett-Packard has notably continued its private cloud focus for customers while also entering the public cloud market, stating publicly that the combination of private and public cloud services—hybrid cloud—is where the industry is headed and customers want to go. Expect systems integrators to continue acquiring cloud management software companies to differentiate themselves. These platforms make up the basis of automation, orchestration, billing, and customer portals deployed by the systems integrators to their customers. In other words, systems integrators will continue to cloud-enable individual enterprise customers or build private/hybrid clouds, but most of them will not become cloud providers themselves.

PRIVATE TO HYBRID CLOUD

Although most cloud consumers want all of the benefits of a public cloud (such as elasticity, low cost, little or no commitment, pay-as-you-go, etc.), the ability to customize a cloud and implement specialized security controls has made private cloud more popular.

The industry-wide trend points to private cloud customers using one or more Anything as a Service (XaaS) products from public cloud providers, as well; so the hybrid cloud model is looking to be the most common form of cloud in the coming years. The next generation of customer clouds will be a primarily hybrid cloud model whereby customers own and operate a private cloud—having modernized legacy datacenters—and use the private cloud management platform to broker out selected services to third-party public cloud IaaS, PaaS, or SaaS providers. These hybrid clouds will become the norm in the industry, so much so, in fact, that even pure public cloud providers will adapt and offer more hybrid and brokering-type cloud integration to other cloud providers and partners through application programming interfaces (APIs) and online marketplaces.

Key Take-Away

The next generation of enterprise clouds will be primarily hybrids whereby customers own and operate a private cloud—usually by first modernizing legacy datacenters—and use the cloud management platform to broker selected services to third-party public cloud IaaS, PaaS, or SaaS providers.

SMALL BUSINESS

Small businesses—typically those that have fewer than 100 employees—are more likely to consume public cloud services over the Internet. These companies have little or no IT department but still want to benefit from IaaS and SaaS providers to reduce the costs and burdens of in-house computing. Many small-business startups have no internal IT personnel and must completely outsource their needs to public cloud providers. Private clouds are often out of the question for small businesses due to the cost, complexity, and lack of adequate IT skills (or willingness to establish an IT department).

PURCHASING CLOUD SERVICES

Small and medium-sized organizations often utilize credit cards for their cloud service purchases. The largest customers, and particularly public sector government customers, tend to use purchase orders submitted to the cloud provider with invoices sent by the cloud provider back to the customer at the end of each billing period. A clearly observable trend is that credit card–based purchases are often associated with rogue or shadow IT—when individuals or teams within an organization purchase a cloud offering on their own, often to reduce the time and complexity of acquiring new IT assets through internal company processes.

CLOUD DEPLOYMENT MODELS

Government customers tend to deploy mostly private clouds for the majority of their services, whereas public cloud is often used for limited use cases such as development and testing or for relatively static public websites. Private and hybrid clouds often require more capital investment or commitment on behalf of the customer organization but gain increased customization capabilities. Community clouds, with multiple cooperative peer organizations sharing a common cloud ecosystem, are not very popular so far, because peer organizations often have difficulty agreeing among themselves on governance, funding, roles and responsibilities, as well as the significant concern that any individual peer's future funding, mission, or leadership changes could disrupt the community.

Key Take-Away

Community clouds have inherent organizational, financial, political, and long-term viability complications. A community cloud is a lot like a marriage: a great idea at the beginning, but will it hold up over time if and when peer agencies change leadership, mission, or funding?

The Future of Cloud Computing

The theme throughout this book has been to analyze lessons learned in the first generation of the cloud and to provide best practices with a focus on technology and business for the next generation. Based on lessons learned, industry trends, and customer-demand signals, the next-generation clouds will focus on a new style of delivering IT rather than the technology itself.

Key Take-Away

The next-generation clouds will focus on a new style of delivering IT rather than the technology itself. The business outcomes and focus on customer demands will clearly be the nexus point, whereas the underlying technologies will still be important but no longer the business justification.

Although the first generation of clouds focused on basic concepts such as pay-as-you-go, elasticity, ubiquitous access, and ease of use, next-generation clouds will expand this list of characteristics for all clouds—essentially expanding the baseline standards and expectations for future clouds.

THE HYBRID CLOUD

Public and private cloud deployment models are currently the most popular choices for customers. Based on lessons learned and customer-demand signals, private clouds are favored for their customization and parallel migration paths for legacy datacenters. Soon after organizations begin their transition to the cloud, clarified requirements and legacy application needs often cause the organization to consider using a combination of on-premises and private cloud services along with external public clouds for selective XaaS needs. This combination is, by definition, a hybrid cloud—the ability to use selected public cloud XaaS offerings through the same private cloud management portal.

The trend continues toward private cloud as the baseline service for many organizations with the ability to burst or hybrid provision to selected public cloud services on demand. This hybrid cloud requires new focus on automated and dynamic provisioning of cloud services across multiple cloud providers and legacy datacenters. The ability to provision in this next generation of cloud requires new technology and tools to perform service aggregation and arbitration of XaaS, which is the basic technology behind hybrid and cloud service brokering.

Key Take-Away

Hybrid clouds will become so common that the term "hybrid cloud" might fade away, because it will be the norm for modern IT delivery.

Most customers—the larger organizations and government entities in particular—want all of the characteristics and benefits of public cloud offerings. As detailed requirements are evaluated, these large organizations quite often determine that they would prefer a private cloud. The primary benefits of private clouds include customizations to the procurements, security, operations, reporting, and governance processes. Keep in mind that public cloud services provide 90% of their services as standardized products, with limited customization. Only private cloud deployments have the ability to customize some or all aspects of the service to meet customer requirements. Private clouds also best facilitate the modernization and migration to cloud transformation for datacenters on a slower transition schedule. So, each organization is left with the decision to sacrifice their customization needs and go with a public cloud or embrace their uniqueness and move to a private cloud.

Key Take-Away

Many customers say they want the features and benefits of a public cloud. After discussing detailed customization, security, and other requirements. though, it often becomes clear that a private cloud model is really the more appropriate one.

As stated earlier, public cloud providers are also creating hybrid services whereby the public cloud integrates back to legacy enterprise datacenters—essentially the opposite of hosting your own private cloud management platform and extending it to public cloud XaaS. I expect to see a massive uptake in the sophistication and quantity of these public-to-enterprise integration tools to further blur the line between on-premises enterprise datacenters and public cloud services.

BRIDGING PUBLIC CLOUD TO ENTERPRISE DATACENTERS

A new and powerful capability being introduced by some public cloud providers is the ability to reach back into a customer's enterprise datacenter. This is done by federating the authentication system (such as Active Directory) and connecting the public cloud provider's network with the customer's network. These network connections can be made through the Internet by using a virtual private network (VPN) or a dedicated wide area network (WAN) communications circuit. After the public cloud and enterprise cloud are connected, consumers of the cloud can then use any combination of pubic and legacy applications, log on using the corporate directory password, and synchronize data across the cloud and the legacy datacenter.

This approach—in which a public cloud provider enables a hybrid cloud—is very new in the industry but shows a significant potential to provide the following hybrid services:

- Backup of enterprise on-premises servers to the cloud
- Federated identity management and authentication between the cloud and enterprise directory
- Cloud-based mobile device management
- Remote application publishing from the cloud to any end-user desktop or mobile device
- Synchronization of cloud and enterprise data that can be accessed from any device and any location via the cloud
- Redundancy and failover of enterprise servers to cloud-hosted VMs

SOFTWARE-DEFINED DATACENTERS

The software-defined datacenter (SDDC) is an approach to configuring IT infrastructure through virtualization of servers, networks, and storage. All of these infrastructure services are pooled and the individual hardware components abstracted behind virtualization software. In an SDDC, the server, storage, and network resources are managed by a cloud management platform that performs automated configuration, provisioning, and allocation of resources.

The three core technologies in an SDDC are virtualization of servers, storage, and networking. Technically, many other components of the infrastructure can be virtualized and automated, such as security, operations, and even components of the physical datacenter facility. As is covered in Chapter 3, the virtualization of physical servers is already commonplace for modern datacenters and cloud environments. The focus in the future will be on virtualizing of storage and networking.

Network virtualization involves pooling all network switches, routers, firewalls (along with IP addressing), DNS, and other network-related services. The cloud automation software automatically configures network segments, routing paths, and firewall rules on demand as customers order their cloud services. The physical network cabling does not run from a server network card directly to a central switch, as in a traditional datacenter; instead, multiple server blades are concentrated into a high-density server chassis, with the chassis or server cabinet having multiple shared high-speed connections to the network. Then, one or more virtual connections are made, through software, to create the virtual network path between the server and the rest of the network, to a specific subnetwork, or other infrastructure components. So, the physical network is configured in an *any-to-any* configuration so that the software is used to actually connect the networks paths, creating and changing these paths through the automation software to keep things manageable. You can create, change, or remove these software-defined paths dynamically through the network via the cloud automation software as needed. The same is true for storage virtualization where server farms are not necessarily directly connected to a SAN; instead, the automation software creates a virtual path between the server(s) and the abstracted pooled storage system(s).

The benefits to these software-defined techniques are numerous. The primary reason is to enable a large quantity of servers, network, and storage infrastructure to be physically deployed and ready for automated configuration just in time upon a cloud service being ordered. The automated provisioning systems actually assign processors, memory, storage, and network configurations to each server or virtual server. One server might be configured to host IaaS virtual machines (VMs), whereas another might be configured to run an enterprise SaaS application—all depending on customer demand and what is ordered. In this example, servers are no longer preconfigured with application software but are instead left in a generic "blank" state, ready for instructions on what hypervisors, operating systems (OSs), and applications to load after a customer places an order.

Key Take-Away

The concept of manually configuring every server with network, storage, OS, and applications is now antiquated. Automation tools now create virtual servers, network, and storage paths on demand, as customers order services. Essentially all things are now dynamic and software defined rather than static, hardcoded, or manually configured.

Some other benefits to "software-defined everything" is that you can swap out servers easily and the replacement server automatically inherits the characteristics and configuration of the original. And as more capacity is needed for the cloud infrastructure, you can add more unconfigured servers, network, and storage devices into the datacenter with the automated and software-defined configurations automatically applied as customer orders arrive and begin to utilize the newly installed capacity.

Finally, the SDDC give you the ability to span services across multiple data-centers for extra capacity and redundancy. The applications and end users of the cloud have no knowledge that the cloud services, storage, and networking spans one or more datacenters or when a failover to a disaster recovery facility has occurred. This technique also makes a cloud service portable—you can move it from one cloud provider to another with the software-defined network redirecting all users to the new provider or datacenter with little or no service interruption.

Taking the software-defined concept to the datacenter level, you can dynami-cally control traditional physical systems such as HVAC, fans, and lighting via software. Imagine datacenter facilities automatically adapting to increases in cus-tomer demand by adjusting environmental settings and fans to maintain proper, balanced temperatures. Or perhaps turning power on or off to entire sections of the facility as needed, to save enrgy costs. One example of this is to use large commercial containers, such as those used on cargo ships, full of computers that can be quickly plugged in at a datacenter but only turned on and activated when demand or capacity is needed. All network switches, routers, server farms, and applications in the container or "datacenter in a pod" are configured via software for a particular customer or to increase capacity on demand only when needed. This isn't science fiction; it is already happening today in some of the latest, most modern datacenters.

CLOUD SERVICE BROKERING

As I detailed in Chapter 8, cloud service brokering refers to the role that an orga-nization or cloud provider can take in delivering to customers a variety of cloud services from multiple providers. I expect a number of commercial community or public providers to launch cloud brokering services in the coming years in addition to large enterprise customers that are already planning this form of internal IT service aggregation.

Public sector government customers have shown a significant interest in cloud brokering. Many state and federal government customers already have the responsibility for consolidating IT purchasing—providing IT services or access to third-party vendors on behalf of entire government entity. Cloud brokering is simply a new style of delivering IT with responsibilities for evaluating which cloud providers are contracted, aggregating all service catalogs, consolidating bill-ing across all providers, and governing the procurement and chargeback process to the consuming organizations.

A theme throughout this book is the future adoption of the hybrid cloud. Cloud brokering will be a method by which large organizations and public cloud providers deliver hybrid multiprovider functionality. Expect to see a significant rise in the popularity of and new services focused on hybrid clouds and cloud brokering very soon. Of course, as I stated earlier, many customers have a tendency to confuse the two delivery methods because each involves similar automated provisioning processes and technology.

Transforming Applications

As detailed in Chapter 4, every modernized datacenter or cloud provides, at a minimum, the basic infrastructure VM, storage, and network services. When you transform enterprise applications to the cloud, you can take advantage of the unique benefits of the cloud such as performance, elasticity, stability, and improved return on investment. Purchasing or deploying a cloud service is just the first step: application porting or redevelopment will become the long-term path to complete the transition to cloud.

There are not many applications that truly utilize the full potential of cloud computing at this time. Most of todays' applications were created long before the cloud became popular and accepted, and it will take more time to reprogram or transform complex applications into the cloud. This transformation also means changing the applications so that they can split all processing and calculations into multiple threads or work streams to provide the dynamic scalability, performance, and reliability. Using multithreading, the application can spread its processing workload across numerous cloud compute devices, thus speeding up the application's response to the customer. As the amount of data grows and application complexity grows, applications will need this capability to scale-out with cloud computers, forming clusters of thousands of computers. Many traditional enterprise IT functions and applications are expected to become cloud-based systems in the future. Inevitably, the cloud will become the first choice for application hosting and cloud native characteristics will be commonplace.

CONTINUOUS APPLICATION DEVELOPMENT (CONTINUOUS DELIVERY)

The integration of continuous application development (also known as continuous delivery) automation, which is described in Chapter 4, will be a key differentiator for the leading public cloud providers and private cloud platforms. Most current cloud providers and management platforms support Development/Testing as a Service (Dev/Test) activities but do not truly implement the full continuous delivery model at this time. When continuous delivery is incorporated into the cloud portals and self-service control panels, Dev/Test will truly take advantage of cloud automation, software-defined networking, and drastically improve the application development lifecycle.

APPLICATION PUBLISHING

Application publishing (detailed in Chapter 1) is expected to increase in popularity, particularly for mobile and laptop devices and users. Although virtual desktops have their place and purpose in the industry, it is application publishing of individual enterprise applications to a large number of users that will soon become a standard method for application management and distribution. Application publishing provides remote execution of applications that are hosted in the cloud, but the crucial capability is the ability to download the latest application version (in the background without the user's knowledge) to each desktop or mobile device for use when offline from the network.

OPEN SOURCE APPLICATION DEVELOPMENT

The development of cloud-native applications is complicated because of the numerous programming languages and application platforms common in the industry. The latest trend, which is expected to greatly expand, is to use open source application development platforms to create multilanguage, multiplatform, portable cloud-native applications. Rather than supporting the traditional method of staging separate development environment for Java and another for .NET (to name just two platforms), new open source cloud development platforms such as Cloud Foundry support dozens of simultaneous languages and platforms. Add in cloud-based database/middleware platform automation and continuous application delivery automation tools, and the entire application development lifecycle will be truly revolutionized. Although these tools are individually available now, the combination of open source, cloud-native, multiplatform, continuous delivery, and automation is still a couple of years away from reality.

Further benefits of open source application development platforms are when you combine it with open source cloud platforms such as OpenStack. Using the same Cloud Foundry example, deployed on top of an OpenStack cloud platform, you now have an environment in which you can readily port any applications created within it to many other industry-standard cloud platform, application environment, or cloud provider that supports these open systems. The industry is a few years from this reality, but organizations should seriously consider using open source cloud platforms—certainly application development platforms—over proprietary systems and cloud providers to position themselves for future interoperability, cloud-native hybrid applications, and portability between cloud providers.

APPLICATION APIS

The industry is well on its way to implementing APIs into every aspect of cloud services, cloud management tools, and application development. The future of cloud computing, integration of applications, connectivity of applications to external services and other providers, and portability of cloud services between providers is all hinged on APIs. The industry is already seeing some of the world's largest systems integrators, software developers, and cloud providers shift to industry or open source standards for APIs rather than proprietary APIs created by every provider (which is how the cloud industry first started). The quantity and level of sophistication of these APIs is where cloud computing will extend its reach into everyday business, consumer, and personal devices and applications. For more on this, see "The Internet of Things" on page 349 later in the chapter.

APPLICATION CONTAINERS

One of the latest trends in cloud computing is application containers. This technology has actually been around for many years and is not specific to the cloud, but it has taken on new forms and popularity through open source products such as Docker. With the application container concept, you can "package" applications into self-contained executable programs that you can deploy onto multiple servers and even onto different OSs. These applications actually run in their own memory space and execute separately from one another because they share a common underlying application platform service, such as the Docker Engine in this example. This "Dockerized" application can run on any server or OS that has the Docker Engine, without needing unique versions or recompiling the app for every unique server or host, or cloud.

This concept of application containers might not be an entirely new technology; however, given the current and future demand for open source and hybrid clouds, expect Docker and similar application containerization tools to become even more popular.

Self-Service Administration and Control Panels

Future clouds will have a significantly enhanced focus on customer-facing self-service control panels—well beyond the basic service administration tools available in current clouds. Cloud management systems not only handle customer orders, orchestration, and provisioning functions of the cloud, but also provide a web-based portal from which customers can manage their cloud applications. Given the basic premise that cloud applications are hosted by a centralized provider (often a third-party), the administration of the applications also needs to be cloud enabled. Whether internal support personnel or a third-party contractor provides the application and day-to-day user administration functions, there are significant benefits to managing all of the cloud applications through a consolidated, consistent user interface or self-service control panel.

As mentioned in Chapter 7, most cloud management portals enable only limited IaaS-centric self-service capabilities, such as the ability to restart or reboot VMs. As the next generation of clouds focus on migrating more applications (not just IaaS), the cloud management portals will need to improve significantly in the area of self-service control panels because applications have significantly more settings and administrative tasks than fairly simple IaaS VMs.

With self-service control panels, you can define multiple roles for customer support staff and optionally end users, with each role assigned unique permissions and abilities to customize or manage applications. Customer support staff might perform tasks such as user account management, configuring applications, resetting passwords, changing mailbox features, adding new websites, enabling smartphones, starting and stopping VMs, or any other administrative functions the cloud provider allows. Or, the end user might be restricted to only changing her name, address, phone number, and password for an application.

The provider and/or customer administrators control what permissions or self-service capabilities are available for each role and users assigned to those roles. Many cloud platforms have a unified multitenant portal to which all customers can log on. Depending on the logon ID, the customer will only be able to see and manage their organization, their user accounts, and their applications; no customer can see or manipulate any other customer's account. The cloud service provider support staff themselves also use the same management portal, but their logon ID permits more capabilities in the system. This does not mean that the cloud support personnel can see any customer private data; they just have the ability to make configuration changes to applications (not data) on behalf of the customer when requested. All changes made to services or configurations are fully logged for auditing purposes.

These are just a few examples of how customers can administer their applications and cloud service subscriptions. If the cloud provider does not have this capability, customers have no choice but to submit a traditional helpdesk support ticket and wait for the work to be done. This forces customers to place a call for every minor administrative task, which is neither cost effective nor a good customer experience.

Key Take-Away

An application self-service control panel is very often overlooked or not available from traditional IaaS-focused cloud providers. Just as you need to manage and configure VMs in an IaaS application (for which most cloud providers do offer a web portal), cloud consumers need SaaS management capabilities to centrally administer cloud-based applications. Future cloud deployments will have significantly more self-service administration capabilities to match the growing number of enterprise applications running to the cloud.

Big Data and Analytics

Big Data refers to the gathering of large amounts of data, often from various sources in the cloud, and storing this data into large databases. These databases and methods of collecting data are a perfect fit for a scalable, elastic cloud-hosted service—it provides customers with access to data that would have been impossible or impractical to gather or host within a legacy IT environment. It is when this data is processed through analytic tools that statistics, trends, and intuitive searching is accomplished—providing business intelligence that organizations have never had in such as useful form until now.

There are two primary categories of data: structured and unstructured. A database with defined fields (e.g., name, address, and phone number) is an example of structured data, whereas unstructured data might be emails or social media for which the actual data is rather random in form and content. Tools to analyze structured data have been available and used across multiple industries for many years. Unstructured data is the most common and fastest growing form of data, so analysis has been difficult. Previously, it could be performed only at a basic level, manually, by humans. When you combine a huge amount of data from multiple sources, both structured and unstructured, this is Big Data. Analytics is the process and tools that you use to work the data into usable views and reports.

Some real-world use cases for big data analytics include the following:

Retail products

You can perform real-time data gathering and create dashboard views of customer sentiment for a new product launch by gathering purchasing, social media, email, user forums, and customer service ticketing systems.

Analytics tools can produce intelligent reports to manufacturers on customer acceptance or complaints almost immediately after a new product launch. You can use *data trending* to improve future products and customer service.

Security and intelligence

Audio, video, social media, email, or logged sensor data gathered from multiple sources can be analyzed to correlate (sometimes seemingly unrelated) events to proactively identify potential threats or criminal activity. The most advanced video processing, combined with analytics, can even detect potential terrorist threats, such as if someone enters a subway station with a briefcase and then later leaves another station without the briefcase. Government intelligence agencies worldwide are also known to use collected audio, email, and website data to identify potential threats or trends. Although this level of surveillance and analytics is usually reserved to intelligence agencies and the military today; it is only a matter of time before this technology is widely used by commercial organizations, or someday even end consumers.

Heathcare

Researchers can use long-term gathering of healthcare data from thousands or millions of patients to determine trends and patterns that no individual hospital, doctor, or research firm could gather and analyze manually or in isolation. Using real-time data gathering from personal wristwatches or medical devices embedded in patients, virus outbreaks, epidemics, and other events could be detected almost immediately.

It goes without saying that all of this structured and unstructured data gathering, along with the analysis output, can represent privacy issues. Ideally, the output data analysis would only represent an aggregated report and statistics without any personally identifiable information (PII). While it is relatively easy to implement PII data isolation and only show the consolidated statistics, the fact that the raw data is collected and stored online also means there is always a potential for data leakage due to security flaws or hackers.

Big Data and analytics are already here to stay in the industry. In the very near future, we will see huge advances in the sophistication of analytics tools and an explosion in the number and diversity of worldwide business consuming or subscribing to this business intelligence data. Everything from customer sentiment, products and prices at retail stores, social media reaction to events and television shows, to commuter traffic will generate data with ever-improving analytical tools producing intelligent reports to business (and consumers) via the cloud—even more exciting is that this will be done in near real time.

The Internet of Things

The *Internet of Things* (IoT)—or, as its sometimes called, the *Internet of Everything* —has recently been discussed in the industry. This essentially means that there will be a drastic increase in the number and type of devices that are interconnected to one another and to the cloud. The key to this IoT is that it will go well beyond business uses and eventually affect just about every aspect of human life, from healthcare to home automation to automobiles. Using APIs and improved standardization, many different devices from all manufacturers will be able to communicate. While I could write an entire book on this topic alone, I will focus instead on how cloud computing will soon be part of most daily tasks and devices you use.

THE IOT, THE CLOUD, AND YOUR HOME

We are already seeing home appliances such as televisions, digital video recorders (DVRs), and even refrigerators that communicate with one another via a wireless home network or the Internet. They also communicate via cable, satellite, and cloud-based content providers such as Netflix. Now take this even further into the home automation trend where a centralized computer (within the home or in the cloud) controls the lights, entertainment devices, appliances, heating and cooling, security sensors, and even the lock on the front door. All of these devices, and the entire home, can be controlled via your smartphone or by any computing device connected to the cloud. This gives it the ability to sense when you or a family member arrives home, automatically adjust the air conditioner, disarm the security system, turn on lights, and notify other family members of movement or activities sensed within the home.

One excellent example is the standard alarm clock that is a thing of the past. The future alarm clock (actually already available today) will be fully integrated into your home, detecting sunrise, adjusting room temperatures just before you wake up, slowly fading up the lights, opening window shades, and starting your preferred music playlist. Taking this alarm clock example even further, imagine just reaching over and pressing a button that automatically emails your office that you will be late or are sick and not coming to work today—shutting the lights and window shades so that you can go back to sleep.

Combine this automated home with the cloud and you get even more capabilities such as automatic updating of firmware in your appliances, unlimited music and video selections to download, visibility or awareness of home activities with an elderly family member across the country, and even synchronization of the home with your automobile. Using the alarm clock example again, imagine the home automation system waking you earlier than normal when abnormal traffic conditions exist on your normal commuter route. The cloud makes this and countless other scenarios possible when integrated into your home, automobile, and personal life.

THE IOT AND CLOUD IN YOUR AUTOMOBILE

Most modern automobiles have internal software (called *firmware*) that runs everything from the engine management system to the radio or entertainment devices. Extending the reach of your automobile to the cloud and to other devices such as your home, smartphone, and even other vehicles will bring a new driving experience that you can customize and integrate with the rest of your daily routine.

Let's look more closely at your cars firmware. Presently you must visit your local dealer or manufacturer to troubleshoot a problem or update the internal computer software. The newest trend—some could say started by Tesla Motors— is to design the cars with self-service or automatically upgradeable software as a core feature. With this functionality, the dealer can update the car with new features or improvements via the cloud even while you're driving down the road. So the days of just having satellite or streaming radio to the car from the cloud are evolving to cars that are permanently connected to the Internet and cloud.

When your car is connected to the cloud, it will take on significant new features, customization, entertainment, navigation, and even engine monitoring and troubleshooting capabilities. Imagine your car dealer or manufacturer automatically monitoring your car's performance, efficiency, or event logs and calling you when a problem is detected or even fixing the problem without you even noticing something was wrong in the first place. Now *that* is true customer service. Realize that this benefits the auto dealer and manufacturer, as well, with reduced visits to the service center and continuous improvements to their products by collecting and analyzing all the data from other customers of the same vehicle type. Yes, there are security and privacy concerns to be worked out, but we'll leave that topic for another book.

Now, let's take your cloud-connected automobile and integrate it with your home. Imagine that your home will sense that your vehicle has pulled into the driveway or garage and then automatically turns on lights or performs other customized tasks within your home. Take this a step further and let's have your home computer's music library automatically update wirelessly to your car so that you never have to put your music on a USB stick (or stream from your smartphone which drains the battery). Performance and efficiency data could also be synchronized automatically to your home computer for long-term trending and reports. You could also send navigation instructions or your favorite restaurants to your car, ready for your use via the onboard vehicle navigation system later. And, of course, real-time monitoring and tracking of your teenager as he drives: how fast is he going and where he is going is always popular (with parents at least...).

Although not yet a reality, one of the most exciting areas in the confluence of automobile and cloud is the interaction with other vehicles, other people, stoplights, even the road itself; that will be the next evolution for the auto industry. There are already applications for your smartphone with which you can see and interact with other drivers to determine how fast traffic is moving and redirect your navigation system to find the fastest route. Currently, these peer-to-peer applications are based on smartphones communicating with one another, but this will soon be a part of the automobile's internal capabilities. Also consider the progress being made in autonomous vehicles that drive themselves by using continuous data from roads, sensors, and other nearby vehicles to help navigate and avoid one another.

The point to all of this is that the cloud is what enables all of these possibilities. Whether the cloud is used just as a communication channel (e.g., streaming music from the cloud), or as method of data transfer and interaction with other devices, it is the software APIs that makes possible the interaction with other cars and devices in the world, and that makes this a very exciting future.

PERSONAL

Let's not forget personal devices and how they will interact with the cloud in the near future. We already have smartphones connecting to the cloud, but the number and diversity of personal devices that also integrate with the cloud is about to explode. Watches are now being developed that monitor your pulse, blood pressure, oxygen saturation, and blood-sugar levels to name just a few. There are glasses that are now connected to the cloud, wristbands for fitness tracking, and even GPS tracking chips that you can embed in your pet. Key areas in which the cloud will change daily life include (but certainly are not limited to) the following:

Healthcare

Cloud-enabled monitoring devices will not only track the health of you or your family, but automatically notify your doctor or even emergency services during certain health-related events. Fitness tracking, today often using wristbands, is already commonplace. Given the vast amount of continuous data, your doctor will have an exponentially increased capability to analyze trends, see how medication is working, and even call you to come into the office before you know there is even a potential problem. These capabilities are even more effective and important for elderly family members—sharing information with doctors but also key family members if desired. Using Big Data and analytics, as described earlier, will revolutionize the healthcare industry when combined with the cloud and personal health monitoring.

Presence awareness

The ability to track family member locations anywhere in the world or just within your home or neighborhood will have a significant impact in your life. Just as you could embed a location-tracking device in your pet, you could track a person's location by their wristwatch, smartphone, or potentially a human-ready form of embedded chip. Take this even further and use these personally worn devices to automatically open or unlock doors, start your car, turn on lights at home, or change music and digital pictures on the wall to your personal liking by sensing your presence—even as you move from room to room within your own home. Tracking this data and integrating with the cloud had almost infinite possibilities for convenience, lifestyle, and security.

Perhaps the scariest part of personal devices and cloud-based integration is the privacy. There will be privacy issues that we will all need to deal with and solve, but most of these technological capabilities will be optional for you and configurable in what data is held private versus what is shared to others (for instance, your doctor). One area you may not be aware of is the value of this personal health, activity, and presence awareness data to businesses. Businesses gathering and analyzing personal data at this level of detail can gain vast knowledge of habits and trends—personally or as a demographic. This data would be invaluable for companies to create and adjust their service or product offerings, safety, quality, and so on. This analytical data is not new; it is already common practice for most retail stores, healthcare providers, and even your Internet provider. When the data gets as detailed and personally identifiable as the wristwatch, embedded chips, and healthcare is where most people draw the line today on privacy. Ensuring privacy while still benefiting from these new technologies will be (already is) a significant challenge for personal interactions and the cloud.

Closing Comments

Throughout this book, I have analyzed lessons learned and best practices for cloud computing based on experience from early-adopter customers and industry cloud providers from 2010 until now. The cloud computing industry has matured at a pace even faster than anyone predicted. As I look back on the first generation of clouds, it is clear that some concepts now so critical to success were not well understood or even thought of back then.

As we study the lessons learned from the industry and first generation of cloud customers, I can clearly see new trends, technologies, and business processes that will be a focus for the next generation of the cloud. The future of the cloud is not just about technology or transforming legacy enterprise IT; it's also about your business—prioritizing what business needs should be addressed first and potentially transitioned to the cloud. Using guidance provided in this book, organizations and business executives can take advantage of this knowledge to better plan, deploy, and complete their transition to cloud. It is no longer a matter of convincing you of the benefits of cloud computing; it is now time to consider when and how you will make the transition from enterprise IT to cloud-based IT service delivery.

Glossary

The definitions in this glossary are intentionally not "straight from a dictionary." Rather, they are intended to provide more clarity and relevance to cloud computing within the context of this book.

Accreditation

The process by which an organization evaluates the security of a computer system against one or more security standards or policies. An accredited system is one that is "certified" to have successfully completed this process.

Agile

A software development and delivery methodology based on iterative and incremental improvements for software releases. Agile is intended to speed time-to-market of software updates, new features, or patches on a continuous basis, usually measured in weeks or months.

Allocated services

The practice of selling resources such as processors, memory, storage, or network based on a fixed prepaid amount or ceiling. Customers pay a fixed price for services, even if their actual utilization is less. *See also* Metering.

Application service provider

Internet-based provider of application hosting services. A precursor to today's more popular term, Software as a Service (SaaS), whereby applications are hosted, managed, and licensed by the provider, often charging customers on a per-user or per-month basis.

Application transformation

The process of adapting or rewriting an application so that it can be hosted in a cloud deployment model. Specific features of cloud-enabled software include elasticity, resiliency, and micro-application services running across one or more computers or virtual machines.

Automation

The process of computer scripting, programming, and other tools deployed to perform a series of processes without human intervention. By programming software and tools to allocate processors, storage, network, and applications, cloud services can be deployed and ready for use within minutes rather than hours, days, or weeks if deployed manually by traditional means. Automation is particularly important in cloud computing, because many cloud providers process hundreds or thousands of orders for new services each hour.

Availability

Refers to the amount of time a computing resource, application, or data is available for use or is online for use, as opposed to being offline for maintenance or in a failed state. Availability is often measured as a percentage of time that services are available compared to the amount of time in a specified period of time.

Backup/Recovery as a Service

A cloud service offering which provides data backup and recovery. This service might include a certain frequency and data retention level included in price by default, with optional enhancements to these defaults at additional cost.

Broker (cloud broker)

A function or role in cloud management that integrates multiple Anything as a Service (XaaS) cloud providers into a single cloud management system. The broker performs aggregation of services offered by multiple cloud providers, centralized cloud management portals, reporting, and system and data portability between downstream cloud providers.

CIPA

Children's Internet Protection Act. This is a federal law enacted by U.S. Congress to address concerns about access to offensive content over the Internet on school and library computers. CIPA imposes certain types of requirements on any school or library that receives funding for Internet access or internal connections from the E-rate program, which is a program that makes certain communications technology more affordable for eligible schools and libraries.

Cloud compute

This refers to the processor, memory, storage, and networking resources provided to customers, typically via a virtual machine.

Cloud-native application

An application that is designed specifically to run in and take advantage of a cloud infrastructure. Characteristics of cloud-native applications include elasticity, composability, and resilience.

Commercial-off-the-shelf (COTS)

Software packaged and sold via retail channels and widely available from major software vendors.

Common Criteria/ISO 15408

A framework that provides assurance that the process of specification, implementation, and evaluation of a computer security product has been conducted in a rigorous and standard manner. The Common Criteria for Information Technology Security Evaluation (*http://bit.ly/1b4si6b*) (CC) and its companion Common Methodology for Information Technology Security Evaluation (*http://bit.ly/1b4si6b*) (CEM) are the technical basis for an international agreement, the Common Criteria Recognition Arrangement (*http://bit.ly/1aDtIno*) (CCRA).

Community cloud

A cloud service that provides for a community of consumers or organizations with shared interest or concerns. The system is managed by one or more of the organizations, by a central provider, or a combination. Organizations utilizing this cloud service have a shared mission, governance, security requirements, and policies.

Continuity of operations (CoO)

The concept of offering services even after a significant failure or disaster. The dictionary definition is more generic, stating that CoO is the ability to continue performing essential functions under a broad range of circumstances. For the purposes of being a cloud provider, CoO is a series of failover techniques to keep networks, servers, storage, and applications running and available to your customers.

Continuous delivery

Also referred to as continuous application development. A software development and delivery approach used to automate and improve the process of software releases to production. Automated processes are used for testing and promotion of software code from development to testing, quality assurance, and production, which improves consistency and reduces overall cost. Continuous delivery is often combined with the Agile approach to software development delivery.

COPPA

Children's Online Privacy Protection Act. Effective April 21, 2000, this law applies to the online collection of personal information from children under the age of 13. The new rules stipulate what a website operator must include in a privacy policy, when and how to seek verifiable consent from a parent, and what responsibilities an operator has to protect children's privacy and safety online.

Data as a Service

Similar to Platform and Software as a Service, Data as a Service is the hosting of a centralized repository of data. This data, often in the form of a large searchable database, is gathered by the provider, often from numerous sources. The service offering is provided to customers that need to access, search, view, and download the data.

Data sovereignty

The concept that computer data is subject to the laws of the country in which it is located, thus preventing foreign governments from subpoenaing the host country and cloud provider where the datacenter is located.

Development/Testing as a Service (Dev/Test)

A cloud service often considered a PaaS offering with IaaS-type compute services being offered along with numerous application lifecycle management (ALM) tools, code libraries, and developer tools.

DIACAP

DoD Information Assurance Certification and Accreditation Process. This is the U.S. Department of Defense (DoD) process to ensure that risk management is applied on information systems. DIACAP defines a DoD-wide formal and standard set of activities, general tasks and a management structure process for the certification and accreditation (C&A) of a DoD information system that will maintain the information assurance (IA) posture throughout the system's lifecycle.

DISA

Defense Information Systems Agency. This is the U.S. government agency that governs IT standards, guidance, and provides some centralized IT services to U.S. Department of Defense organizations. DISA has produced several cloud security guidelines with the latest called Department of Defense (DoD) Cloud Computing Security Requirements Guide (SRG) initially published in January 2015, which replaces the previous Cloud Security Model (CSM). The SRG defines roles, and standard for private cloud and external cloud service providers based on four Impact Levels. This is a relatively new standard and likely to mature over time, this DISA SRG is more specific to cloud than the DIACAP standard for overall DoD IT. Refer to DoD Cloud Computing SRG at www.disa.gov (*http://www.disa*).

This DISA standard is intended for DoD organizations and it contains more security controls and requirements than FedRAMP or FISMA. The four SRG levels are described in Chapter 6.

Disaster recovery

Process, policies, and procedures for recovering from a natural or human-induced disaster. This is a subset of the continuity of operations plan focused on how to restore systems and services to an operational level.

Elastic or elasticity

Refers to the ability of a computing resource or application to automatically scale out (adding more compute resources or additional virtual machines) to handle an increase in workload/utilization.

FedRAMP

Federal Risk and Authorization Management Program. This is a government-wide program in the United States that provides a standardized approach to security assessment, authorization, and continuous monitoring for cloud products and services. FedRAMP is a set of cloud security standards followed by most civilian (non-DoD) United States Government agencies and their certified public cloud providers.

FERPA

Family Educational Rights and Privacy Act. The Education Department is releasing a Notice of Proposed Rule Making (NPRM) under the Family Educational Rights and Privacy Act. The proposed regulations would give states the flexibility to share data to ensure that taxpayer funds are invested wisely in effective programs.

FIPS

Federal Information Processing Standards. 140-2 standards provide guidance and minimums characteristics for data encryption. Many U.S. federal government agencies are required to adhere to this policy for protected data.

FISMA

Federal Information Security Management Act. Title III of the E-Government Act. This requires each federal agency to develop, document, and implement an agency-wide program to provide information security for information systems that support the operations and assets of the agency, including those provided or managed by another agency, contractor, or other source.

Geographically diverse

Refers to having datacenters and cloud compute server farms in different physical locations from each other. The separation of datacenters is usually 500 miles or more so that any regional disasters (natural or intentional) are unlikely to affect both datacenters. Ideally, geographically diverse datacenters are more than 1,500 miles apart, and neither datacenter is in an earthquake or flood-prone area. Note that having datacenters in different countries is also common, but this presents additional issues as some customers need guarantees that their data is not hosted in certain countries (*see also* data sovereignty).

High availability

Refers to percentages of how much time a system is online versus unscheduled outages. High availability is also something you design and build in to your cloud solution using redundant components and continuity of operations to achieve a high level of availability measured by system availability to the customer.

HIPAA

Health Insurance Portability and Accountability Act of 1996. Legislation that provides privacy and security protection of individually identifiable health information.

Hybrid cloud

A cloud service that is a combination of two or more cloud deployment models. Cloud systems are managed through standardized or proprietary technologies often called the broker system, or broker provider. *See also* Broker.

Hypervisor

A software system that is installed on a physical server and then creates multiple virtual machines, each having a configurable amount of processor, memory, storage, and network resources.

Infrastructure as a Service (IaaS)

Cloud compute services, normally in the form of virtual machines, with configurable processor, memory, storage, and networking. Infrastructure as a Service often includes other cloud services such as Storage as a Service, Backup/Recovery as a Service and Development/Test as a Service.

ISO

International Organization for Standardization. A standards organization that plays a role similar to that of the National Institute for Standards and Technology (NIST); however, ISO is an international, nongovernment entity that is widely accepted or adopted worldwide. NIST is primarily followed by U.S. government organizations.

ISO 27002

This document provides best-practice recommendations on information security management for use by those responsible for initiating, implementing, or maintaining Information Security Management Systems (*http://bit.ly/1ERh1Sx*) (ISMS). Information security is defined within the standard in the context of the C-I-A triad (*http://bit.ly/1E9EPSZ*). The C-I-A triad is the preservation of confidentiality (*http://bit.ly/1G3YHaA*) (ensuring that information is accessible only to those authorized to have access); integrity (*http://bit.ly/1IS3mgA*) (safeguarding the accuracy and completeness of information and processing methods), and availability (*http://bit.ly/1HftBeE*) (ensuring that authorized users have access to information and associated assets when required).

LDAP

Lightweight Directory Access Protocol. This is a standard API for accessing and distributing directory/identity services. *See also* SAML.

Load balancing

A load balancer distributes workloads (network traffic) across multiple computing resources or applications. The load balancer attempts to equally use each computing resource, balancing the utilization of each; however, it also monitors availability and will automatically redirect traffic should one or more computing devices go offline due to maintenance or failure.

Managed cloud

A cloud environment where systems management, upgrades, and support are performed by a third party provider on behalf of the customer organization—usually under contract and governed by a service agreement. A managed cloud can be hosted at a customer, provider, or third-party data center. Managed cloud normally associated with a private or virtual private cloud where the routine management is outsourced to a third party.

Managed services model

In this model, subscribers pay a fee to an IT service integrator or outsourcing provider to perform day-to-day computer management, operations, and support services.

Metering (metered services)

The practice of measuring resources (processors, memory, storage, and networking) consumer and billing for actual utilization of these services. Metering is the opposite of allocated services within the cloud computing industry.

Mission critical

Services or functions of the business that are essential for the success of the business or customers. mission-critical refers to computer systems and applications that are considered vital and must maintain a high-availability rating. Failures of mission-critical systems are catastrophic to the organization or customer.

Multitenant (multitenancy)

Software architecture in which multiple customers use a shared system but are separated from one another. Customers share the resources but are prevented from interacting or seeing other customers in the environment.

NIST

The National Institute of Standards and Technology. This agency is responsible for publishing computer standards and guidance under the Federal Information Security Management Act (FISMA) of 2002, Public Law 107-347.

OBM A-130

The Office of Management and Budget (OMB) through Circular A-130, Appendix III, Security of Federal Automated Information Resources, requires executive agencies within the federal government to (a) plan for security; (b) ensure that appropriate officials are assigned security responsibility; (c) periodically review the security controls in their information systems; and (d) authorize system processing prior to operations and, periodically, thereafter.

Open source

Computer software that is available in source code form. An open-license allows users to study, change, improve, and sometime distribute the software. Open source software is often improved upon by many individuals, universities, and other organizations for the benefit of all users or the system.

PCI DSS

A multifaceted security standard that includes requirements for security management, policies, procedures, network architecture, software design, and other critical protective measures. This comprehensive standard is intended to help organizations proactively protect customer account data.

Platform as a Service (PaaS)

Cloud service providing a set of applications, tools, and potentially database system to the consumer. Provider manages all underlying server farms, networking, storage, operating system, and core applications. PaaS is similar to IaaS, but the provider has preconfigured and is responsible for not only the compute infrastructure but also the applications, tools, and resources.

Private cloud

Cloud services offered exclusively to a single consumer at either a provider's facilities, a consumer's own facilities, or a third party. Multiple business units within the consumer organization can access the system. Management of the system can be performed by the provider, consumer organization, or third party, regardless of where the physical resources are located.

Public cloud

Cloud service offered to the general public. The provider owns, manages, and operates all compute resources located within the provider's facilities. Resources available to consumers are shared across all customers.

Redundancy

The concept of duplicating components or systems with the purpose of keeping the system online and available should a single component fail.

Resilient

Normally refers to a characteristic of cloud-native applications that can sustain errors or failures in the cloud infrastructure and still function. A resilient application will have embedded self-healing logic to retry, reroute, throttle, and queue failed transactions rather than generate a user-facing error. *See also* cloud-native.

Return on investment (ROI)

A measurement used to evaluate the efficiency gained or effect of a given investment. ROI is calculated by taking the gain from the investment minus the cost of the investment, then dividing by the cost of the investment.

SAML

Security Assertion Markup Language. An XML (*http://bit.ly/18RFKaW*) standard for authentication considered an industry standard for cloud computing single sign-on, federated identity authentication.

Scale down

The concept of reducing computer instances, after a scale out has occurred, when peak utilization has subsided and the additional computing resources are no longer needed.

Scale out

The concept of adding additional computers, usually virtual machines, in a cloud environment to handle more workload or peak utilization. Scale out is not the same as scale up, but these terms are often misused.

Scale up

The concept of increasing the size of computing resources such as memory or processors to handle more workload or utilization.

Scaling

The concept of resizing computing resources to handle increases or decreases in workload or utilization. *See also* scale-up, scale-down, and scale-out.

Software as a Service (SaaS)

Cloud service offering that provides one or more applications to the consumer. Applications are hosted and managed by the provider in the cloud, with the consumer accessing the application services from various end-computing devices such as PCs, laptops, tablets, smartphones, or web browsers.

STIG

Security Technical Implementation Guide. A methodology for standardized secure installation and maintenance of computer software (*http://bit.ly/1cCLtFo*) and hardware (*http://bit.ly/1PXVxYA*). The term was coined by DISA (*http://bit.ly/1PXVAUa*), which creates configuration documents in support of the U.S. Department of Defense (*http://bit.ly/1ERgkZw*). The implementation guidelines include recommended administrative processes and span the device's lifecycle.

Storage area network (SAN)

A dedicated network that provides block-level data storage. A SAN is typically a large consolidated system, with one or more head units and numerous disk drives. Sophisticated RAID, striping, cache, and processing algorithms are used to maximize storage performance and reliability.

Storage as a Service

Cloud service, often part of IaaS, that provides storage on demand. This service often involves multiple levels of storage performance, as well as block and network-attached storage (NAS) types. Customers are normally charged for the amount of allocated or metered per gigabyte or terabyte.

Thin client

An end-user computing device that has only a portion of a typical desktop computer's processing power, memory, and storage. The thin end device often does not have internal storage, so a minimal operating system is stored in read-only, nonvolatile memory. Thin-client devices—similar to dumb terminals use in mainframe environments—need to connect to a larger computer environment through the network in order to run software applications. Thin-client devices are similar to zero-client devices, with the difference being that zero-client devices have no local operating system or software and can only be used when connected to a larger computer network.

Virtual machine (VM)

An isolated guest computer and operating system running within a physical computer's hypervisor. One physical server running a hypervisor can host numerous virtual machines, each having a configurable amount of processor, memory, storage, and network allocated.

Virtual machine image (or template)

A file that contains a snapshot or copy of a preconfigured operating system and potentially some applications. This image file is used to instantiate or create a new virtual machine quickly rather than having to run an operating system installation process for every new virtual machine.

Virtual private cloud (VPC)

A variation of public cloud where a segmented compartment of an otherwise public cloud infrastructure is dedicated to one customer. VPC offerings bring some of the price advantages of a large cloud provider, but with a bit more customization, security, and segmentation of VMs, storage, and networking.

Virtualization

Virtualization of computing resources is defined as a virtual machine. Virtualization can also have an extended meaning, whereby networking, storage, and applications are no longer hardcoded or assigned to specific compute devices. Resources as mapped in a logical manner then can be changed easily, often while systems are still online, rather than hardcoding, cabling, or allocated resources to an individual compute device.

Workplace/Virtual Desktop as a Service (WPaaS)

Cloud service providing a remotely hosted desktop operating system, commonly Microsoft Windows or Linux, and applications to consumer end-users. Some cloud providers categorize this as part of IaaS or PaaS, but many utilize a unique name for this service to differentiate this virtual desktop offering from other products.

XaaS

Anything as a Service (X = anything). Could be any IaaS, PaaS, SaaS, or future unknown cloud-based service.

Index

About the Author

James Bond has more than 25 years' experience in the IT industry and has designed and deployed countless datacenters, server farms, networks, and enterprise applications for large commercial and public sector government clients—he was building hosted application services long before the term "cloud" was first used in the industry. Mr. Bond is a business and technical cloud subject matter expert, providing cloud strategy, guidance, and implementation planning to C-level executives seeking to transition from legacy enterprise IT to cloud computing.

Mr. Bond currently works for Hewlett-Packard as a cloud chief technologist. He routinely presents executive briefings at industry conferences and in-depth consulting workshops on lessons learned to large commercial and government organizations. His specialties are enterprise IT transformation to private and hybrid cloud as well as cloud brokering. Prior to Hewlett-Packard, Mr. Bond built numerous cloud computing companies and practices serving in the roles of chief technology officer, product vice president, chief architect, and software development management.

Mr. Bond has a bachelor's degree in information technology from the University of Maryland and has received numerous industry certifications and awards throughout his career. He is a well-respected industry leader and long-time contributor to numerous trade magazines and a featured speaker at IT conferences. This is his first published book.

Colophon

The cover fonts are Gotham, the text font is Scala Pro, and the heading font is Benton Sans.

Get even more for your money.

Join the O'Reilly Community, and register the O'Reilly books you own. It's free, and you'll get:

- $4.99 ebook upgrade offer
- 40% upgrade offer on O'Reilly print books
- Membership discounts on books and events
- Free lifetime updates to ebooks and videos
- Multiple ebook formats, DRM FREE
- Participation in the O'Reilly community
- Newsletters
- Account management
- 100% Satisfaction Guarantee

Signing up is easy:

1. Go to: oreilly.com/go/register
2. Create an O'Reilly login.
3. Provide your address.
4. Register your books.

Note: English-language books only

To order books online:
oreilly.com/store

For questions about products or an order:
orders@oreilly.com

To sign up to get topic-specific email announcements and/or news about upcoming books, conferences, special offers, and new technologies:
elists@oreilly.com

For technical questions about book content:
booktech@oreilly.com

To submit new book proposals to our editors:
proposals@oreilly.com

O'Reilly books are available in multiple DRM-free ebook formats. For more information:
oreilly.com/ebooks